# Jami Lin's Books, Videos, Programs, and Feng Shui Design

## Books

Feng Shui Today: Earth Design the Added Dimension
*its universal roots to practical, decorative Feng Shui: "an absolute necessity to read!"*

The Feng Shui Anthology: Contemporary Earth Design
*40 top world-wide practitioners share secrets and solutions, "a literary masterpiece!"*

The Essence of Feng Shui: Balancing Your Body, Home, and Life with Fragrance
*"Jami's work in using aromatherapy in good Feng Shui is fascinating!."*

Spirit in the Bedroom: The True Lover's Guide to Relationship (release late millennium/early next)

## Videos

Feng Shui Today: Enrich Your Life by Design
*Feng Shui in 3-D: Tour Jami's frequently published home, walk through a consultation!*

## Essential Oils

Feng Shui Essentialsc: Chakra/Bagua Blendsc
*"Eyes closed, I identified which oil was which by the way it effected my energy. Using the Root/Career blend, a client immediately grounded herself which resulted in greater clarity and insight."*

## Music

Sound Chi: Feng Shui Music to Heal the Home and Spirit with Steven Halpern
*Steven's musical genius and Jami's expertise, "it's a melodic chi- enhancing delight!"*

## EarthDesign™ Practitioners Training Certification & Special Programs

- EarthDesign™ Practitioners Training Certification & Weekend Feng Shui Workshops
- Continuing Education programs for Interior Design, Architecture, and Real Estate
- Inspirational, motivational, and highly informative talks, lectures, seminars, and workshops: design/architecture, real estate, landscape, builder, & spiritual
- Custom lectures, workshops, and intensives: available upon request

## Feng Shui Consultations

Personalized Feng Shui site or phone consultations for residential, corporate, healthcare, retail, hospitality facilities, and developers. Consultations are available for all stages of Feng Shui design: pre-development and site consideration through existing structures.

## Feng Shui Interior Design

From pre-development, space planning, architectural detailing, finishes, furnishings, and accessories, Jami Lin and her staff of professional interior designers will co-create your complete Feng Shui environment. Residential, corporate, healthcare, retail, and hospitality facilities.

Professor Lin Yun,
the Grand Master of Black Sect Tantric Buddhism Fourth Stage,
writes the following Chinese proverb in cinnabar
while holding the blessing mudra.

With this blessing, the readers of Contemporary Earth Design
will receive increased wealth, wisdom, and prosperity,
while evil and sickness will be expelled.

"Whenever you open a book, you will receive benefits."

Master Lin Yun can be reached at The Yun Lin Temple
2959 Russell Street, Berkeley, CA 94705 USA T: 510-841-2347 F: 510-548-2621

# The Feng Shui Anthology
## Contemporary Earth Design

**Jami Lin**

Earth Design Incorporated, Literary Division
Miami, Florida

**The Feng Shui Anthology: Contemporary Earth Design**
Published by: Earth Design, Incorporated
Copyright ©1997 by Earth Design, Incorporated

00 99          4 5 6

**ISBN: 0-9643060-8-5**

Earth Design is registered in the U. S. Patent and Trademark Office

*For information:*
Earth Design, Incorporated, Literary Division
P.O. Box 530725
Miami Shores, Florida 33138
Tel:  (305) 756-6426
Fax:  (305) 751-9995
E-mail: earthdes@gate.net
Web: http:\\www.gate.net\~earthdes

Cover Design/Graphics:        Jami Lin, Paul Kane, Ardis Heiman
Editors:                      Jami Lin, Maggie Leyes, Rita Lewison-Singer

**Publisher's Cataloging-in-Publication**

Contemporary Earth Design: A Feng Shui Anthology / [compiled and
   edited by] Jami Lin.
        P. cm.
        Includes bibliographical reference and index.
        ISBN 0-9643060-8-5


        1. Feng-Shui. 2. Interior Decoration. 3. Spiritual Direction
   I. Lin, Jami.

BF1779.F4C66 1996                       133.3'33
                                        QBI96-40625

*I wish to honor my Feng Shui colleagues,
my friends,
whose individual support and love
have made this anthology possible.*

### A Special Thanks to My Family:  I Love You!

Joel Alan Levy

Ardis Heiman

### I couldn't have done it without you, thank you!

Master Lin Yun
Crystal Chu and the entire staff of the Lin Yun Temple

Maggie Leyes
Elizabeth Pierra-Quintana
Rita Lewison-Singer
Marilyn Camero

### Thanks for your help!

Mitzi and Eddy Levy, Art and Susan Rochlin, Ranzi Vallecorse,
Wilfredo Agurto, Lori Hodges, Lance Stelzer, Carlos Correa,
Rick Spisak, Alex Corgelas, James Allyn Moser, Bill Hall,
Bob Kirsh, and Ellen Whitehurst.

*You are the vessel in which
your essence is poured.*

*You choose
how it is to be filled.*

The original cover of **The Feng Shui Anthology** suggests that while seated in your sacred space, you have the ability to fill yourself with all the abundance and grace life has to offer: a secure sense of self and spirit, good health, a loving life partner, family and friends, recognition of your efforts, and the joy of being alive.

# How to Use the Anthology

Read the book cover to cover as a comprehensive book on Feng Shui, written by all the experts.

If you chose, select the articles of most interest first. As you read, there are footnotes that will lead you to related articles. Eventually, you will receive all the benefits from reading the entire anthology because, everything is a part of everything else, and all the articles are interwoven.

Footnotes have been added by individual authors in the standard text, or by Jami Lin, in the italicized text, to add further information, definition, or clarity.

# Contents

# Preface

A life-time ago, I was sitting in a comparative religion class and my mind started to drift. I thought, "One day, I would like to write a book that pulls spiritual concepts together."

Many teachers and classes later, I realized that spirit is of one essence, with many paths to get there. As an interior designer, I became intrigued with the path of Feng Shui. I resonated deeply with it, as it was the added dimension to my interior design work; it enhanced the body, the creativity of the mind and spirit, along with enhancing the environment. I also knew that Feng Shui was much more than the "Chinese art of placement;" it had global implications for spiritual renewal, and I called this universal concept, "Earth Design."

When I began writing my first book, Earth Design: The Added Dimension, I was reminded of my fleeting thoughts in that university course and realized that I had begun to fulfill my vision. I wrote about the universal and comparative nature of Earth Design and how universal geomancy and Feng Shui can be brought into everyone's lives, into their interiors - both their homes and their hearts.

With this anthology, I am continuing to live according to the destiny confirmed in my college daydream. I have chosen, or have been chosen, to bring together a collection of universal Feng Shui ideas from today's best practitioners. Through their individual consultation and design experience, these Feng Shui experts from around the world are giving you their best ideas and philosophies so you can move forward on your spiritual journey with greater peace and harmony. I am grateful to all these special people, these pioneers in Feng Shui, who have helped me to follow my dream for a more loving Earth. It is with great pleasure that I again share practical Feng Shui that you can apply to your home, office, and life. To begin the book, I will share my favorite Chinese proverb:

*If there is harmony in the house, there is peace in the nation.*
*If there is order in the nation, there will be peace in the world.*

Jami Lin

Since I am not Asian, I am often asked about my name and its spelling. Jami Lin is my first and middle name, spelled the exact karmic way my Mother gave it to me on the day I was born.

# Foreword
## Feng Shui Grand Master Lin Yun

In eager anticipation, <u>Contemporary Earth Design: A Feng Shui Anthology</u>, compiled and edited by Jami Lin, is finally being published! Not only is this book a masterpiece of the Feng Shui world, it is also a rainbow soaring across the publishing industry. The knowledge this book contains will help us attain wonderful, desirable, comfortable, and pleasurable living and working environments.

This book is also a collection of great writing by Feng Shui experts from around the world. Combining the ideology behind spirituality, aesthetics, fine arts, and religion, and using various aspects, perspectives, and themes, this book explains in everyday language the result of profound research. It lets us know that if we begin to understand and emphasize this ancient and matchless art of Feng Shui, our powers of creativity, analysis, judgement, and cognition will naturally be enhanced. This understanding will reinforce our mental and physical health, as well as elevate the interior and exterior spatial order in relation to creativity, design, and decoration. The *living conditions* where we reside and work will be well-adjusted.

Feng Shui has no nationality. Even though it originated in ancient Chinese culture, Feng Shui is no longer just an art of ancient Chinese architecture and placement. It has already established its place in the world and can be used by every ethnic group on Earth.

For this collection, in addition to the efforts of Jami Lin, whose distribution of good karma and kindness knows no bounds, more appreciation goes out to all of the contributing authors. With each author's fluent literary talent, superb wisdom, valuable experiences, and most of all, ardent and enthusiastic heart, we are able to share, through <u>Contemporary Earth Design</u>, the results of many years of studying Feng Shui.

This book guides the reader through eight main sections: Feng Shui Basics, Feng Shui Schools, Architecture and Landscape, Decorative Feng Shui, Feng Shui for the Healthy Body, Feng Shui for the Healthy Home, Feng Shui for the Spirit, and The Divine Plan. Described in great detail, are Feng Shui's wonder and function, design and effect, development and tolerance, in topics such as the Bagua, Chi, energy, portents, classical traditions, East-West ideologies, new cures, contemporary architectural design, landscape design, interior/exterior design, real estate values, using existing resources, first impressions, inspiring arrangements, personal relationships, and ancient Chinese wisdom.

To attain perfect health, in body, spirit, and at home, this book offers insights into life healing, physical health, the five elements, scents, energy fields, children, place of mind, Feng Shui traits in the Age of Aquarius, spiritual cultivation, color and chakra, and much more. Each topic is discussed from the basic level to the more advanced. Nothing is left out. Most notable is that the most difficult and most comprehensive theories of Feng Shui are explained, from the mundane to the transcendental, as well as from the psychological, physiological, and spiritual aspects.

From its contents, it is clear that Jami Lin, who excels in morals as well as academics, has gone through great difficulties in compiling this book, and we can now witness the splendid result of her accomplishment. There is a Chinese proverb that says, "Whenever you open a book, you will receive benefits." This perfectly describes the ultimate value of this book.

Lin Yun

November 1996


Translation by Mary R. Hsu

# Introduction

## Sarah Rossbach

In the past decade, Feng Shui, the ancient Chinese art of placement has made the journey from East to West and has entered not only the Western mind but also Western design, spirituality, and practices. <u>Contemporary Earth Design: A Feng Shui Anthology</u> presents the diversity of thought, approaches, and practices of Western Feng Shui.

This diversity appropriately reflects back to Feng Shui in ancient China. For in China, there existed a great range of not only Feng Shui schools but also Feng Shui expertise. These experts ranged from semi-literates and scholars to Buddhist and Taoist priests. They ran the gamut from wise man to charlatan. Their training ranged from the Nine Star School to the School of Forms to the Black Sect and others. Some used the "loupan," the Chinese cosmic compass, and astrology; others examined the forms of the earth, waterways, and vegetation, and others employed a mixture of practices plus intuition and common sense.

Today, Feng Shui has been adapted to the West and is used Western design, architecture, and life. Western Feng Shui includes many different approaches and varying levels of knowledge, creativity, perspective, spiritual depth, and expertise. In its journey through time and space, Feng Shui is ever-changing and evolving, but the goal remains the same: the creation of a positive and harmonious environment to enhance the lives and fortunes of its occupants.

Feng Shui incorporates so much that is human, bridging practical and mystical, spiritual and material, mundane and transcendental. This book marries these seemingly contrasting qualities, and so read each chapter with an open mind and heart.

As they say in France, "Vive la difference!" or in China: "Bu yi-yang, de shr-ching-Wan suai!"

# Contributing Authors

**Juan Alvarez** is a consulting engineer, licensed general contractor, mortgage/real estate broker, and well-known astronomer. He is Grand Councilor Emeritus of AMORC, one of the oldest philosophical fraternities in the world. A student of Professor Lin Yun, Juan has been lecturing, consulting, and conducting Feng Shui seminars in Spanish communities in the U.S., Panama, and Curaçao. Juan has published a book on Feng Shui in Spanish, *Feng Shui, Harmonia Del Vivir*, and can be reached at the Fairy's Ring Bookstore: 75 Merrick Way, Coral Gables, FL 33134, ph: 305-446-9315 or fax: 305-448-5956.

**Mary Buckley** is a musician, gardener, and mother of two daughters. She has studied Feng Shui with teachers of several traditions, including Professor Lin Yun. She is a Feng Shui consultant, associate producer for New Dimensions Radio, and the originator of "Chi Dancing," a form of improvisational Tai Chi. She has practiced various Eastern healing arts professionally since 1984 and has been an associate teacher with Paul Pitchford of the Heartwood Institute. Mary can be reached at PO Box 642, Ukiah, CA 95482-0642, ph: 707-462-5971, Email: mary_buckley@redwoodfn.org.

**Carol Bridges** is the author of *A Soul in Place, Reclaiming Home A Sacred Space*, (ISBN 00-945111-11-8, Earth Nation Publishing, PO Box 743, Nashville, IN 47448.) She teaches at the Nine Harmonies School of Feng Shui in Nashville, IN, a manifestation of her dream. She also does individual Feng Shui consultations and workshops throughout the U.S. Call Carol at 812-988-0873 to receive her current schedule or for books and information on the next Sacred Place Practitioner Training.

**Crystal Chu**, Chief Executive Officer of Yun Lin Temple, holds a Bachelor of Arts degree in Sociology and a Master degree in Business Administration. She has learned from and worked closely with Master Lin Yun for over fifteen years. Assisting Master Lin, Crystal has traveled extensively and has gained a wide range of exposure and varied experiences in Feng Shui which have enriched her teaching, writing, and practice of Feng Shui. She may be reached at the Yun Lin Temple 2959 Russell Street, Berkeley CA 94705, ph: 510-841-2347.

**Terah Kathryn Collins** is a nationally known consultant, speaker, and teacher of Feng Shui. She is author of *The Western Guide to Feng Shui* (Hay House Publishers, 1996), co-founder of the Western School of Feng Shui in Solana Beach, CA, and originator of Essential Feng Shui™ Practitioners training program. She has an extensive background in communications as a neurolinguistic programmer and in the field of holistic health as a polarity therapy teacher/practitioner. For information on consultations and training programs, contact Terah at 437 South Highway 101, Suite 752, Solana Beach, CA 92075, ph: 619-793-0945.

**Jeanne D'Brant, D.C., D.A.C.B.N.** is a holistic health practitioner, chiropractor, clinical nutritionist, and co-director of D'Brant Holistic Health Clinic. Jeanne has traveled to more than forty countries studying healing traditions, including Traditional Chinese Medicine, Ayurveda, and homeopathy. She has been featured on radio and television, has written for several Feng Shui publications, and is co-authoring *Woman's Wellness: A Guide for the New Millennium*, (fall, 1997.) Jeanne is available for consultations and workshops. She can be reached at 103 Fort Salonga Road, Northport, NY 11768, ph: 516-757-1324 or fax: 516-757-1368.

**Dennis Fairchild** is a leading Feng Shui instructor and the author of several books, including *Healing Homes: Feng Shui - Here & Now* (WaveField Books; PO Box 1781; Birmingham MI 48012-17819 ISBN: 0-9649981-0-6.) He can be reached at 1025 East Maple, Suite 105, Birmingham, MI 48009-6435.

**Andrew and Sally Fretwell** teach and consult on Feng Shui throughout the U.S. and Europe. Andy is a qualified continuing education teacher for interior designers and architects in Florida. He has studied with Master Mantak Chia for many years and is himself a teacher of the Taoist healing arts and Tai Chi. For details of courses or to schedule a consultation: 1329 Rugby Rd, Charlottesville, VA 22903, ph: 1-800-954-5602 or 804-970-1860, fax 804-970-1993, Email: andrew23.ix.netcom.com.

**Shera Gabriel** is a licensed, certified real estate appraiser, property rehabilitation consultant, and Feng Shui practitioner. She has studied Feng Shui with James Allyn Moser, Seann Xenja, and Professor Lin Yun. Shera does consultations for home buyers as well as for investors and residential property owners who are interested in using Feng Shui to rehabilitate distressed homes. For information on workshops and consultations, Shera can be reached at Box 89, Charlo, MT 59824, ph: 1-800-406-3930 or on her Internet web site, http://www.fengshuitoday.com.

**Lillian Lesefko Garnier** is an internationally recognized expert on five element Feng Shui and facial diagnosis. As a professor of Oriental medicine, she teaches/lectures at universities, business associations, and to the general public. She learned the ancient art of Feng Shui from her Chinese mother's family and has combined these teachings with her research and education in psychology, Traditional Chinese medicine, ergonomics, color, and symbolism. Lillian can be reached at The Lotus Center, 1100 S. Coast Highway, Suite 212, Laguna Beach, CA 92651, ph: 714-497-8729, fax: 714-376-2265.

**Hope Karan Gerecht** discovered Feng Shui toward the end of her studies in Interior Design and realized that it should be the basis of all design. She was the first interior designer to study BTB Feng Shui with Professor Lin Yun. He told Hope, "You will be creating homes which are not only beautiful, but that will heal as well." Her practice includes the Form and Compass schools of Feng Shui. Hope is the author of two books: *Harmonious Homes* and *Healing Design*. She can be reached at Feng Shui Interior Design, PO Box 196, Stevenson, MD 21153, ph: 410-486-6086.

**Johndennis Kaiten Govert, Roshi**, is a Soto Zen priest and founder/spiritual director of Daikakuji, Great Enlightenment Temple. He holds an MBA from Northwestern University in planning and organizational design and does consultations applying Zen insight, Feng Shui, and American management science for improving homes and businesses. He is author of *Feng Shui: the Art and Harmony of Place* and *Zen Feng Shui: Finding Place of Mind*. For books, training programs, seminars, and consultations: Daikakuji Publications, PO Box 44035, Phoenix, AZ 85064-4035, ph: 602-788-3398, fax: 602-788-8555.

**Helen and James Jay** are Feng Shui practitioners and offer training at their Feng Shui Designs Learning Center in Nevada City, California. They were featured in the critically acclaimed video production, *Feng Shui: The Chinese Art of Design and Placement*, produced by Mirror Images. They are currently working on their next video release. For information on their programs, or to order joss paper and other supplies, call 1-800-551-2482 or on the Internet at http://www.fengshuidesigns.com, Email: fengshui@oro.net.

**Linda M. Johnson, FSIC, FSIA, MSC** is the co-founder of Feng Shui International Concepts. Linda is internationally renown, has appeared on radio and television, and is a popular presenter at conferences and conventions. She is available for workshops, speaking engagements, and private consultations. Her clients have included multi-million dollar corporations, psychologists, retail business owners and advertising agencies. Linda can be reached at Feng Shui International Concepts, PO Box 94 Mariposa, CA 95338, ph: 209-966-4011 or Email: fngshui@sierratel.com.

**Mark Johnson** started his Compass School Feng Shui studies in 1970 in Pasadena, CA, with Professor Hua. He furthered his studies with a one-year sabbatical in Taiwan in 1974. He has taught Feng Shui seminars across the U.S. and has written several feature articles on the subject in prominent publications. He can be reached at 1-800-497-4244. Internet web site, www.chi-kung.com

**Katrine T. Karley** is a Feng Shui practitioner who has worked extensively in the holistic design of real estate, developing land in accordance to the principles of Feng Shui. Gifted with extrasensory perception, she uses Feng Shui as a focus for her talent of imparting beauty and harmony to all spaces. She continues to study with Professor Lin Yun and is at work on a multi-media project. For a consultation or a copy of her audiotape, *The Basics of Feng Shui*, please contact Katrine at PO Box 3934, Sarasota, FL 34230-3934, ph: 941-351-9150, fax 941-359-8344.

**David Daniel Kennedy** is a Feng Shui practitioner and teacher. He founded Feng Shui International, a professional consulting firm, and the Feng Shui Design Access Catalog. which offers designer quality Feng Shui items for home and business use. Through his consultations and seminars, David has assisted hundreds of home and business owners in dramatically improving their wealth, career, relationships, and personal energy. For information on consultations, seminars, and Feng Shui Design Access, contact Feng Shui International, 1563 Solano Avenue, Suite 127, Berkeley, CA 94707, ph: 1-800-962-4457.

**Kirsten Lagatree** has been a broadcast and print journalist for the past 15 years, but the article she wrote about Feng Shui for *The Los Angeles Times* changed her life. Not only did it begin her interest in Feng Shui, but it launched her career as the best selling author of *Feng Shui, Arranging Your Home to Change Your Life*. Kirsten has a Master of Arts degree in Humanities from The University of Chicago. She currently lives in Northern Virginia and can be reached at ph: 703-573-8789, Email: Klagatree@aol.com.

**Pamela Laurence** is a sculptor who works with wood, metal, and clay. She recently designed "Tantric Falls," an exclusive line of fountains. She is an active Feng Shui consultant in the New York area and is the director of the Metropolitan Institute of Interior Design, where she is offering the country's first licensed Feng Shui Certificate Program. For further information on Pamela's sculpture, Feng Shui products, classes and consultations call ph: 516-845-4033 or see our web site at www.met-design.com.

**Toni Lefler**, trained in BTB Feng Shui, founded Symmetry Designs in 1992. She provides Feng Shui consultations for relocations, renovations, and new buildings, custom placement design, move-in assistance, and real estate staging and evaluations for residential and commercial sites. Toni is a member of the Feng Shui Guild and Interior Arrangement & Design Assn. (IADA). She is available for seminars and lectures. *Staging Your Home to Sell*, a guide book to preparing homes for optimum sale, and other publications are available through: Symmetry Designs, 3582 Carlton Road, Lake Worth, FL, ph: 561-439-1231. Email: SYMMETRYDESIGN@Compuserve.com

**Melanie Lewandowski**, President of Phoenix Design Associates, is a lecturer, consultant, and Feng Shui expert in the tradition of BTB Feng Shui. A disciple and senior student of Master Thomas Lin Yun, Melanie has spent more than 25 years working with individuals and organizations in the area of personal effectiveness. Melanie has a B.S. in Computer Science and a M.S. in Management. Her work is dedicated to blending ancient and contemporary modalities for personal and social transformation. She can be reached at Phoenix Design Assn. PO Box 407, Bensalem, PA 19020, ph: 215-633-0589, fax: 215-633-0386.

**Maggie Leyes** is a professional writer and eternal student of such spiritual and healing arts as Feng Shui, acupuncture, numerology, astrology, vibrational medicine, oracle reading, and yoga. As an editor and contributor to *Contemporary Earth Design: A Feng Shui Anthology*, she would like to thank Jami Lin for sharing her vision, knowledge, and wisdom with her and the world. Maggie can be reached at PO Box 414192, Miami Beach, Fl 33141-9998, ph: 305-867-7943, Email: cheman@netrunner.net.
 -- Maggie, Thank you for everything, especially your friendship! xo, JL

**Jami Lin**, graduate of the University of Florida School of Architecture, and is an internationally renown lecturer and consultant on Feng Shui. Jami's first book, *Feng Shui Today: Earth Design the Added Dimension* forged new territory in the field of Feng Shui and was heralded as "a breakthrough; an absolute necessity to read." Her video *Feng Shui Today: Enrich Your Life by Design* is already recognized as, "the finest on the market." With over twenty years of experience as a professional interior designer, Jami has pioneered the transformation of Feng Shui by integrating practical interior decorating and self-development that brings EarthDesign™ home to the spirit. Watch for her new video, *The Essence of Feng Shui: Balance your Chakras, Home and Your Life with Aromatherapy*, along with her new *Feng Shui Essentials: Chakra/Bagua Essential Oil Blends*™. For information on consultations, workshops, lectures, continuing education classes (CEU's) for interior designers and architects, and book/video orders, visit her web site: http://www.netrunner.net/~earthdes or contact Earth Design, PO Box 530725, Miami Shores, FL 33153, ph: 305-756-6426 fax: 305- 751-9995. For Jami's favorite Feng Shui/Earth Design tips, send a first class stamp and mailing label to the above address.

**Grand Master Lin Yun** (Professor Thomas Lin Yun), spiritual leader of the fourth stage of Tantric Buddhism, Black Sect, is regarded as one of the most renowned Chinese philosophers today and the foremost authority on Feng Shui. After years of study and meditation, he has attained a profound level of spiritual ability. Through this ability, Master Lin has helped numerous people by means of transcendental cures, making him an especially sought after advisor, spiritual teacher, and Feng Shui expert world-wide. He has lectured at the invitation of many academic institutions, religious organizations, and other groups. He currently holds the position of adjunct Professor at San Diego State University and leads workshops in the San Francisco Bay Area and other major cities. For more information, please call the Yun Lin Temple at 510-841-2347.

**Bob Longacre** is an educator, carpenter, color therapist, and professional Feng Shui practitioner. Bob has traveled to over 35 countries helping to heal and synchronize sacred places. He has designed, built, and retrofitted many structures. Bob studied Western sacred design methods at the Findhorn Foundation, Feng Shui with Professor Lin Yun, and color therapy with Gimbel, Brayere and Hitchens. He is co-publisher of *Sweet Fern magazine* (RRI Box 566, Walpole, NH 03608, $14 year), a wholeness/wellness quarterly, with a major column on Feng Shui/sacred architecture. He can be contacted at 603-756-4152, Email: sweetfern@top.monadinet, website: www.echoroom.com/home/sweetfern

**Ho Lynn** (Lynn Ho Tu) is a disciple and senior student of Master Lin Yun. She has been teaching Lin Yun studies and conducting weekly Black Sect Tantric Buddhist School meditation sessions at the Yun Shui Jing Center since 1989. She was founder and editor-in-chief of the *Yun Lin Temple News*, a quarterly publication in English devoted to Black Sect Tantric Buddhist activities and Master Lin's teachings, and currently writes the Q&A section. Ho is the Chairperson and CEO of the World Lin Yun Educational Foundation and travels extensively giving speeches on Lin Yun studies. She may be reached at the Yun Lin Temple: 510-841-2347, Yun Shi Jing She Center: 415-341-3544, or at the Foundation: 415-794-3149.

**A. T. Mann** has written fourteen books (translated into twelve languages), including *Sacred Architecture* and *Sacred Sexuality*. Tad has taught at the Manchester Metropolitan University Department of Architecture and the Danish Design School and participated in major info-eco design conferences in Europe. He lives and works in Copenhagen, Denmark with his wife Lise-Lotte. He is an astrologer, architect, graphic designer, author, and illustrator. He is currently writing **The Sacred Garden** and a first novel about an esoteric detective. Tad can be reached at: Tel/Fax: +45 3157 3788, Email: atmann@dk-online.dk.

**Kathy Mann** is a Feng Shui consultant trained in the school of Black Hat Sect Tibetan Buddhism. She is a Master Reiki healer and has pursued a metaphysical transformative path for the last eleven years. Kathy is a member of the Feng Shui Guild and the Feng Shui Professional Society of Florida. A New Jersey native, she has practiced Feng Shui across the country and is available for consultations on site or by mail and fax. For information on consultations, lectures, workshops, and seminars, she can be reached in Tampa, FL at ph: 813-831-0263, fax: 813-837-5214, Email: kmanfeng@gte.net.

**Cynthia Murray** has a strong background in communications, Feng Shui, 9 Star Ki, and macrobiotic theory. Her approach to Feng Shui includes a full-spectrum approach to living well in the Aquarian Age. She was a presenter at the First International Feng Shui Conference and has contributed to the *Feng Shui Journal*. Cynthia does consultations and conducts classes and workshops in Colorado and New Mexico. She currently lives in Boulder, CO, and can be reached at ph: 303-543-2230.

**Elaine Paris** is a Feng Shui consultant, Reiki Master, and Master Dowser. Elaine teaches dowsing and has traveled extensively using it as a tool for awakening communication with the higher self and for locating water and noxious energy lines. Elaine has also studied sacred geometry, aromatherapy, and sound therapy, incorporating them into her Feng Shui work. Elaine studies with Professor Lin Yun and is one of his disciples. She can be reached at Feng Shui, Etc., 200 South winds Rd, Farmington, AR 72730, ph: 1-800-606-5029 or 501-267-4809, fax: 501-267-4802.

**Richard L. Phillips**, B.S.C.E., M.B.A., is a designer specializing in the effects that color, lighting, and space have on behavior. For over a decade, he has done consultations with homeowners and businesses to improve their health and bottom line through good design. His designs, renovations, and articles have been published in regional and national publications. Richard does consultations with individuals, companies, and other designers nationwide; he can be contacted at ph: 918-744-1916, fax: 918-744-1948, Email rlpdesign@aol.com.

**Hank Reisen** is a Feng Shui consultant and architect with a master's degree from MIT. Who has studied traditional schools of Chinese and Japanese Feng Shui since 1979, most recently with Wang Yu Te in China. He is also a senior student of Professor Lin Yun since 1987. Many of his architectural designs incorporate the principles of Feng Shui, and has lectured and consulted on numerous projects throughout the U.S., Canada, and Japan. Hank can be reached at his offices in Cambridge, Massachusetts at ph: 617-661-3181.

**Sarah Rossbach** is the author of *Feng Shui: The Chinese Art of Placement, Interior Design with Feng Shui*, and is co-author with Master Lin Yun of *Living Color: Master Lin Yun's Guide to Feng Shui and the Art of Color*. She has studied with Master Lin Yun since 1977 and has written a new book to be released in fall, 1997. She graduated from Barnard College and Columbia University Graduate School of Journalism. Sarah lives in the New York area where her bed and desk are in lucky positions.

**Susan H. Ruzickza, Ed.D.**, an ordained minister, has been practicing Feng Shui full-time for over four years. She is a disciple of Professor Lin Yun. Prior to her work in Feng Shui, Susan was a bioaucoustic therapist, conducting research on the effects of music, sound, and electromagnetic fields on the frequencies of the human body. She also worked with special children for over 20 years as a recreation therapist and special educator. She can be reached at Feng Shui, Etc., 200 South winds Rd, Farmington, AR 72730,
ph: 1-800-606-5029 or 501-267-4809, fax: 501-267-4802.

**Nancy SantoPietro** is a full time Feng Shui specialist and teacher. She has studied BTB Feng Shui with Professor Lin Yun. Nancy is Chairperson of the Feng Shui Studies Dept. of the Metropolitan Institute of Interior Design, in Plainview, NY. Her company, Nancy SantoPietro & Associates, with offices in Brooklyn and Hunting, NY, and Seattle, WA, provides consultation and educational services for homes and businesses throughout the country. Nancy authored *Feng Shui: Harmony by Design*. For information, ph: 718-256-2640, WA at 206-784-9840, or her free catalog of Feng Shui products call 718-256-8773.

**Shelley Sparks** has been a Feng Shui practitioner for more than three years. She uses Feng Shui to extend harmony, healing, and beneficial qualities to the gardens she creates as a landscape architect for residential and commercial clients. She is available for workshops, lectures, and private consultations. Shelley can be reached at Harmony Gardens, 12224 Addison Street, Valley Village, CA 91607, ph: 818-505-9783.

**William Spear** is an internationally recognized educator, consultant, and writer on Feng Shui, including his book, *Feng Shui Made Easy,* the I Ching, oriental philosophy, and macrobiotic medicine. He has appeared on radio and television and has spoken at such venues as the United Nations and The National Academy of Sciences in St. Petersburg, Russia. He conducts a five-day intensive workshop: The Passage: life's transformational journey. William has a Feng Shui practice in NY, CT, and London and can be reached at 24 Village Green Dr., Litchfield, CT 06759, ph: 860-567-8801, fax: 860-567-3304 Email: fengshuime@aol.com. Web: http://members.aol.com/fengshuime/wmhtml.

**Angel Thompson** is a well-known astrologer and Feng Shui practitioner. Her approach to Feng Shui combines the location techniques of astrology with the solutions and cures of the East to create a system that exemplifies the power of placement. For more information on her lectures, seminars, audio tapes, and book: *Feng Shui, How to Achieve the Most Harmonious Arrangement of Your Home and Office* (St. Martin's Press, 1996) Angel can be contacted at 1809 Washington Way, Venice, CA 90291, ph: 310-821-2527, fax: 310-822-9846, Email: Feng ShuiLA@aol.com.

**Pamela Tollefson** is the president of Feng Shui Design and is a Feng Shui pioneer in the Midwest. Her background is in interior design, and she is also trained in metaphysics, astrology, and energy work. As a senior student of Professor Lin Yun, she works according to BTB Feng Shui. Since 1992, she has been consulting, lecturing, and teaching Feng Shui in the U.S. and abroad. Pamela can be reached at 129 W Brown Deer Rd, Bayside, WI 53217, ph: 312-527-9919 or ph: 414-228-9877,
fax: 414-228-9876, Email: fengshui@execpc.com or Pamela@fengshui-design.
Web site: www.fengshui-design.com

**Derek Walters** has followed a varied career path as science teacher, classical musician, and author. He is an internationally recognized pioneer and authority on Chinese astrology and Feng Shui. He lives in Manchester, England, but spends much of his time outside the country leading seminars and giving consultations. He can be contacted at 23 Polefield Road, Black Ley, Manchester, M9 6FN; ph/fax: 44-161-740-1926.

**Angi Ma Wong** is an intercultural consultant, corporate trainer, Feng Shui teacher, and practitioner. She is the award-winning author of *TARGET: The U.S. Asian Market, A Practical Guide to Doing Business, The Practical Feng Shui Chart Kit,* and *The Wind/Water Wheel: A Feng Shui Tool for Transforming Your Life*. She has been featured on radio and television, including the Oprah Winfrey Show, and in publications: *The New York Times, Los Angeles Times, Chicago Tribune*, among others. She can be reached at Pacific Heritage Books, PO Box 3967-JL, Palos Verdes, CA 90274, ph: 310-541-8818, fax: 310-541-7178, Email: amawong@worldnet.att.net, Internet web site: www.wind-water.com.

**Seann Xenja** is a Feng Shui practitioner providing site analyses internationally. A construction and design professional, his work has been featured on CNN, in the *New Age Journal, The San Francisco Chronicle*, among others. He is the author of two best-selling videos: *Feng Shui: The Ancient Chinese Art of Placement*, and *Advanced Feng Shui Techniques for Your Home or Office.* He offers an advanced, five-day intensive course: Feng Shui Techniques for Practitioners. Seann can be reached at PO Box 3508, Yountville, CA 94599-3508, ph: 707-255-6306, fax: 707-226-2248,
Email: SGXenja@aol.com.

**Kathy Zimmerman**'s interest in Feng Shui began during her travels in Asia, and she went on to become an advanced graduate of the American Feng Shui Institute. She lectures on Feng Shui and was a featured speaker at the First International Feng Shui Conference in April, 1996. Kathy is available for lectures and consultations on all stages of property development as well with existing businesses and homes. She can be reached at P.O. Box 39713, Los Angeles, CA 90039-0713, ph: 213-661-1435,
fax: 213-666-2302

Black Hat Sect Tibetan Tantric Buddhist Feng Shui has been abbreviated as BTB Feng Shui.(Please turn to next page for additional information.)

Graphics have been supplied by individual authors unless otherwise noted at the end of article or in a footnote. *Public Domain* art has been supplied by Dover Publications.

# Black Sect Tantric Buddhism

*Crystal Chu, assistant to Feng Shui Grand Master Lin Yun, provides clarity to the terms, Black Hat, Black Sect, Black Hat Sect, and Black Sect Tantric Buddhism.*

The historical development of Black Sect Tantric Buddhism can be seen as a succession of four stages, according to Professor Thomas Lin-Yun, leader of the religion at its present fourth stage.

Black Sect Tantric Buddhism originated from the indigenous Bon religion of Tibet before the introduction of Buddhism. The primitive first stage emerged into its second phase through exposure to the Tibetan Tantric Buddhism and spread to China. In the process, the Black Sect, already a mixture of religions, continued to encompass traditional Chinese philosophies and folklore, such as Confucianism, Taoism, Yin-Yang philosophy, Eclecticism, I-Ching, Feng Shui, holistic healing, and Exoteric Buddhism.

The fourth stage of the religion, Black Sect Tantric Buddhism, was introduced to the West, and was reinterpreted in terms of modern knowledge, such as philosophy, medicine, psychology, architecture, ecology, and social sciences. The Lin Yun Temple was founded in 1986, in Berkeley, California, as the first temple of the fourth stage of Black Sect Tantric Buddhism. It encourages people to actively participate in society through their own professions, rather than advocate the rigors of a secluded monastic life.

The concept of a "colored hat" emerged as follows.

As the Black Sect Tantric Buddhism developed into the third and forth stages, it also acquired the title Black Hat. In Black Sect Tantric Buddhism, the level of the spiritual power is divided into six levels according to the Six Syllable Mantra -- Om Ma Ni Pad Me Hum. These six levels are represented by six different colors. By the same token, Black Sect Tantric Buddhism has a unique Six Section Chi Cultivation Exercise. This special meditation exercise is also divided into six levels. The color representation from the lowest to the highest level is white, red, yellow, green, blue, and black respectively. Thus, the "hat" colors can also be differentiated by these six levels, with the Black Hat having the highest status as well as spiritual power.

Some people may confuse the "Black Hat" designation of the spiritual order Kagyu (also known as the White Sect Tantric Buddhism) with that of Black Sect Tantric Buddhism but it is not the same. "Black Hat" may be used by many spiritual traditions in the same way that "captain" may be used for as a chief airplane pilot, U.S. Navy officer, or the head waiter in a restaurant; they need not refer to the same designation.

Although Professor Lin Yun prefers the term Black Sect instead of Black Hat Sect to avoid confusion with any other tradition or definition, it does not imply that Black Hat Sect is an incorrect term for Black Sect Tantric Buddhism.

# Feng Shui Basics

# Earth Design: The Roots of Our Nature

## Jami Lin

With so much media attention, you have probably heard of Feng Shui. It is also likely that this Chinese concept is as hard for you to grasp as it is to pronounce. Earth Design incorporates the principles of Feng Shui, natural laws, and mythology to create greater health, wealth and happiness.

**You can use Earth Design as a method to align your environment with the natural laws so you can benefit from their perfection.**

For as long as he has needed shelter, man has been affected by his space. Ancient man was sensitive to his surroundings and his connection to the earth.

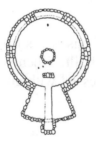

**Native American Kiva**

**The Roman Pantheon**

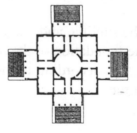

**Villa Capra Palladio**

Using the same natural instincts as his animal brothers, he intuitively understood the lay of the land. He could feel when a space was magnetically hot and over-stimulating to the body and the senses or when a site was so special that it was honored and shared with all clan members for ceremony or hunt. Observing nature and using her secrets for personal enrichment has been used by man since the beginning of time. This practice has reached modern day through mythology.

## Mythology and Earth Design

Mythology is the intuitive explanation of the workings of nature and her cycles. History has proven that when these cycles are represented in the design of buildings and their interiors, abundance and well-being are enhanced. Ancient Earth Designers across the globe constructed sacred structures in auspicious locations to honor their spiritual expression as well as their cultural mythology.

The Egyptian pyramids were constructed to house the spirit of Osiris for all eternity, and Greek temples were the gods' earthly homes when they ventured from Mount Olympus. When the gods were pleased, visionaries advised that man would be blessed with good fortune.

The sublime and enduring beauty of these sacred buildings arises from the foundation of the natural laws on which they were built. When you design according to the same laws, you too will be blessed with good fortune.

### The Cycle of Personal Mythology

*The Force* has been defined and explored at great length in Hollywood's science-fiction mythology, "Star Wars." The force or Chi (the Chinese word for energy) is the momentum of life. Scientifically, energy is the attraction of molecular structure; it is the glue that holds the cycles of nature together. Like the blood that circulates and nourishes your body, Chi is the life force that circulates through everything, natural and man-made, including your home and office.

You are part of nature's wholeness. The same energy that holds the earth's cycles together also holds your personal energetic cycle together.

 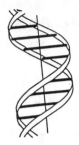 

Water is a beautiful example of an earth cycle: water falls to earth through precipitation; it is absorbed by the earth, plants, and animals; it evaporates into the air and continues to cycle because of the earth's force.

The mind-body-spirit triad, physically represented by the pyramid, is your personal energetic cycle. This cycle is what gives you your humanness and reason for being. Each element in the pyramid supports and nourishes the others.

A focused mind directs the body to do remarkable tasks, and the body increases in strength. A strong body supports the mind and spirit. The mind grows in confidence, and humankind reaches for higher goals. An open mind has the ability to receive expanded knowledge, which cultivates growth of the spirit. Through spiritual awareness, mental and physical sensibilities become more finely developed.

**Intuition is the added dimension that exponentially evolves the personal triad.**

Earth Design is a tool to help you unite the three dimensions of the triad. It grounds you in your surroundings and increases your sensitivity to how space affects you. You can then intuitively make energetic adjustments in your environment to create balance and harmony of mind, body, and spirit.

Earth Design teaches you to use nature's perfect cycles as a model for your own energetic cycle. As you refine your cycle, you begin creating a personal mythology in your own sacred space, your home. You become the protagonist, creating and living your own mythology.

**Earth Design is a tool for planning your environment to evolve your personal mythology: your own success stories.**[1]

There are issues throughout your life that define your myth. Marriage, career, childbirth, and the death of a loved one can all be vehicles of transformation.[2] A clear example in today's society of how personal myth, cycles, and Earth Design are played out is the American woman reaching mid-life changes.

I had three women clients who had all reached an archetypal rite of passage, a mid-life cross-roads. One cycle of their lives had ended, and they were all looking to make changes to continue on their life path.

> *The first had put her career on hold to raise her children and was now ready to get back to the work she loved. Forty and divorced, the second woman had a solid and successful business but was looking for a fulfilling life partner. The last had given herself away as a caretaker to her husband and mother to her children. At fifty-five, her children had families of their own, and her husband had left her for a younger woman. She was alone, without a sense of identity.*

Through Earth Design, I was able to help each of them identify blockages in their sacred spaces, their homes, and to suggest adjustments for making the necessary energetic shifts. By implementing Earth Design solutions in their lives, they were able to take control of their situations. They realized that they were the hero of their own lives and myths!

---

[1] I would be honored to think that Joseph Campbell, who spent his life defining universal myth, would wholly agree.

[2] The Bagua uses eight of these life defining areas. *Please refer to "The Bagua,"* p 35.

At whatever stage you find yourself, you too can use your personal energetic cycle and Earth Design to make the energetic shift. It is time to evolve and take control of your own destiny. Spirit tells you that guidance and strength come from beyond yourself; as the hero, you have what it takes to transcend all odds. Most myths end with a variation of "...and the world was peaceful again." or "...and they lived happily ever after." Earth Design solutions can help bring that balance into your life.

Like an archetypal "Star Wars" hero, man and mythology continue to evolve, like the ever-expanding sacred geometry of the pi spiral.

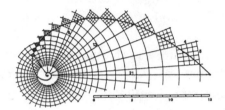

## Nature as the Supreme Model

Throughout history, Earth Design has been the physical manifestation of man's spiritual evolution. With intuitive observation and spiritual awareness, Plato and Pythagoras validated Earth Design through mathematics and science. More recent Earth Designers also applied their intuition to interpreting nature's laws. Frank Lloyd Wright explored the cantilever by imitating how a tree branch extended off its deeply rooted trunk.

Buckminster Fuller designed the Geodesic Dome according to the magnetic grid lines[3] of the earth and The Platonic Solids.

---

[3] *Please refer to "Energy Systems and Feng Shui," p. 275, and* <u>Earth Design: The Added Dimension</u>, *Chapter 3.*

You do not have to be a masterful designer to start developing your own intuitive sensitivity.

> *One day, I was hiking in the Canadian Rockies, and I gradually came to recognize that Johnson Canyon was constructed by fire (igneous) and earth (rock), magnificently chiseled by water (glacial runoff) and air (winds). Because I had a working knowledge of Feng Shui, I realized that if the natural five elements[4] had the power to create such wonder, it would be easy to understand how using representations of the five elements in our homes and offices could make a significant impact on our lives.*

Use nature's perfection as a model; she is rich and abundant. As part of the natural order, you are also perfect and have the opportunity, when you combine it with motivation and hard work, to grow in wealth. By wealth, I am referring to the humanness of being, which *is* the joy of life: rich in respect, love, and health, ready to give to each other and back to the earth.

The spiritual aspect of Earth Design is the most exciting part. The more your physical environment provides a conscious or unconscious base of comfort and beauty for your body, the more your mind and spirit are free to reach great heights.

The physical manifestation of this concept is beautifully represented by the entrance to the Louvre Museum. It masterfully expresses global spiritual evolution and is displayed for the whole world to experience.

The entryway, which is the most important part of any space,[5] is a large crystal pyramid. When you look at this sacred shape,[6] you are reminded of all the pyramids throughout time. How is this sacred pyramid any

---

[4]   *Please refer to the "Five Phases of Energy," p. 81, and Earth Design: The Added Dimension.*

[5]   *Please refer to "Utilize all Your Resources," p.189 and "The Room of First Impression," p.207.*

[6]   Please see Earth Design: The Added Dimension for information on sacred structures based on Pythagorean Mathematics and Plato's Solids. *Please refer to editor's note in "The Five Phases of Energy," p. 81.*

different from those of the Egyptians and the Mayans, or of the steeple of a church or mosque?

They are all physical representation of man's quest for ascension.

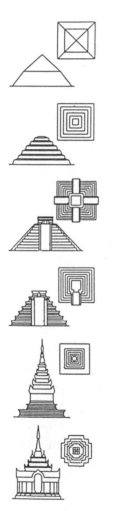

Mr. I. M. Pei, who designed this recent addition to the Louvre, used today's technology and building materials to design a pyramid of light. What does that concept mean to you?

Standing under the street level, in the belly of the pyramid, you can look up through the glass at three different building facades. The spirit of today's architectural contribution serves to connect the buildings that were constructed over the centuries. Each has a unique facade, reflecting the architectural style of the period it was constructed. In the womb, you can look up at design history.

**Through the light, you experience evolution through Earth Design.**

*I experienced pure magic when I entered this light pyramid. I descended from street level on a beautiful spiral staircase. All of a sudden, through the middle of this spiral, a stainless-steel cylinder started to rise from its base; I realized this was the elevator. When fully extended, I saw the double helix of DNA, and the universal mathematic proportion of pi.* **Evolution**.

Like traditional pyramids, there are underground passages that connect the pyramid to the various wings of the museum. One passage terminates at the subway. At the entry to the terminal, there is a marble pyramid four feet square at the base. Right above its apex is an inverted glass pyramid of the same proportion: apex to apex. Above the double pyramid, as part of the building structure, is one of the three pyramid-shaped sky lights that surround the larger main entry pyramid. (Aren't there also three smaller pyramids at Giza?)

Here I was greeted (at a subway entrance no less!) by the hermetic wisdom: "As above; So below." Through the funnel of the glass pyramid, light fills the solid and stable earth plane for universal balance. Where the pyramids merge, looking almost as if they had been computer generated, a three-dimensional Star of David is created connecting heaven and earth.

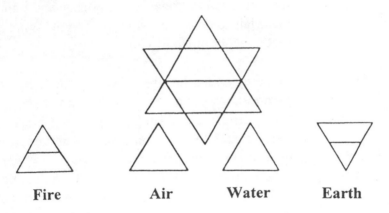

**Fire          Air          Water          Earth**

### All roads lead to Paris

In Paris, there are no straight streets, except for the Champs Elysées. This magnificent street connects such spiritual structures as The Louvre Museum, the Egyptian Obelisk, and the Arch de Triumph.[7] It terminates with the modern sacred structure, La Grande Arche, located in the La Defense section. With only *one* straight street and so many important monuments on it, could it be that the Parisian Earth Designers intuitively knew how to lay out the city to connect this important street to a ley line and the earth's energy?[8]

---

[7]     For me, the Champs Elysées and its monuments are energetically sacred. It is your own experience in a space or structure that determines whether you can personally classify it as having a sacred quality.

[8]     As ley lines are part of the earth's energetic body, "proof" that the Champs Elysées was originally built on a ley line is difficult to come by, but intuitively it seems right. *Please refer to "Energy Systems and Feng Shui," p.275.*

*I wanted to get close to La Grande Arche, not only because it is architecturally interesting, or because it has a geodesic type structure, but because it intuitively called to me. Not taking my intuition lightly, I knew it was time to be lead on a journey.*

*Ascending in the exterior glass elevator, I went up to the rooftop observation deck. As I walked out, a roof-sized astrological chart greeted me. It was cloudy that day, but it seemed to me like a gigantic sun-dial. I suspect when there are shadows, they indicate where the sun is positioned in the heavens, and if the date were April 20, the Spring equinox, shadows would indicate the sun entering Aries.*

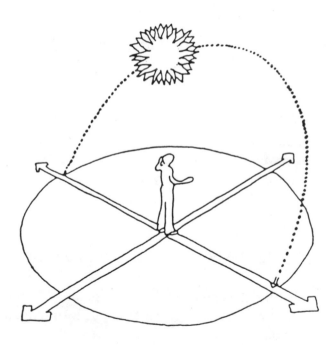

**Sacred Modern Architecture Is Alive!**
**Man Is an Integral Part of the Heavens! And of the Universe!**

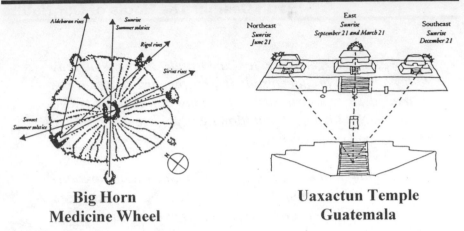

**Big Horn
Medicine Wheel**

**Uaxactun Temple
Guatemala**

The architect had used the heavens[9] as a design tool, just as ancient Egyptian, Greek, Mayan, Aztec, and other cross-cultural Earth Designers have done since man began constructing buildings.

## From Stone Age to New Age, Earth Design is about vision.

As you begin to use Earth Design and develop sensitivity to the principles of nature, you *light*-en up. You are gentler with yourself and the people around you. You become more at ease with life. Your new perceptions enable you to make better decisions. People enter your life with a willingness to support your goals, knowing that in turn you will help them reach theirs. You work smarter, not harder, leaving more time for the other joys of life.

## Now, isn't Earth Design easier to grasp and pronounce?

When life is full, all riches come with greater grace. When you are rich in your complete humanness, you set an example, inspiring others to live to their full and balanced potential.

---

9      Astrology refers to planetary magnetics, time, which is based upon the heavenly cycles, and its relationship to human evolution. It is for this reason I included personal astrology as part of decorating your home and office in Earth Design: The Added Dimension. I have also included several astrologically-oriented Feng Shui articles in this anthology.

# The Bagua
## Master Lin Yun's Innovative Approach to Feng Shui

## Ho Lynn

Feng Shui, the ancient Chinese art of placement, was a foreign concept to the Western mind just ten years ago. Grand Master Lin Yun,[1] considered by many as the foremost Feng Shui master of our time, was instrumental in introducing the concept throughout the world. As the spiritual leader of the reformed, contemporary Tantric Buddhist Black Sect, he has founded a new, highly accessible school of Feng Shui. This Tantric Buddhist School combines traditional concepts, contemporary thought, and philosophy into its Dharma[2] practices. At the heart of his teachings is Master Lin's revolutionary concept of the Bagua, a fundamental energetic tool of Feng Shui.

To understand the basis of Tantric Buddhist Black Sect Feng Shui and Master Lin's revolutionary Bagua, it is vital to look at some basic philosophical concepts:

---

[1] Master Lin Yun is a distinguished scholar and teacher with over forty years of work and research in Feng Shui. In 1986, he founded Yun Lin Temple, the first temple of the current Tantric Buddhism, Black Sect, in Berkeley, California. He teaches and lectures extensively in the United States, Europe, and Asia. Please refer to the end of the article for a complete biography on Master Lin Yun.

[2] *Dharma on one level means the Sacred Law, the Buddhist Cannon; it also means that man's internal nature is a model for his external life, which is expressed in thoughts, words, and actions.*

## Yin/Yang and Tai Chi

### Evolution of the Universe
### The Tai Chi Symbol

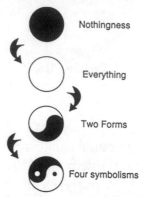

The image of the Tai Chi symbol is the entire universe and all phenomena depicted by two inseparable elements: the yin and the yang. Yin symbolizes nothingness and stillness and yang symbolizes everything, substance, and dynamic force.

Yin and yang are inseparable elements; within yin there is yang and within yang there is yin. Master Lin illustrates this point by using the example of a child observing the sky. If a child merely scans the sky, he says there is nothing to see. If he is given a powerful telescope with which to view the heavens, he marvels at the wonders in the sky because there is so much to see. Therefore the sky is both nothing - yin and everything - yang. All things follow this same principle.

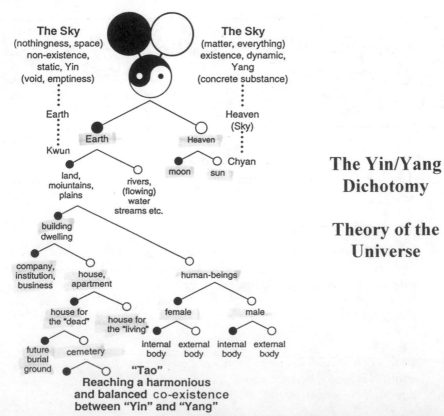

### The Yin/Yang Dichotomy

### Theory of the Universe

In Chinese, the character Tao means *the way, the path* that leads you from the start to an end without obstruction.

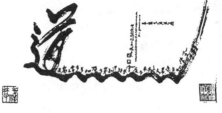

Professor Lin Yun's
Calligraphy of Tao

Yin

Yang

The two elements form into one entity

in ceaseless formation, continuously evolving

Following the law of "nature"

According to Professor Lin, the two strokes on top represent the yin and yang elements in life; the horizontal line beneath the two strokes means the two elements united into one entity; the character under the horizontal line is the law of nature, and symbolizes a forever movement.

Following the concept of the Tai Chi symbol of a Bagua, where yin and yang are viewed as one entity and co-exist in balanced harmony, Master Lin theorized that, like the character Tao, only when the yin and the yang reach a state of balanced co-existence can everything in life and all universal phenomena move on in ceaseless formation, peace, and harmony.  From this view, he developed three theories of how this balance can be applied to various aspects of our lives.

**Tao of Marriage**

Master Lin says it takes a woman (yin) and a man (yang) to form a family. Following this law of nature, when the two can cohabit in balance, their union will continue in eternal harmony.

## Tao of Heaven and Earth

Each day is formed by the constant cycle between the sun (yang) and the moon (yin), which follows the laws of nature and allows the universe we live in to continue into eternal existence.

## Tao of Life

In life, good luck (yang) and bad luck (yin) are interwoven throughout a lifetime, which creates an up and down, *roller coaster* life path. This universal law of nature produces an eventful life.

Based on these theories of Tao, Master Lin brings an important influence to our lives. He has put the yin/yang concept of the Bagua into practical application, including his many innovative thoughts on Feng Shui. According to Master Lin, Feng Shui can be viewed as a field of study that brings harmonious relationships between man (yang) and the dwellings (yin) he lives or works in; it is a discipline of finding the Tao between man and his environment.

## I Ching

The I Ching[3] (Book of Changes), is a book of ancient wisdom and philosophy written about 3000 years ago in China. It is based on the symbolism of eight basic trigrams.

The trigrams are composed of a series of three lines, either yin (dark, passive, female principle) or yang (light, active, male principle).

---

[3]  The I Ching is attributed to sage-kings Fu-Hsi, the creator of Bagua (the Eight-Trigrams), King Wen, Duke Chou, and Confucius.

These eight trigrams are seen as primordial symbols by which all phenomena and life can be understood. They were originally associated with eight archetypal natural phenomena: heaven, earth, water, fire, lake, mountain, thunder and wind.

Over time, these trigrams have taken on additional symbolism, corresponding to directions, seasons, life areas, and the body. These trigrams are then combined in pairs to make a hexagram. There are a total of 64 possible combinations or mutations that represent all situations, both human and cosmic. They are the moving, changing permutations of the basic eight trigrams. They illustrate the flow, the yielding and the active cycles of change and transformation that all life experiences on this plane.

| **Chyan** | **Kan** | **Gen** | **Jen** |
| *Heaven* | *Water* | *Mountain* | *Thunder* |

| **Syun** | **Li** | **Kwun** | **Dwei** |
| *Wind* | *Fire* | *Earth* | *Lake* |

Scholars have studied the I Ching from a variety of perspectives. Some focus on its academic merit, studying its writing style, philosophical implications, and literary value, while others have become experts in textual and syntactic analysis. There are many editions of the I Ching, and consequently, the authenticity of a particular book, chapter, sentence, and word becomes an important issue for scholars to explore.

Historically, no punctuation marks were used in Chinese texts, and as a result, interpretations of a text or paragraph could differ greatly from one individual to another. Master Lin has a wonderful story to illustrate this point. King Wen used four words with no punctuation to describe the first hexagram Chyan of the I Ching. The words in Chinese read 元亨利貞. If a punctuation mark is placed after each character, it illustrates 元 (a beginning), 亨 (smooth development), 利 (prosperous), and 貞

(persisting.) Together the phrase means *taking off smoothly and prospering persistently*, a very good reading indeed. However, if it is punctuated after the first and third, it becomes 元 (Yuan Dynasty),亨利(Henry the man), 貞 (chaste). As Master Lin would playfully suggest, this oracle would be translated literally as, *In the Yuan Dynasty, there was a man named Henry who was a very chaste person*. This example certainly underlines the importance of syntax.

Master Lin wished to remove the common perception that the I Ching was too difficult to comprehend by anyone but scholars. He has analyzed the various meanings of the title, and added his own interpretation.[4] He explains that the character "I" of I Ching, by itself means *changes*, but it can be further understood as: *changeable* (always changing), *simple changes*, and *unchangeable* (never changing).

Illustrating his views about the *changeable* aspect of "I," Master Lin explains that a life consists of a beginning, a process, and an end. A baby does not stay young forever; he grows taller, becomes wiser, and he continues to change until he grows old and weak and his life ends. Nature also mirrors this process; a flower will bud, blossom, and finally wilt and die. This *changeable* aspect of "I" means that nothing on earth stays constant, that everything goes through changes. At the same time, all phenomena go through this same process of change regardless of time and place; this is the *unchangeable* meaning of "I." Therefore, where there is *changeable,* there is also *unchangeable.* In addition, the *changeable* and *unchangeable* parts contain a simple pattern of: a beginning, a process, and an end; this is the third meaning of "I" or *simple changes.*

Master Lin gives "I" a fourth interpretation, *easy*: the character for easy consists of the same character as "I." Synchronistically, this fits with Master Lin's approach to both the I Ching and Feng Shui. He encourages a practical approach, which combines academic interest with transcendental application.

---

4     Master Lin describes the book's title as consisting of two characters: the top is the character for *sun*, and the bottom *moon*, which essentially makes it the study of yin and yang.

## The Bagua

The eight trigrams of the <u>I Ching</u> are also used in a mystical octagon or Bagua. The eight principle trigrams that make up the Bagua can be further understood as *changeable* and *unchangeable*. There are four unchangeable trigrams or yin Guas. They do not possess direction; their meaning remains *unchanged,* whether they are viewed right side up or upside down.

| | | | |
|---|---|---|---|
| **Chyan** | **Kwun** | **Kan** | **Li** |
| *Heaven* | *Earth* | *Water* | *Fire* |

The other four trigrams or Guas clearly possess a quality of absolute direction. They become different trigrams, and their meanings change when viewed from the opposite direction. For example, Syun becomes Dwei when reversed. These are the changeable or yang Guas.

| | | | |
|---|---|---|---|
| **Dwei** | **Syun** | **Jen** | **Gen** |
| *Lake* | *Wind* | *Thunder* | *Mountain* |

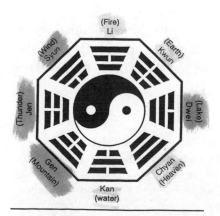

Traditional scholars viewed the direction of Tai Chi, or center of the Bagua, as fixed or unchanged with the trigrams moving away from it or dispersing energy.[6]

---

6    Based on the traditional Bagua of King Wen.

The Bagua of Tantric Buddhism, Black Sect, developed by Professor Lin, views the Tai Chi in a different manner. It is an ever changing, ever-moving entity composed of yin and yang; it has no beginning, no end, no clear top or defined bottom. Tai Chi is a non-directional entity.

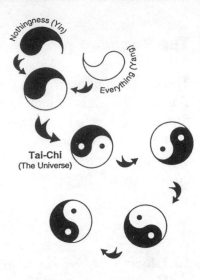

Master Lin reverses the directions of the four changeable yang trigrams so the Chi (energy) of the Bagua flows toward the Tai Chi or center.

**Master Lin's Bagua reflects a focused, inward-gathering energy.**

This change was a revolutionary contribution to the academic world. Master Lin's revision shows the primordial forces moving toward the center of the Tai Chi or universe, giving a strong sense of these powerful dynamic forces gathered at the Tai Chi.[6]

---

6   *The editors suggest that we might view Master Lin's new Bagua as a symbol representing the change in cycle through which humankind is moving. The ancient Bagua was appropriate for its time, leading people through the necessary cycle of expansion outward, toward materialism. The new Bagua, with its energy moving back to the center, is a tool for our times. It can guide us back to our source and to a higher level of energetic being, which can only be found in the core of ourselves.*

## The Placement of the Eight Trigrams of the Bagua

Each of the eight trigrams or locations correlate to a specific aspect of our lives. Master Lin's Feng Shui practice uses the concept of the *Moving Eight Trigrams*.[7] The Bagua is superimposed onto a house oriented by the location of the entrance that leads into the house. The figure of the Bagua can be superimposed on a house, yard, office building, apartment complex, commercial building, or any room of a living or working environment.[8]

The entryway, or *mouth of Chi* which will always be in one of three areas:

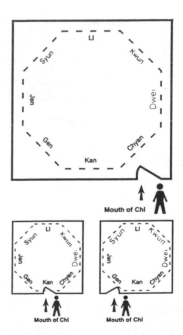

| | |
|---|---|
| **Chyan:** | benefactor[9]<br>helpful people<br>traveling, brother<br>father |
| **Kan:** | career<br>ancestor<br>foundation |
| **Gen:** | knowledge<br>education<br>self-cultivation |

---

7   The traditional schools, who use the fixed direction of the Tai Chi employ a loupan or compass to determine an absolute direction of a position and overlay the Bagua based on that finding.

8   Since using this Bagua does not rely on outside tools such as a compass, it can be carried with you in your heart wherever you go.

9   Each of the eight trigrams represent eight fundamental life conditions or situations. When a Feng Shui cure or adjustment is made to the area of your home represented by the Bagua, it can bring positive transformation to that specific area of life.

From there, the other areas can be easily located.

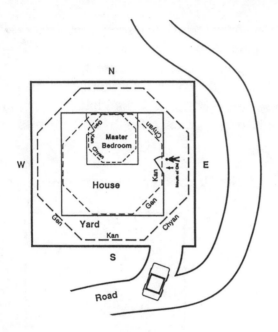

The ever changing Bagua: Placement of the eight trigrams relative to the position of the mouth of Chi.

When there is a regular shaped house, the eight positions of the Bagua can be easily identified.

When a house has an irregular shape, an area may be *missing,* which creates a negative force. In some instances, an area can *protrude,* which provides · a strengthening force to the corresponding area of life.

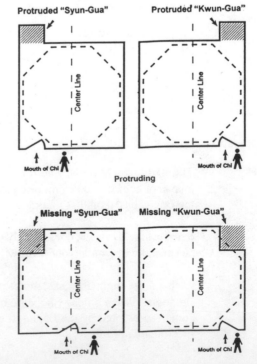

Master Lin has made the Bagua an easy, practical tool so that people can apply the knowledge to many areas of their lives, including divination, palmistry, physiognomy, secret cures, Feng Shui, holistic healing, Chi, spiritual cultivation, and meditation.

Holistic healing can be achieved by implementing Feng Shui adjustments to positions in the house or bed that correlate to the Bagua of the body parts.

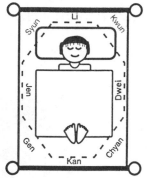

The Bagua on a Bed
Transcendental Solution
(Secret Cure)

For instance, when you superimpose the Bagua on your body, the head relates to Chyan (fame) Gua. If you suffer from migraine headaches, in addition to searching for traditional medical treatment, you can apply a Feng Shui adjustment to the Chyan area of a house, your bed, master bedroom, or other important living space.

The Bagua can also be superimposed onto an individual's face, palm, or entire body.

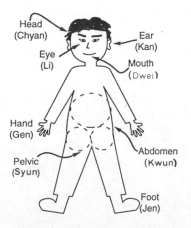

On a Body
Holistic Healing

On a Face
Physiognomy

A protruding, distinct jaw
may indicate a
distinguished career.

A round, shiny forehead
may be associated
with fame and prosperity.

Superimposing the Bagua onto the palm of your hand can give you a
wealth of knowledge. A concave shape in a Bagua area means difficulties
in the corresponding life area; a convex shape indicates that fortunate
events may arise. The types of lines  present in certain areas of the palm
may produce an impact on the area of life that the Gua represents. In
general, vertical and regular shaped lines that form squares, rectangles,
and circles are generally positive; as are other unusual lines like: ⌗ , ✳
and ⊞, ✛ . Horizontal lines, triangular and irregular shaped lines such as
⌓ , ✗ , △ _____ are generally negative.

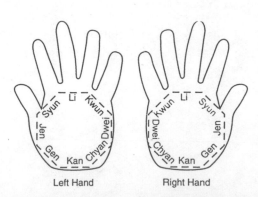

**On a Palm
Palmistry**

The application on  Master Lin Yun's studies are limitless. Elements such as the color of the flesh, Chi readings, intuition, and other correlating factors should all be taken into account for a deeper understanding of the subject.

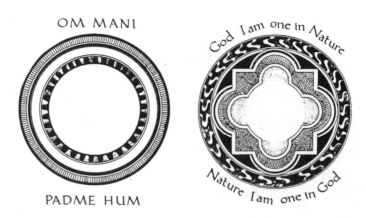

OM MANI

PADME HUM

God I am one in Nature

Nature I am one in God

## Grand Master Lin Yun

Lin Yun has made the Bagua an accessible tool that anyone who has a true desire to learn Feng Shui can use. Based on his innovative views, he has introduced the importance of reaching harmony through the concept of Tao: achieving a balance between yin and  yang. The Bagua, under Master Lin's studies, has brought the East one step closer to the West.

Grand Master Lin Yun is an adjunct Professor at San Diego State University. Formerly he taught at Yale in China at the Chinese University of Hong Kong, the University of San Francisco (1980-81), Stanford University (1981-82), and as a research professor at the Institute for Far Eastern Studies of Seton Hall University (1982-85). For the past twenty years, he has traveled and spoken about Feng Shui throughout Europe, Asia and Australia. He has been a lecturer at such distinguished organizations and institutions as the Library of Congress, the American Institute of Architects, the Parapsychology Society of the United Nations, Harvard, Yale, Princeton, M.I.T., Dartmouth, Stanford, UC Berkeley, UCLA, Cornell, Duke University, and many other schools. In addition, he was the keynote speaker at the first International Feng Shui conference held in San Diego, CA., in April, 1996.

# The Power of Chi

## Angel Thompson

In ancient times, people believed the world and everything in it was inhabited by an indefinable quality that infused and animated all life. It was known as breath, air, energy, spirit, soul, *prana* to the Hindus, *spiritus* to Catholics, *pneuma* to the Greeks, *ruah* to the Hebrews, and *Chi* to the Chinese.[1]

Chi is an energetic, formative principle that is spontaneously expressed through life. It gives life to the elements of nature in their various forms, shapes, colors, odors, and tastes. Chi is the unifying principle of energy, linking all things, from a grain of sand to a tear on a baby's cheek.

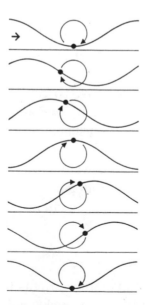

This life force energy is carried by currents of Feng (wind) and Shui (water). Rain, snow, hurricanes, tornadoes, and sunlight bring Chi to the earth from the cosmos, while the earth releases it in the form of wave action, natural springs, geysers, volcanoes, and earthquakes. The earth gives signals about its supply of Chi. If vegetation is lush, the surface has abundant Chi; where the land is dry and cracked, Chi resides deep within the earth and is harder to access.

---

1    The Chinese philosopher Hsu said that Chi comes from "ling," which are tiny, airborne particles or molecular charges that in circulate the universe and enter the womb at conception. When we are born, ling becomes Chi; when we die, our Chi returns to the limitless universal ling.

## The Cycle of Chi

The cycle of Chi can be compared to the act of filling a balloon with air. The first phase is abundant and strong, like breath forcing air into the balloon and giving it form. The second phase or breath is not as strong, but it pushes more air into the balloon. The third strains to complete the task; the balloon is full and has reached its potential. The fourth phase marks the end of the cycle. Having reached its potential, the balloon must eventually deflate or burst; in essence, it must die, thus completing the cycle.

### Chi in Motion

Chi flows fast, slow, up, down, in, out, high, low, and deep or shallow. It rises, falls, inflates, deflates, sinks, rises, bends, twists, and curls. It travels along curved, crooked, wavy, winding or straight lines, in spirals, mazes, and labyrinths. It disperses into the wind and pulses through electrical lines.

Chi instigates motion, while gravity holds objects to the earth. Thus, Chi and gravity are partners, working together to maintain stability in the midst of motion. The presence of sufficient, balanced, and active Chi promotes a healthy environment and a healthy body. To get a true feeling for this magical energy, draw the following lines and note how you *feel* as you create each shape:

straight ● crooked ● crossing ●meandering lines ● wavy lines,
lines passing through a point ● lines radiating from a point
lines converging on a point ● tangent lines creating a circle

## Negative Chi

Negative Chi is called *Sha*. It is the carrier of unfavorable currents that adversely affect you. Sha seeps, drips, and oozes through cracks, holes, and broken windows. It accumulates and stagnates in dead corners and sharp angles. It gains speed when it is forced into straight lines. It occurs in places dense with people, animals, or things, like barnyards, overcrowded elevators, trains, planes, and rooms.

Sha is aggravated by bad smells, bright glaring lights, and loud irritating noises. It is the cold wind blowing at night and the aura surrounding dead or dying things. It can be seen, smelled, heard, felt, tasted, and sensed by intuition. It is sharp, rotten, contaminated, polluted, toxic, vile, painful, and dangerous. It is external or internal, apparent or hidden, and it affects physical, mental, spiritual, and social conditions.

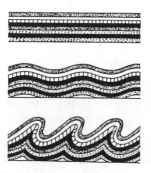

Sha is also produced on a grand scale by geographical faults and fissures in the earth. Tension rises to the surface and escapes in the form of earthquakes, shaking, and splitting. These fault lines exist across the globe; no place is immune to Sha.

Known fault lines lie in geographical areas with a specific pattern of human behavior. Tension-filled lives are common to those who live near the fault in New York City. Southern Californians living near the San Andreas fault line are subject to shaky standards; the rich and famous come and go as quickly as the latest trends. San Francisco, located on the same fault, has a dynamic, *ground-breaking* tension. This tension was first expressed by the gold prospectors of 1849, and it still is today by those who lead the way in promoting gay rights.

**Secret Arrows**

Chi travels in a curve. When it is forced into a straight line, it acts like a bullet from a gun or an arrow from a bow that threatens to wound anything at the receiving end. Feng Shui strives to protect a space or site from these secret arrows.[2]

Urban environments are filled with secret arrows, as most cities and structures are built on the principles of straight lines. Roads, driveways,

---

[2]   *Please refer to "Contemporary Architectural Design," p. 143.*

pathways, walkways, and sidewalks are usually straight. Buildings are crowded together so their roof lines point at each other. There is a profusion of corners, walls, poles, television antennas, billboards, tunnels, railroad tracks, trees, signposts, crosses on churches, and other straight or angular features capable of producing secret arrows.

Any straight line leading towards the front door of a house, directs Sha to the site. Straight lines that lead directly towards a main entry or that come almost to the entry and then turn to make a sharp right angle are especially dangerous as they combine the effects of Sha and secret arrows. The energy becomes confused and congested.[3]

Inside, straight lines come from the corners of other desks, cabinets or tables and can also come from long, narrow corridors or from the corners of hallways. These straight lines or secret arrows stab at anything in their path, creating a feeling of pressure, tension, conflict, and anxiety.

*The manager of a busy bookstore reported that she was under constant pressure. The customers, her friends, and everyone who came into the store seemed to take their complaints to her. Her desk was squeezed into a narrow corner, so she had no maneuvering ability. Even worse were the secret arrows pointing from a half wall on one side and the edge of a copy machine on the other. Both were aimed at her desk and stabbing her in the middle of her back.*

Make sure no straight lines, sharp angles, or points are directed toward your desk, bed, or major sitting area. It is fairly easy to find and protect a space from secret arrows. If you can, remove the arrow. If it is not architecturally or logically possible, create a barrier between you and the arrow. Use artwork, plants, objects, pots, boxes, or anything that is appropriate to the space and is pleasing to you.

---

3    *For solutions to secret arrows, please refer to* Earth Design: The Added Dimension.

You can also neutralize, deflect, and send the arrow back to its source by placing a mirror with the reflective side towards the offending angle. The best shield is an element that controls the element of the arrow.[4] If you cannot move, shield, deflect or cover the arrow, move your body to a less vulnerable space.

## Factors Affecting Chi

Chi is affected by the abstract: form, shape, reflection, shadow, color, or pattern, and by the tangible: objects and all forms of matter. Chi is also transmitted through media: sound, light, heat, electricity, and weather conditions such as temperature, moisture, wind, thunder, lightning, rain, and snow.

Things you do not see or seldom notice can cause distortions that affect Chi: a smudge on a window, furniture placed half off a rug, a messy closet, accumulated garbage, a warped mirror that splits images, a broken chair, a blank wall, a cracked ceiling, and an uneven floor.

Chi influences your perception of reality and how you view the world. This influence, in turn, determines how others see and relate to you.

## Excessive Chi

Feng Shui advocates moderation over excess, a good maxim for life as well. Too much of anything, including Chi, causes an imbalance.

Did you ever think that having a spectacular view could be a problem? When the view extends 180 degrees or more, excessive, strong Chi floods the space, overpowering the interior. If your home or office has such a view, you may feel bewildered, confused about goals, relationships, your direction in life, or anxious and stressed by too much seeing, doing, going, talking, visiting, gossiping, thinking, reading, processing, or taking

---

4  *Please refer to "The Five Phases of Energy," p. 81.*

on too many responsibilities. If the excess is caused by a view of nature, place elements of nature between you and the Chi. If the view is of the city and its buildings, create barriers with layers of glass, crystals, water, lighting, and dark red or black colors.

Excess Chi is often found where the forces of elements meet. Mountain top homes are a good example. The wind, rain, and snow bombard the peaks, and you may feel as if you are being blown away. Active water near your house, such as the crashing surf, a rushing river, or a booming waterfall, can also be problematic. The atmosphere is charged with negative ions, which might throw off the electromagnetic field of the body, making you feel awash and adrift with energy.[5] A lot of glass should not be used in these settings. Wood or earth materials, colors, and shapes will mitigate the force of the Chi.[6]

If there is an excess of Chi from external influences that you cannot change, create layers or barriers between you and the oncoming Chi. Place plants, furniture, statues, baskets, or other decorative objects in three or five rows with larger objects in front of smaller ones to create the illusion of depth. Do this in a subtle, artistic way. Do not stack furniture against the windows as if you were barricading the space. Even if there is a fabulous view, consider covering the window with transparent fabric,[7] paper, or other materials that let in light but block out excessive Chi.

## Insufficient or Weak Chi

It is easy to spot where the Chi is weak, unavailable, or inaccessible. The environment is dark, dim, cold, moist, damp, silent, still, vague, diffused, confused, gloomy, irritating, spooky, empty, barren, broken, or dirty. Here you will find isolation, cold wind, clouds covering the sun, barren

---

[5]    *Please refer to "Energy Fields, Fragrance, and Feng Shui," p. 339 and "The Energetic Basis of Good Health," p. 293.*

[6]    *Please refer to "The Five Phases of Energy," p. 81.*

[7]    *One of my favorite decorative solutions is translucent pleated-shaped shades with a solar back. They control heat and still allow for the vista.*

gardens, and sick, depressed people. When there is insufficient or weak Chi, there is no energy for life. Health, business, love, and every area of life is diminished. It is not a good idea to build or live where Chi is weak or inaccessible because there is not enough energy to support life.

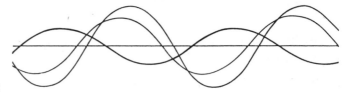

## The Flow of Chi

In Feng Shui, as in life, the first consideration is Chi. Chi is life and you want healthy, moving Chi in your home. To discover how Chi moves through a space, do this exercise: walk slowly from your driveway or path to your entryway, through your home and out the back door. As you move, be directed by your intuitive flow.

Once you have determined the flow of traffic, you will be able to tell how Chi flows in your home. If there are obstacles of any kind, Chi flow is negatively affected. People adapt immediately to environments, and so they tend to step over boxes, shove bags aside, or leave clothes lying around. All these habits inhibit, obstruct, or block the flow of Chi, causing tension, poor health, or worse for the inhabitants.

Remove obstacles from the flow of Chi or re-direct it by using lights, mirrors, colors, symbols, or other accessories that attract Chi. Then cover, block, deflect, disburse, break-up, or remove any secret arrows caused by corners, angles, straight lines, beams, poles, trees, blank walls, or narrow corridors. Create a traffic pattern natural to Chi.

## Bringing Chi into Your Space

When Chi is not accessible, you must invite it into your space and encourage it to stay. Chi is attracted by light, living things, and objects that catch your eye, like a beautiful painting. It is attracted to bold colors, pleasant sounds, running water, plants, and flowers. Whatever pleasantly attracts your attention, attracts Chi.

Movement stimulates Chi. Anything that moves can be used to stimulate Chi. When Chi gets stuck, it gets heavy and dense. Use something sharp, like a pointed leaf plant or a lamp on a tall, thin pole to stimulate Chi; the concept is similar to acupuncture.[8] Be careful with the placement of this object because the points can also act like secret arrows, attacking anyone who is seated or walking through its vicinity. Mirrors, glass, or shiny objects also stimulate Chi by sending light into dark corners where Chi often gets stuck.

Chi likes plants, water, light, heat, safety, color, reflection, movement, and especially curved spaces where it can circulate and then move on. Straight corridors, walkways, traffic patterns, and straight edges can be coaxed into curves with round occasional tables, round vases, round pillows, circular patterned materials, or round rugs. The maxim to remember is:

**If you are attracted to a space, Chi will be too.**

Free-flowing Chi is like a river stocked with the gifts of long life, prosperity, and health. Make sure there is plentiful Chi that flows freely through your space. It will bring you every rich treasure you deserve.

---

8   *Please refer to "Energy Systems and Feng Shui," p 275.*

# Drawing on Chi

## Seann Xenja

*If I give a student one-fourth of what he should know, I expect him to get the other three-fourths himself, otherwise I do not want him as a student.*
Confucius

Throughout Chinese history, teachers and scholars have followed the example of Confucius to varying degrees. Written information is presented incompletely, often with key parts left out. Over time, the student is expected to search out what he or she needs to know, thus supplementing the instruction of teachers and growing with the experience. This process of learning can be very frustrating for the Western mind. In Western society, information is disseminated quickly, systematically, and completely in a well-packaged form. Its methodology is based on facts, details, and scientific inquiry.

As a student of Feng Shui, you are faced with a unique challenge. If you approach the intuitive art of Feng Shui as a list of external or internal factors, you do not get very far. By trying to follow the traditional methods, you come up against a culture gap. Without clear, comprehensive guidelines, you begin to learn in bits and pieces and to practice in fits and starts. Often you know only a minimal portion of *how* and *what* and even less of *why*. But what appears as a frustration may, in fact, be a blessing. With no guidelines or rules, you become free to experiment, learn, practice, and most of all, to discover new ways to deepen your understanding of Feng Shui.

Where do you start?

> **The essentials of Feng Shui can be felt, perceived, noticed,
> and most easily accessed through intuition.**

Getting to a place where you can feel and understand Feng Shui in your body[1] gives you the ability to always return there for the answers. Remember:

> **The essential truth is inside you.**

## The Flow of Chi

An appreciation of the all-pervasive nature and power of Chi [2] is central to understanding Feng Shui. Chi underlies all life and all realms of existence. The more clearly you perceive the quality, flow, and interplay of personal and environmental Chi, the easier it is to practice Feng Shui. Chi can rise and fall, disperse, pool, or settle. Its flow can be fast, slow, or static. Cross currents of Chi can generate energetic patterns of conflict. Chi can be of the earth, the atmosphere, or of people. The quality of Chi is expressed through form, shape, color, or the feeling it generates.

To experience the spirit of Chi, you can use an approach that integrates your body, mind, and intuition. This method involves making a series of drawings. You will need five or six large sheets of paper, a crayon, a small mirror, and a round cut glass crystal.

Do not simply read these exercises. Do them! This is the interactive age, so let's see what the process reveals. Pick a spot where you can stand and draw with ease along with full body motion.

---

[1]    *Please refer to "Utilize All Your Resources," p. 189.*

[2]    *Please refer to "The Power of Chi," p. 49.*

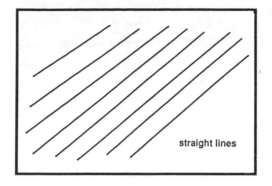

straight lines

Start by drawing a straight line of Chi across your paper. Notice your feelings and sensations. Then draw a series of straight lines. These could be lines of Chi flowing down a long corridor or straight street.

The experience of freedom, acceleration, and purposeful direction is characteristic of this Chi flow pattern, which is so common in our modern world.

If your paper is filled, turn it over. Draw a point; this is, in its essence, a unique place on the time/space continuum.

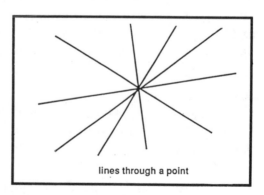

lines through a point

Now draw a line through the point. Do you have trouble hitting it? As you get closer to the point, there is often a sensation of slowing down.

You may feel this sensation in your body near your navel. This is the Tai Chi of your body. As the line moves away, you may feel an increase of energy. Lines of Chi interact with the places they pass through.

Imagine this point as your house, and the line is a long stream of traffic coming toward you. This is when the mirror and crystal save the day. Hold the mirror so it touches the paper and faces the line just before it reaches your point. Looking in the mirror, you can see how that line is reflected away. Using the crystal instead of the mirror, place its bottom point on the line, and look through the top of the crystal. You can see the line split into many little lines that all go in separate directions. This is how a crystal works to redirect and disperse Chi. If you prefer an alternate solution, draw a wall, a row of trees, or a horse-shoe shaped path to redirect the flow. Remember that every point in time and space receives energy flowing to, through, and around it. The nature and quality of the various energies determine the outside influences on the site.

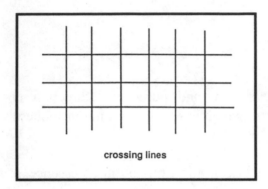

crossing lines

Lines of Chi can also cross and intersect. Starting with a new sheet of paper, draw a series of parallel straight lines. Then draw a second set of parallel lines at right angles to the first.

You have created a grid pattern similar to the layout of many cities, office buildings, and even the interiors of some homes. Again, notice your feelings and bodily sensations as the lines cross and the grid takes shape. Some people feel discomfort when creating the intersections while others may feel relief from the sense of order and control the grid gives them.

Crossing lines of Chi can generate conflict and friction. On busy streets, this energy is controlled by traffic lights and signs, which is not by any means a perfect system as car accident statistics and grid lock problems show. The resulting energy patterns affect the buildings and people located in and around these intersections. Similar energies occur within buildings when doors oppose each other or where hallways intersect. By holding your crystal over an intersection and looking through it, you can see why it is often chosen as an interior remedy to disperse potentially conflicting flows of Chi.

Angled lines are very common in modern design and have a unique effect. To experience the sensation they create, begin drawing a series of angled lines.

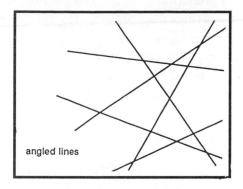

angled lines

Notice how one or two send energy in new directions, but as the numbers increase, the resulting corners, shapes, and pattern complexity can quickly become overwhelming and unpleasant.

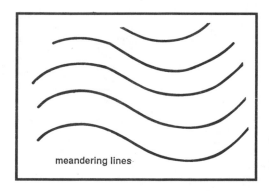

meandering lines

Keeping in mind that straight lines are rarely found in the natural world, discover the feeling of drawing curved or meandering lines. Begin by drawing a gently curved or wavy line.

This has a very soothing and calming effect. It is the natural form of a stream, river, or pleasant-feeling pathway. No mirrors or crystals are needed here.

## Shape, Design, and Arrangement

You can also approach the study of Feng Shui by examining the perceptual and psychological effects of shape, design, and arrangement. Physical conditions which result in unbalanced perceptions are often negatively manifested in your life. Having your back to a door, a split view, angled or blocking walls, and sloped ceilings can destablize your nervous system. Odd or incomplete shapes can create a sense that something is missing. Mundane factors such as the first room you see when entering a home can have behavioral effects.[3] The transcendental domain of ghosts, spirit, and thought energies also plays an important role.[4]

To give a sense of how some of these variables operate within the framework of Feng Shui, use the drawing tools again. Objects attract and radiate the same Chi as the shape they resemble or symbolize.[5]

Draw a columnar shape and sketch curved lines of Chi radiating off the curved surface. How do these lines feel when they are coming toward you? How do they feel when you draw them moving away from you? This is the same energetic condition found in such natural forms as trees or in man-made objects like round tables or walls with rounded corners.

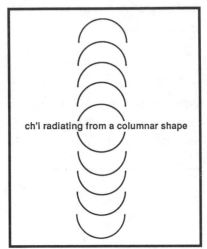

ch'i radiating from a columnar shape

Objects and forms with square, acute and, to a lesser degree, obtuse angles, create a completely different feeling.

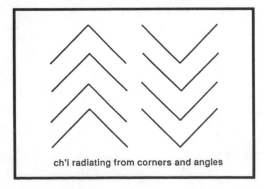

ch'i radiating from corners and angles

Again, start with an angle corner, and draw lines of angled Chi. Draw them coming toward you. This is the classic cutting and dividing energy, and in Feng Shui, it is associated with a variety of ailments and problems.

---

[3]    *Please refer to "The Room of First Impression," p. 207.*

[4]    *Please refer to "The Bones of Your Home," p. 399.*

[5]    *Please refer to "The Five Phases of Energy," p. 81.*

Wind chimes or strings of bells are often used to deflect or disperse this energy. Experiment with your crystal to discover[6] its dispersing ability. Watch the ease with which a mirror reflects an equal set of angles to meet and cancel the negative of the original angles. Angled Chi drawn with the points heading away from you will have a very different feel than those which are drawn toward you.

Using Chi flow drawing techniques also allows you to experience the effects of wall and doorway alignment.

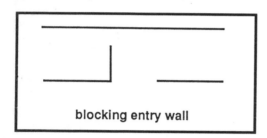

**blocking entry wall**

Draw a blocked entry, one with very little distance between the doorway and the first wall seen beyond the threshold.

Notice how the energy stops abruptly and then must change direction. No wonder people who have this problem in their home or office have trouble making progress. Now place the edge of your mirror on the line representing the blocking wall. Instantly you have twice as much space.

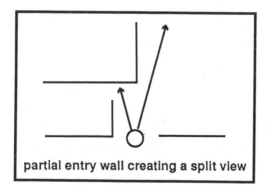

**partial entry wall creating a split view**

Another problematic configuration is an entry wall that obstructs part of the view of a room's interior. This arrangement creates a split view and causes an imbalance between the information received by the visual fields.

---

6    Dowsers have discovered that positive ions radiate off the pointed portion of an angled shape or wall corner and that negative ions or life enhancing energy radiate from the wide portion backward.

Because the left and right portions of your visual field are processed respectively by the right and left halves of the brain, this condition can lead to mental destabilization. As with the blocking wall, see how your mirror can even out the depth of field.

To complete this section, draw two pathways, one with only straight and right-angled lines, and a second with gentle, meandering curves. Now trace the path of a person walking or of Chi flowing on the path. Which feels best for your journey through life?

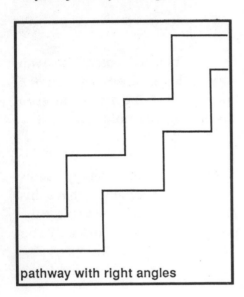

**pathway with right angles**

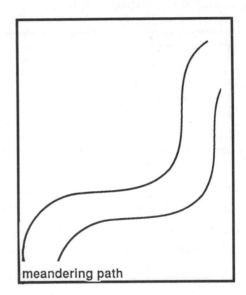

**meandering path**

I encourage you to use Chi flow drawing as a tool to help you analyze and understand the energy of life in its many forms of expression. By feeling the flow of Chi within your body, you can sense and determine problems and generate solutions without having to know Feng Shui rules or principles. After all, that is what the first Feng Shui practitioners did. They had no written language, no books, videos, or workshops - just Chi, people, the spirit of place, and the ability to discern and encourage the best ways for Chi to flow.

# Using the Components of Feng Shui Cures
## Create New Cures for Greater Success

### David Daniel Kennedy

The culture and history of Chinese civilization has given rise to many different schools of Feng Shui thought and practice. Among these are several schools in the Taoist tradition; others have arisen from Buddhist teachings. In the West, some Feng Shui practitioners are now pioneering their own schools or ways of practicing Feng Shui. One rapidly spreading system of Feng Shui derives from the Black Sect of Tibetan Tantric Buddhism[1] as taught by Professor Lin Yun[2] of Berkeley, CA.

Generally referred to as BTB Feng Shui, the Black Sect method comprises a widely varied body of practical and spiritual knowledge. A continuously evolving system, it contains a multitude of shamanistic practices, wisdom teachings, folk ways, and traditional remedies. Tibetan, Eastern Indian, and Chinese spiritual methods along with many other pieces of religious and cultural lore have been added to the tradition over the years.

Since Professor Lin introduced his Feng Shui to the West in the 1980's, its popularity and influence has spread rapidly due to its effectiveness, accessibility, and emphasis on transcendental solutions to life problems. At the center of this rich and eclectic brew of healing wisdom is the concept of the cure. A cure is a specific change made to the environment[3]

---

[1]   Black Hat Tantric Buddhism is an unorthodox Buddhist religious sect which is now in its fourth stage of evolution: incorporating current knowledge to explain ancient wisdom to bridge the gap between ancient traditions and modern ways of thinking.

[2]   Professor Lin is the Grandmaster of Black Sect Feng Shui, leader of the sect in its fourth stage, and acknowledged world authority on Feng Shui.

[3]   In BTB Feng Shui, cures can be made for the outer environment: home or office, the personal environment: the body/mind complex, or both.

using Feng Shui principles and techniques performed with a certain purpose or goal in mind.

Cures are Feng Shui in action. A cure is not a wind chime, plant or mirror, although these items are often used to create cures.[4] Rather, a cure is the process of creating desired change in your environment and life using Feng Shui principles and techniques. In the Black Sect tradition, many cures have been brought forth by Professor Lin, created by his students, and borrowed from other Feng Shui schools, all for the purpose of greater life transformation, success, and balance.

Feng Shui cures are made up of various components or variables. These components are the specific features of a cure and of the curing process in general. The components are factors which can be individually or collectively varied to ensure that a cure best meets your needs. You can also assemble components to invent an altogether new cure to resolve a life issue. Using the components enables you to approach the curing process from the level of principle, thereby gaining deeper understanding of energy movement and transformation.

BTB Feng Shui is a Tantric art,[5] though the Tantric aspects of Feng Shui have unfortunately been overlooked. Tantric means working purposefully and directly with subtle energy to create balance and dynamic life change. The Tantric masters of ancient times were masterful energy technicians, orchestrating subtle fields with consummate skill, along with transforming seen and unseen realities. The Tantric aspect of Feng Shui concerns aligning subtle energy systems in your environment to trigger desired results.

---

[4]     In this article, the physical items used for cures are simply referred to as cure items or cure objects.

[5]     Tantric refers herein to Tantra as a vast body of spiritual knowledge containing many principles and practices which have the capability of transforming all of life, eventually resulting in enlightenment and other advanced spiritual states. It does not specifically refer herein to Tantra as it is commonly known in the West as a sexual path to higher states of consciousness.

**The Tantric paradigm operates from these belief systems:**

1. All things are energy.
2. Energy can be manipulated endlessly for positive change.
3. The only limitation to positive change is your own choice.

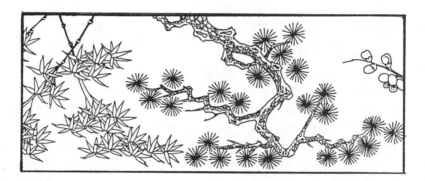

By adopting a Tantric attitude and intuitively using the Feng Shui components, you are able to create a limitless variety of potent life cures. Broadening your capacity to effectively wield components of energy movement also frees you from the illusion that there are official cures which would heal if only someone would give you the secrets.

**A cure is whatever it takes to move the energy to change your life, nothing more or less.**

By cultivating greater awareness of subtle energy and its effects, you gain the ability to manifest your desires. With a Feng Shui cure, this manifestation can happen in a single moment because all relevant aspects of your environment's energy have been properly aligned and balanced to produce a specific result. The use of subtle energy to create results is greatly facilitated if you employ a wide variety of components to create and fine tune your cures.

## The Feng Shui Cure Components

Following are components of the cure process along with examples of their usage. They have been divided for easy reference into main categories:

> **Item Components**
> **Environmental Components**
> **Performance Components**
> **Transcendental Components**
> **Other Components**

The first element in each category is a basic element, one of prime importance in the curing process. This is not an exhaustive list of components. In addition, some components invariably overlap with others. Feel free to add to these components additional variables you discover along the way. Be aware that not all components will apply to all the cures you perform. A good way to start is by adding one additional element to a cure you already know to see its effect. Soon you will be able to mix and match these components and add your own to come up with unique solutions to your needs.

### Have fun with your cures!

 **Item Components**

The components in this section relate to the physical item(s) with which you will perform your cure:

**Objects Used for a Cure:**

> This component refers to the item, object, or materials with which the cure will be performed; these could be crystals, pieces of furniture, or accessories.[6] They are tools to help you create a new pattern of Chi in your environment and life.

**Size of Item:**

> A larger cure item sometimes creates a more powerful effect. In other cases, a very small item may have a special psychological impact.

**Color:**

> The color selected for your cure has a major impact on the cure's effectiveness.[7]

---

[6]    BTB cures do not always entail adding items to your environment. Removing or rearranging items in the environment are also methods of creating cures.

[7]    For extensive information on BTB Feng Shui color, refer to: _Living Color: Master Lin's Guide to Feng Shui and the Art of Color_ by Sarah Rossbach and Lin Yun (Kodansha:New York, 1994). _For extensive information on "Chi and Color," "Feng Shui Astrology and Color," and "Conventional Interior Design and Color," refer to:_ _Earth Design: The Added Dimension._

## Shape of Item:

Shape plays a key role in the energy of a cure. Powerful shapes include octagons, circles, spheres, triangles, pyramids, and many others. Shapes which are personally meaningful can also boost the energy of the cure.

## Number of Items:

Three crystals or nine bells, rather than only one, may be employed to create the needed energetic shift.

## Numerology in Size or Length:

The vibrational frequencies of certain numbers have greater healing power than others. In BTB Feng Shui, the number nine, representing completeness, has special auspiciousness. Additional powerful numbers include 1, 3, 27 and 99. These numbers, as well as any multiple of nine can be used for the size or length measurement of an item, in inches or centimeters. I often suggest clients use mirrors which are 9" octagons or which measure 18" x 27" or 27" x 36" to ensure that the power of this element is included in the cure. If a cure is hung from the ceiling, its ribbon or cord can also be adjusted to an increment of nine.

## Quality:

If the item you use for your cure is of very high quality, this can add special energy to the cure, both psychologically and in the material vibration of the object. If it was made with care and precision, it will reflect the heightened consciousness of the maker.

## Newness:

A newly purchased cure item can also lend powerful distinction to a situation. On a subtle level, being the first to use an item brings significance and freshness to the energy you are creating. If a brand new item is not possible, the newest or nicest one you find can suffice.

## Value/Expense:

A highly valued and/or expensive cure item will focus additional importance and attention on the item and the resulting cure.

## Personal Significance/Symbolism of Item:

Employing an item that has special personal meaning or sentimental value can boost a cure's energy, Examples include an heirloom with strong ancestor energy, a personal medicine bag, or other talismans.

## Personal Connection with Item:

Sleeping with or wearing the cure item can add dramatically to the effectiveness of your cure. Connecting your personal Chi strongly to that of the item will assist in your healing. Placing the item in a personally significant container or location is also a powerful way to use this element.

## Personal Construction/Design:

The object or process used in your cure may be personally created by you to further heighten its significance.

## Blessing by Special Place, Person, or Event:

The cure item can be specially blessed in many different ways: by a qualified spiritual master, priest, or minister; by having a person who has attained the state you desire (wealth, marriage) touch the item; by meditating with the item, and by many other methods. The energy of natural phenomena is another powerful means of charging your cure item before placing it in your home or office.

# Environmental Components

Components in this section concern the environment in which the cure is performed or where the cure item is placed.

## Location of Cure:

The main area or location where the cure is performed is a key factor in determining its success.

## Placement in Environment:

How and exactly where the cures are situated is important: is it invisible or easily seen? Is it placed in the position which feels the most powerful? Is it near another object of importance, adding to its power?

## Placement in Bagua:

This element is a key factor in successful cures. Based on the wisdom of the I Ching, the Bagua[8] (sacred octagon) portrays nine subdivisions: eight sides, plus the center of the space. Each side of the Bagua has a life correspondence which can be enhanced by performing your cure in the appropriate area. The nine life correspondences of the Bagua are: career, knowledge, family, wealth, fame, partnership, children, helpful people, and health.

## Geometry:

In addition to the geometry of placement, the geometry of the cure object's shape can be employed. For example, a crystal can be placed directly between a window and door, balancing both, and simultaneously be positioned over the center of the foot of the bed to assist in career and movement.

---

8    *Please refer to "The Bagua," p. 35.*

## Performance Components

Performance components are those which concern the actual performance or action of doing the cure.

### Action Performed:

This is one of the prime components which creates a cure. The action for your cure can range from placing a cure item in its appropriate place, to rearranging your furniture, to moving to another country. Actions utilizing cure items include adding objects; removing, clearing, getting rid of items; rearranging existing items, or combinations of these. Other actions include: rituals,[9] visualization, and body movements.

### Special Date:

Performing your cure on a date of significance adds meaning on multiple levels. Special dates can include the new moon, your birthday, New Year's Day, an anniversary, or other special life event. Your special date could be an auspicious number of days before or after a certain date, such as 99 days after moving into a new house.

### Special Timing:

Utilizing special timing in the performance of your cure distinguishes it from everyday actions and further impresses it into your consciousness. In the BTB tradition, 11:00 to 1:00 (p.m. or a.m.) are the two most powerful times to perform cures. These are the time periods when yang and yin energies are at their peak and transforming into their complementary opposites, making them ideal times for personal and environmental transformation. Sunrise and sunset are also good times for performing cures.

---

[9] *Please refer to "The Magic of Rituals and Feng Shui," p. 369.*

## Repetition:

Repetition can be utilized in many different areas of the curing process. The entire cure can also be repeated one or more times for greater impact. An example of adjusting the repetition element: if a cure traditionally calls for nine repetitions of an action, you may boost the number to 18, 27 or a higher multiple of nine.

## Duration/Number of Days:

You may perform the cure or leave it in place[10] for a specific significant duration, such as one week, 9 days, 99 days, one full or half cycle of the moon, one year, until your son returns from college, or any other variation of your choice.

## Special Sensory Input:

Music, sounds, smells and special images can all be employed during the initial performance of a cure or during its entire lifetime to accentuate the cure.

## Commitment/Special Attention:

The level of commitment required to create or maintain the cure as well as the amount of special attention you place on its performance can serve to strongly distinguish the cure from the rest of your life and build its Chi.[11]

---

[10]  In the Black Sect system, some cures involve personal rituals which are performed once or over time; other cures simply involve rearrangement of the environment; still other cures involve both of these methods.

[11]  Life force energy; etheric energy. This is the energy which cures are designed to shift. Out flow of Chi is a key determiner of your life destiny. The more positive Chi generated by a cure the better.

**Ceremony/Ritual/Special Process:**[12]

Closely related to the above element, performing a ceremony or ritual during your cure helps create sacred space and calls in spiritual forces to assist your transformation. The ritual you use can be received from a Feng Shui consultant, obtained from a book of Feng Shui practices, or created by yourself for this particular cure.

**Verbal/Written Affirmation:**

Formulating and using an affirmation which represents the new reality you are choosing is yet another excellent way of sending a message to your environment, to yourself, and to the universe that things are new and different in your life.

# Transcendental Components

Professor Lin teaches that the transcendental components mark the most powerful and effective of those used in BTB Feng Shui cures. For this reason, the Black Sect system emphasizes the importance of transcendental components in each cure you perform to maximize success.

**Transcendental cures work in the unseen realms from which the visible reality is manifested.**

Because they work at the level of Yi,[13] they transform the underlying Chi of a situation that results in transformation of mind, body, emotions, and life events.

---

12    *Please refer to "The Magic of Ritual and Feng Shui," p.369.*

13    More basic even than Chi, Yi is sometimes translated as *intention*. Yi refers to an impulse which on a spiritual level, is usually much deeper than conscious or surface intention. In Chinese philosophy, Chi follows Yi, and physical phenomena follow Chi.

## Intention/Desire:

Intention is the keynote of your cure. It is the reason you are choosing this change in your life. The clarity of your intention, the will to accomplish it, and the desire backing it are the prime factors in the success of a cure. Intention, will, and desire create the energetic space for the other components to play out their roles in shifting the energy.

## Attitude/Faith/Belief:

Your belief and faith in your cure and its effectiveness to make change happen is another fundamentally important aspect of its success. Consciously holding positive thoughts, feelings, and attitudes regarding your cure is very effective and sets many important psychic, emotional, and psychological forces in motion.

## Connecting to Higher Power:

Another vital element in the success of a cure is the invocation of spiritual forces to assist you in your transformation. This is done by consciously opening up to, asking for, and receiving the help you seek. It is helpful to visualize one or more spiritual beings or human beings coming to your aid and performing the needed action both in the physical and spiritual arenas.[14]

## Body Movement:

In BTB Feng Shui, body, speech, and mind movements are used in concert to reinforce all other components of the cure. This combination is called "The Three Secrets Reinforcement."[15] The

---

[14]  *Please refer to "The Bones of Your Home," p.399, for an example of such a ritual.*

[15]  Specific instructions on how to perform the three secrets reinforcement process for your cures is given personally from teacher to student or from practitioner to client. This practice can be performed regardless of religious affiliation or spiritual background; each person's individual religious or atheistic symbolism can be employed effectively for the reinforcement. *Please refer to Spirituality and Feng Shui," p.357.*

Three Secrets Reinforcement is a way to strongly infuse your desire and intention into the cure, imprinting the entire process with your personal desires and Chi. The body movement element involves the performance of spiritual hand gestures (mudras) or other body positions which focus the energy of the body in a spiritual manner.

### Speech Movement:

This element involves spiritual speech, including prayers, chants, and mantras: vibrational sounds chanted to invoke spiritual frequencies and assistance.

### Mind Movement:

The mind movement element incorporates mental visualization of your wish or desire as a means of projecting it into reality.

# Other Components:

There are additional components that influence, affect, and empower cures. The components in this category include both known and unknown factors that constitute the most interesting and effective of all possible cure components. They afford us a rich field for further inquiry into the extraordinary field of Feng Shui.

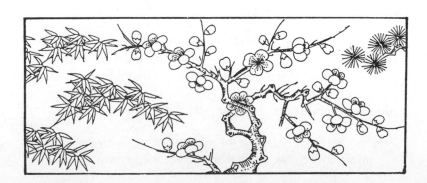

## Dream Transformation

In order to gain insights into a dream or to transform a negative dream, perform the following cure:

1. Record your dream on a piece of paper and review it so it is fresh in your mind. Choose before you begin whether you want to gain insights, transform a negative dream, or retrieve parts of yourself.

2. Sit in a meditative position with an 18" square piece of red cloth on your lap. Repeat a prayer or mantra of your choice nine times.

3. Close your eyes, relax deeply, and allow yourself to reenter the dream situation.

4. Replay your dream inside your awareness. As you do so, perform the following: If you are gaining insights, as you get each insight, gather it with your hands and place it in the red cloth on your lap. If you are transforming a dream, play the dream out in the way which is most healing, balancing or victorious for you. Gather with your hands the positive experience with which you end the dream and place it in the red cloth.

5. After the gathering is completed, create a bundle with the red cloth and tie a bow around the neck of the bundle with a 27" red ribbon.

6. Place this bundle on the floor under the head of your bed. Sleep over the bundle for 9 consecutive nights. Each night as you go to bed, imagine that the positive insights, experiences, or parts are being integrated into yourself completely. Believe and feel that this is happening. You may place a round mirror under the red bundle for stronger effect.

7. On the morning of the tenth day, take the red bundle to a remote place with strong natural energy.

8. Feel that you have now fully and completely integrated all the learning which you needed from this dream. Reciting a prayer or mantra, open the red cloth and shake it in the wind nine times releasing any remaining energies back to the universe. You may take the cloth home and put it in a sacred place or under your pillow if you wish.

9. Perform the three secrets reinforcement or say a prayer with a positive visualization for your current and future life growth.

# Feng Shui Schools

# The Five Phases of Energy

## Mark Johnson

Each person, like all that is manifested in the universe, can be described and understood in terms of five archetypal energies: earth, metal, wood, water, and fire. Though each of these forces is present in everyone, there is usually one elemental phase that predominates a person's make-up. Compass School Feng Shui traditionally uses the Chinese Energy Calendar and various methods of calculation to determine which energy phase is dominant.

Each of these five phases, or the five elements of energy has a corresponding geometric shape that represents and contains its primal energy.

> **Fire** has a pyramidal shape.
> **Earth** has a square or rectangular shape.
> **Metal** (air) has a half of a sphere or is domed shape.
> **Wood** has a cylindrical or any tall, columnar shape.
> **Water** has the lower half of a sphere or any irregular shape.

**These five fundamental shapes concentrate and store the five phases of transformational energy.**

Since these shapes contain elemental energy, they can be used to balance one or more of the energy phases that may be out of sync in your space or your body. Using the knowledge of your dominant energy phase in conjunction with the five fundamental shapes, you can create harmony in your environment.

### The Cycles of Energy

The five primal forces or phases of energy are in constant transformation. They operate and interact in creative, destructive, and moderating cycles.

These three cycles can become useful tools for building energy or for mitigating negative energetic influences.

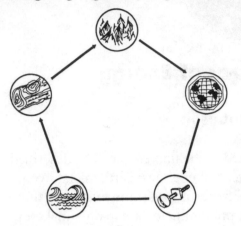

In the **creative cycle,**[1] the wood phase creates or nourishes the fire phase, fire creates the earth phase, earth creates metal, metal creates water, and water creates wood.

So, if you are a wood person, meaning your predominant energy is the archetypal wood force, you can nourish yourself by introducing the water phase into your environment, perhaps in the form of an aquarium, a pool, or a pond

In the **destructive cycle**, the wood phase destroys the earth phase, earth destroys water, water destroys fire, fire destroys metal, and metal destroys wood.

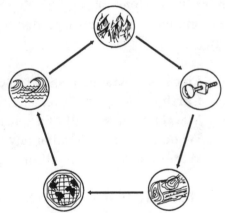

This cycle can be used to neutralize an energy type that may be harming you. If you are predominantly a metal person, a view from your apartment window of a pointed church roof could be a negative energetic influence for you because pointed and pyramidal objects represent fire energy which *destroys* metal. Since water destroys fire, you could place an indoor water fountain in the path of the church view to neutralize its negative effect.

---

1    *Graphics: Earth Design: The Added Dimension*

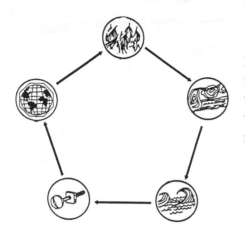

In the **moderating cycle**, earth moderates fire, fire moderates wood, wood moderates water, water moderates metal, and metal moderates earth.

As one energy creates or nourishes another, its energy is weakened in the creative process. Fire creates earth, but loses energy in the process; to replenish itself, it draws more energy from wood. In the moderating cycle, the energy can be drawn from the primal force without destroying it.

*The pointed, fire-shaped Transamerica building in San Francisco was designed according to the principles of Feng Shui. The fire shape draws energy away from the tall, columnar (wood shaped) buildings around it. The architect did not want to destroy the inherent wood energy of the area completely. Instead, he wanted to draw energy from the wood environment over a long period of time, which would have been impossible if he had destroyed it. A building with a metal-shaped, domed structure would have destroyed the energy of the columnar, wood shaped, structures around it.*

## Finding Your Energy Type

Compass School practitioners have traditionally calculated your energy type based on your date of birth, insisiting that your basic energy composition at birth is as fixed and unchanging as your DNA. However, it is my observation that many people have changed their energy composition through substance abuse, near death experiences, mystical experiences, and spiritual cultivation. By using the following in-depth questionnaire and factoring in these changes, you can more accurately determine the predominate energy type *you are now*. If you have had no such life altering experiences, then this method will simply confirm what your birth chart calculations would have been.

The results will give you a clear picture of which element predominates in your makeup and which may be lacking. With this information, you can make the necessary changes in your environment with Feng Shui cures.

The Questionnaire[2]

To get an accurate reading, mark the answers to the questionnaire according to *who you are* not *who you want to be*. Use the following scale:

+2      if the question is **a lot like you**.
+1      if the question it is **somewhat like you.**
--0      if the question is **neutral.**
--1      if the question is **not much like you**.
--2      if the question is **nothing like you.**

Do not look to see what phase you are relating to until after you finish.

---

2       *Apply your phase or element for health-enhancements: Please refer to "Using Feng Shui to Create Health," p. 285, "Five Elements for Better Health," p. 303, and "The Energetic Basis of Good Health," p. 293.*

## Phase I

\_\_Are you a natural born initiator?
\_\_Do you have problems with authority figures?
\_\_Do you suffer from migratory pains?
\_\_Do you act assertively and confidently?
\_\_Does other people's slowness and clumsiness irritate you?
\_\_Do you like struggling against great odds, proving yourself to others?
\_\_Are you always doing something or going somewhere?
\_\_Do you have high blood pressure?
\_\_Have you often been told you don't compromise much?
\_\_Do you always have to be the first and best?
\_\_Does confinement and sitting quietly drive you crazy?
\_\_Do you get frequent muscle cramps?
\_\_Do you like to make all the rules and then break them?
\_\_Are you really passionate about everything you do?
\_\_Do you pioneer new trails wherever you go?
\_\_Do your nails alternate between hard and thick, and dry and brittle?
\_\_Are you intolerant of uncommitted people with no direction?
\_\_Does your own personal freedom reign supreme in your life?
\_\_Are you afraid to show vulnerability?
\_\_Do you love speed and adventure?
\_\_Have you ever had tendinitis?
\_\_Do you manipulate people and situations to get what you want?
\_\_Is controlling your anger one of your biggest problems?
\_\_Do you find any kind of restraint insufferable?
\_\_Do you do your best work under pressure?

## Phase II

\_\_Would you describe yourself as an introspective loner?
\_\_Do you have an exaggerated sex drive?
\_\_Is the search for *truth* a prime motivator in your life?
\_\_Do you hate superficiality more than anything?
\_\_Are you highly creative, imaginative and original?
\_\_Are you modest and do you fear being in the limelight?
\_\_Do you pride yourself on being self contained and self sufficient?

__Is rapid deterioration of teeth and gums a problem?

__Do you seek the deep mystery in everything?

__Are you out of touch with your emotions?

__Do you suffer with backaches frequently?

__Are you tactless and even rude occasionally?

__Do you have a very penetrating and critical mind?

__Do you hate waste and conserve everything?

__Is the desire to stick-to-it one of your strongest virtues?

__Do you have hardening of the arteries?

__Is it hard for you to share with others?

__Do you suffer with isolation and loneliness?

__Are you afraid of loosing yourself in others?

__Are you considered enigmatic and eccentric by your friends?

__Do you have remarkable powers of concentration?

__Are you really awkward in social circumstances?

__Do you have trouble conforming?

__Have you recently had kidney or bladder problems?

__Are you watchful and objective with other people?


**Phase III**

__Are you highly motivated to seek the divine?

__Do you have an enlarged or weak heart?

__Are you charismatic?

__Do you have an extreme aversion to pain?

__Do you love drama, performing, and being in the limelight?

__Are you often spontaneous?

__Do you get sores on your tongue and around your mouth?

__Can't say no to anyone?

__Do you tend to be more sensual than your friends?

__Have you ever had a speech impediment?

__Do you love to give your opinion?

__Do you fear separation above all else?

__Are you clever on your feet?

__Do you desire fulfillment more than almost anything?

__Do you bore easily with the dull and ordinary?

__Do your cheeks turn red easily?

__Could you be described as extravagant?

__Are you bright and scintillating at social gatherings?

___Do you have eczema?
___Do you have trouble with boundaries?
___Is the need for intimacy and merging a strong motivation with you?
___Does sharing come easily?
___Are you mostly optimistic and enthusiastic about life?
___Are you strongly empathetic?
___Do you suffer from anxiety and insomnia?

## Phase IV

___Are you a law and order person?
___Do you hold righteousness and virtue in high regard?
___Are rituals important to you?
___Do you have stiff joints and muscles?
___Is chaos your enemy?
___Do you have no time for nonsense?
___Do you hold very precise standards?
___Are you really sensitive to temperature changes?
___Are you intolerant of disorder and dissonance?
___Is your skin and hair really dry?
___Do you fear intimacy?
___Do you have a strong aesthetic sense?
___Does carelessness in others drive you up a wall?
___Are you considered cool, dispassionate, and distant?
___Do you have a tight chest with dry coughing?
___Are reason and high principles your guiding light?
___Are you a little too strict and nit-picky?
___Do you have very refined tastes?
___Have you been called self-righteous?
___Do you have a lot of moles and warts?
___Is social involvement on the bottom of your list of things do?
___Do you have sinus problems?
___Does your constant self-control drive your spontaneous friends crazy?
___Are you into changing other people?
___Do you suffer from constipation?

**Phase V**

___Do you see yourself as a service oriented person?
___Are you working on being more self-reliant?
___Do your friends often use you as a negotiator?
___Is bloating and water retention a problem?
___Do you struggle with inertia and feel "stuck" sometimes?
___Does nurturing come easy to you?
___Are you haunted with self-doubt?
___Do you like to be in charge but not in the limelight?
___Are you not the most efficient person in the world?
___Does your need to be accommodating result in conformity?
___Are you constantly going through an identity crisis?
___Is a need to belong strong in you?
___Do you suffer with muscle tenderness?
___Are you referred to as a "peacemaker" by your friends?
___Do you regard loyalty as one of the most important traits in a person?
___Are you quite conservative in your thinking?
___Do you have a strong need to be needed?
___Are you always involved in everybody's business?
___Do you suffer with swollen glands and other lymphatic disorders?
___Would you like things to be more predictable?
___Do you tend to be overly protective?
___Do unrealistic expectations leave you disappointed much of the time?
___Do you try to be all things to all people?
___Is there a deep "emptiness" in the pit of your stomach?
___Do you have a squarish, solid physique?

Add up the total score for each of the phases. The phase that has the highest score is your predominant energy type. The phase with the lowest score is the weakest energy.

> **Phase I is the *Wood*[3] type.**
> **Phase II is the *Water* type.**
> **Phase III is the *Fire* type.**
> **Phase IV is the *Metal* type.**
> **Phase V is the *Earth* type.**

Interestingly, a majority of water people take this test and almost no earth people. It seems that earth types do not study Feng Shui in the first place! They are too involved in the practical, tangible aspects of life.

## Using the Five Fundamental Shapes

These five fundamental shapes act not only on an archetypal level, they also gather and concentrate their respective energies enabling you to draw from them. A beautiful example of the inherent power of the geometric shapes is seen in the large structures in Tibet (and the Far East in general) called *stupas*. They meditate in the base of these structures to get a balance of the five energy phases.

Stupas are built by stacking these five geometric shapes one on top of another in certain proportions in order to gather and store a balance of the five phases. People in Tibet believe the shape itself actually accumulates and focuses those forces.

By using the five basic geometric shapes and the cycles of creation, destruction, and moderation in relation to your specific energy type, you can create balance and harmony in your life.

---

3    If you hate questionnaires and refuse to use this one, you are more than likely a wood person!

*To complement the information in this article, interior designer Jami Lin[4] has added the elemental energetics along with practical decorating applications.*

## Fire

The energetic symbolism of fire is action, motivation and intellect.

*If you have an overabundance of fire:*

Use the destructive[5] cycle:    Water: Use glass, a mirror, something with an irregular shape, a photo or painting of the ocean, a fish tank, water fountain, or blue-toned, cool colors.

Use the moderating cycle:    Earth: Use ceramic or stone floor covering, furniture, and accessories, natural-tone colors, or flat-shaped and heavy items.

*If you lack fire: add some*    Fire: Use pointed-shaped items, flame stitch or geometric patterns, red or warm-toned colors, and materials that come from animals, such as leather and wool.

Use the creative cycle:    Wood: Use wood, rattan, hemp, cotton, or sisal furniture, accessories, floor coverings, floral or organic patterns, column shapes, and the color green.

---

4    *Please refer to Earth Design: The Added Dimension, and "Outdoor Feng Shui," p.155 for more information.*

5    *A more appropriate term for this cycle might be "regenerative" as nothing in nature is ever really destroyed; the Chinese knew this as well as any earth people.*

## Earth

The energetic symbolism of earth is stabile, solid, reliable, and confident.

*If you have an overabundance of earth:*

| | |
|---|---|
| Use the destructive cycle: | Wood: Please see previous description. |
| Use the moderating cycle: | Metal: Use metal accessories such as planters, picture frames, and sculptures, round or dome-shaped objects, along with metal, grey, and jewel-tone colors. |
| *If you lack earth: add some* | Earth: Please see previous description. |
| Use the creative cycle: | Fire: Please see previous description. |

## Metal

The energetic symbolism of abundance, wealth, and financial success.

*If you have an overabundance of metal:*

| | |
|---|---|
| Use the destructive cycle: | Fire: Please see previous description. |
| Use the moderating cycle: | Water: Please see previous description. |
| *If you lack metal: add some* | Metal: Please see previous description. |
| Use the creative cycle: | Earth: Please see previous description. |

## Water

The energetic symbolism of water is emotional sensitivity and the ability to go with the flow.

*If you have an overabundance of water:*

Use the destructive cycle:     Earth:  Please see previous description.
Use the moderating cycle:    Wood: Please see previous description.
*If you lack water: add some*   Water: Please see previous description.

Use the creative cycle:          Metal: Please see previous description.

## Wood

The energetic symbolism of Wood is growth, creation, and nourishment.

*If you have an over abundance of wood:*

Use the destructive cycle:     Metal: Please see previous description.
Use the moderating cycle:    Fire:   Please see previous description.

*If you lack wood: add some*   Wood: Please see previous description.

Use the creative cycle:          Water: Please see previous description.

When you design with all of the elements, you not only have well-balanced energy in your environment, you also have good design quality through the representational balance of shape, material, color, and texture.

# The Seven Portents

## Derek Walters

There are three aspects or levels to understanding and using Feng Shui: the practical, the aesthetic, and the mystical. The design of a structure's main entrance, the most important Feng Shui area, will illustrate how each level comes into play. The entrance is important from the practical standpoint of welcoming visitors while deterring burglars. From the aesthetic viewpoint, it must be visually satisfying for both the visitor and the resident. The mystical aspect of Feng Shui views the door as the face of the building, which clearly reveals its personality.

The Chinese are comfortable with the traditional explanations for why Feng Shui cures work: they improve Qi,[1] balance the elements, and deflect evil spirits. Westerners schooled in the rational, dualistic world view prefer a more common sense approach. Increasingly though, they are disappointed if the rational explanation is not tempered with something slightly more esoteric, such as: energy flow improves by suitable interior adjustments.[2]

One branch of Feng Shui offers no rational or aesthetic explanations, only transcendental ones; it is the mysterious location of the Seven Portents: source of Qi, long life, celestial monad, ghosts, accidents, imps, and severance of fate. It identifies which areas of a space have *positive* or *negative* energy and suggests which areas can be used constructively and which should be avoided. It is more esoteric and perhaps more complicated to grasp than the straightforward Bagua system.

**The Seven Portents offers astonishing results.**

---

[1] *Qi is interchangeable with Chi or energy.*

[2] *This may signal that a shift is occurring in Western thought, that we are becoming more aware of unseen forces.*

Unlike the Bagua system, there is not a universal pattern which applies to all room layouts. The Seven Portents have eight different patterns depending on the specific orientation of the building. The pattern does not rotate logically for the eight directions. The Seven Portents change position in relation to the door and to each other. It is necessary to have eight separate charts, one for each of the eight directions: the four cardinal points: north, south, east, and west and the four intermediate, non-cardinal points.

There is no general theory which explains the whole system. Some researchers suggest that the location of good and unfavorable portents is due to the interaction of the two sequences of trigrams in the famous philosophical work, the I Ching. It sounds plausible but does not seem to work in practice. A likely explanation is that this system and body of knowledge developed based on the practical experience and observations of Feng Shui practitioners accumulated over the centuries. The patterns now in use are due more to practical application than to abstract theory.

Looking at examples of two of the portents gives us a glimpse into how they come into play in our lives and the power that they have to influence us.

> One area is called the Imps;[3] it is where annoyances reoccur. Everyone has experienced a situation where the simplest task suddenly develops into a major operation. You pound a nail into the wall to put a picture up; the nail bends. While you are looking for another, you cut your finger on something in the tool box. You go to get a bandage for your finger but cannot find the box, and so on. If this kind of thing has happened to you, it probably happened in the Imps area.

A favorable area is called the *Source of Qi,*[4] it has a beneficial and inspiring atmosphere.

---

[3]  *Also known as the Six Curses in Derek's book, The Feng Shui Handbook and Earth Design: The Added Dimension.*

[4]  *Also known as Generating Breath in The Feng Shui Handbook and Earth Design: The Added Dimension.*

*A woman contacted me because she was feeling very depressed and lacked the motivation to go out. I discovered that the room which housed the Source of Qi was her late husband's office, which she kept locked. I advised her to open up the room so the inspiring Qi could fill the house. She did, and a couple of days later, she called me delightedly to say that she now felt completely revitalized.*

## Determining Your Home's Orientation

You must first determine the direction your main entrance faces as designed by the architect. The front door must be used as the orientation point, even if for convenience and practicality sake, it is not the most utilized entrance. The orientation can be found in one of three ways:

Using a compass to find magnetic north.[5]
Observing the position of the sun at midday, when it is due south.
Using accurate maps and charts.

Each method has its drawbacks. The compass method is the simplest, but magnetic north varies considerably from one place to another and also changes direction over time. The second method is the most accurate, but you need a working knowledge of astronomy and navigation. Maps may be misleading as they are often on too small a scale to read properly. Whichever method you use, check it by using one of the alternative methods. Once you know the orientation of the main entrance, consult the appropriate chart at the end of this article. The portents apply only if they fall within the confines of built walls.

---

[5] *Try standing outside with your back against the front door with a compass in hand. The direction you are facing (where your eyes are looking) is the direction of the chart you use. If you are looking out north, use the north chart.*

# Examining the Seven Portents

**Source of Qi: Generating Breath**

This is one of three very favorable locations. It is the source of all beneficial influences in the building. It is a good place to work, especially for creative fields. While in this area, if you suddenly have an idea, act on it; you can be sure that it will be a good one.

**Long Life: Lengthened Years**

This is another favorable area and a suitable location for the bedroom, dining room, or living room. In a business situation, it would be appropriate for storing perishable goods or the deep freeze but would be a waste of beneficial space to use for everyday cupboards or corridor space.

**Celestial Monad:**

This is the ancient name of the Pole Star. It is regarded as a very beneficial portent with spiritual qualities. It brings happiness and health. The Celestial Monad is never located at the rear of the building.

**Ghosts:**

This area is regarded with superstitious dread by some Chinese. Some ancient Chinese texts say it should be avoided at all costs. Viewed another way, it marks the gateway to the spirit world, the link between this world and the next. Those who are sympathetic to spiritual matters can place their religious symbols in this location, whether a cross, candlesticks, or Buddhist shrine. Placing photographs of past and present generations on the wall or on a small table may insure that the spirits of ancestors look after the living.

**Accidents:**

Do not worry if you keep breaking things in the accident zone. It is far better that a few household objects are broken than someone's limbs. This is not a good area for workshops, kitchens,[6] or any room where people are likely to be dealing with dangerous materials. It is less of a problem when the bedroom is in this area, as most of the furnishings are soft. Houses with balconies here should fill them with plants to prevent children or guests unfamiliar with the area from wandering about and possibly having accidents.

**Imps:**
**The Six Curses**

Constant annoyances reoccur in this area. Make the most of it by performing your most disagreeable chores here. If you dislike ironing, do it here and release all your anger and frustration on the Imps.

**Severance of Fate:**

Avoid this area at all costs. Some people are able to overcome the malign influences inherent in this zone. Test the area by putting a vase of cut flowers here and a similar vase of flowers in the long life area. If both vases of flowers last for the same length of time, it can be assumed that the negative forces have lost their malign influences, and the room is safe to be used. Using it for storage is a safe recommendation. Avoid building an extension in this area.

---

6   *If your kitchen falls into this area, it may be helpful to design with earth and water elements to minimize accidents by "putting out the fire." If the bathroom falls here, use earth elements to ground possible mishaps.*

## Using the Seven Portents System

Buildings with an irregular-shaped floor plan may be more or less favorable than those with a rectangular shape.[7] Whichever portent falls outside the structure's design is no longer a factor and does not influence the occupant. This may or may not be good depending on whether the missing section was a favorable or an unfavorable portent. The same is true if the main entrance is not centrally located with rooms on each side of the door. In this case, the wall at the side of the door shuts out that particular portent. The area immediately in front of the door and the central core of the building have no portent.[8]

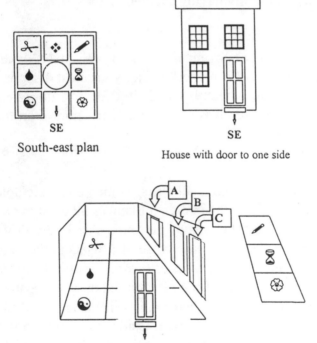

South-east plan

House with door to one side

**A**

This area behind the wall would be favorable, *Source of Qi.* Hang a landscape or mirror here.

**B**

This area is unfavorable, *Severance of Fate.* It would be better to hang a portrait or architectural picture rather than a mirror.

**C**

*Celestial Monad,* another favorable area. Hang a mirror or landscape here.

---

7    *Some traditional Feng Shui schools view L-shaped buildings and those that are not a complete rectangle as unfavorable.*

8    *The area immediately inside the front door is known as the Favorable Welcome area in __The Feng Shui Handbook__ and __Earth Design: The Added Dimension.__ This area should be open, expansive, and inviting. The central core, the Tai Chi, of the household is also favorable and is a good position for the living room.*

In the building on page 98, the portents marked B are considered to be outside the house and have no effect on it. If there were to be new construction in those areas, the influence of the portent would be introduced.

When the portent beyond the wall is a favorable one such as Source of Qi, its beneficial influences can be coaxed into the building by placing a mirror on the wall. This gives the impression that there is another room behind the wall in a favorable location. Alternatively, you could place a picture with a long distance vista or an expansive ocean view. On the other hand, if there is an unfavorable portent (Accidents) beyond the wall, shut it out with a picture that has no depth, perhaps an architectural engraving, a building, a still life, or even a portrait.

## The Charts

The accompanying eight charts of the Seven Portents show where they can be found in buildings facing each of the eight directions. For people not used to working with a magnetic compass, the center of each chart has an indicator showing the position of north. Simply note the position of the needle when standing by the main entrance, and consult the chart it matches.

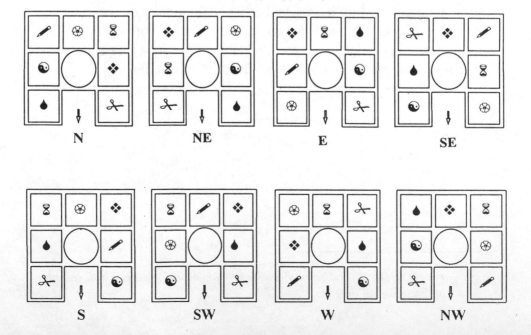

N      NE      E      SE

S      SW      W      NW

| | **Source of Qi** | *Inspiration* |
|---|---|---|
| | **Long Life** | *Healthy Constitution* |
| | **Celestial Monad** | *Recuperation and Healing* |
| | **Ghosts** | *Gateway to the Spirit World* |
| | **Accidents** | *Not a Place to Have a Workshop or Balconies* |
| | **Imps** | *Recurrent Annoyances* |
| | **Severance of Fate** | *Time Runs Out* |

Using a transcendental branch of Feng Shui like the Seven Portents seems intimidating at first, but these seven areas begin to take on meaning and come into focus more clearly as you begin to assess your home and start making the appropriate changes. When you begin experiencing the benefits of your cures, you will be a Seven Portents convert.[9]

---

[9]  *Thanks to Derek, The Seven Portents provide my clients and I with valuable information all the time.*

# Riding the Wind and Harnessing the Water

## Angi Ma Wong

The house had been vacant for three weeks. Even in the twilight, there was no reason for the pervasive eeriness I felt as I slowly pushed the door open. I wanted to turn around and run out. Several steps led me into the foyer and the feeling persisted. I could not put my finger on it, but the house felt lifeless. Normally it would have been bustling with the sounds of four teenagers and two adults going about their business; now it was silent.

As I walked through the familiar halls and rooms, checking here and there, my footsteps echoed on the hardwood floors, muffling a bit as the flooring changed to tile, and finally swishing on the plushness of the carpeting. Nothing was amiss, and yet I sensed that the house was disturbed in some way and did not welcome my presence. It was not a good feeling, especially since the house was my own.

Perhaps you have been in someone's house or apartment and shared this same feeling. Instinctively, you sensed that something did not feel right. When you first moved into your own new home or office, it may have taken weeks or months of rearranging furnishings until your surroundings felt comfortable. You probably did not know it then, but you were already practicing Feng Shui.

**Those of us of Chinese heritage are taught that there are five things that determine our destiny: fate, luck, philanthropy, education, and Feng Shui.**

**Fate**:  Your fate is decided by heaven. It is your fate to be born into affluence or poverty, to be the first or fifteenth born in your family, to be an Italian industrialist's daughter, a British prince, or a beggar on the streets of Bombay. Fate influences about 70% of your destiny.[1]

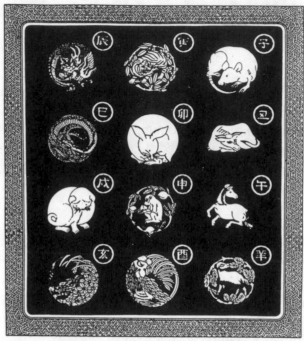

The next four elements comprise the remaining 30% of your destiny and are the areas where you can take proactive steps to change the course of your life.

**Luck:**  You can always better your luck by improving your odds. Joining the neighborhood bingo game instead of buying a lottery ticket along with 6 million other people in your state is a clear example.

**Philanthropy:**

Doing compassionate acts of charity is certainly within everyone's ability. It does not take any money to smile, pay a compliment, or give back to your community by volunteering your time.

---

[1]  *Please refer to "Classical Feng Shui," p.109, and to learn about fate from a western astrological perspective, see "Family and Space Relationships," p. 249.*

### Education:

You can be actively involved in self improvement in many ways: read, listen to tapes, take a class or trip, learn a new skill, or experience something you have never done before.

### Feng Shui:

Feng Shui originated in China as a means for the living to remain connected to and in communication with their departed ancestors. The compass[2] was invented, not as a navigational tool, but to insure the proper placement of grave sites to maintain this connection.[3] Locating the most ideal grave site would insure that the descendants would be rewarded with good fortune, health, business success, large families, and prosperity. This is definitely powerful *destiny improving* help.

The same care involved in proper placement is still used today in Chinese communities and families throughout the world, whether it is finding a grave site for grandfather, an office for mother, or a new home for the newlyweds.

**Once a closely guarded secret of holy men and mystics of China,
the centuries-old practice of Feng Shui
is now accessible to everyone.**

---

[2]    The Chinese compass, called the "loupan," has up to 24 concentric bands of mystical markings.

[3]    *Please refer to "Energy Systems and Feng Shui," p. 275.*

Practicing modern Feng Shui techniques gives you the power to change your environment and consequently to change your life. You are surrounded by the universe and its magnificence. Although you cannot see its cosmic energy, you can feel it each time you take a walk in the woods, paddle down a river, or wade in the surf. It is this same energy that binds and bonds you to all people and things.

### What do you want to change or improve in your life?

Each of the eight directions or compass points is associated with specific areas of life:

| | |
|---|---|
| **North:** | Business Success or Career |
| **South:** | Fame and Fortune |
| **East:** | Family Life or Health |
| **West:** | Children and their Fame |
| **Northwest:** | Helpful People and Travel |
| **Northeast:** | Knowledge and Intelligence |
| **Southeast:** | Wealth |
| **Southwest:** | Marriage, Relationships, and Motherhood |

These points are also associated with symbols, colors, animals, and elements. You can enhance and harmonize your environment by adding an area's corresponding element or color. To help you remember them, use the acronym **CANE** (Color, Animal, Number, Element).

# Practical Feng Shui Chart [4]

**NORTH (1)**

Career
Business success
Black
Water
Consequence of man
Death
Mourning
Penance
Calamity
Guilt
Evil Influence
Tortoise
Ears

**NORTHWEST (6)**

Father
Trips
International trade
and travel
Interests outside
the home
Helpers
Head
Grey

**NORTHEAST (8)**

Knowledge
Intelligence
Scholarly success
Turquoise
Hands
Door of the devil

**WEST (7)**

Children
Children's fame
White
Metal
Purity
Autumn
Tiger
Mouth

**EAST (3)**

Health
Family life
Green
Wood
Growth
Youth
Prosperity
Harmony
Dragon
Feet

**SOUTHWEST (2)**

Marriage
Spouse
Mother
Abdomen
Yellow
Back door of devil

**SOUTHEAST (4)**

Wealth
Fortune
Purple
Hip

**SOUTH (9)**

Fame
Red
Fire
Longevity
Festivity
Fortune
Sincerity
Used to ward
off evil
Bird
Eyes

---

[4] *Please do not confuse Angi's Feng Shui lineage and Bagua with that of Black Hat Sect Feng Shui, which does not use compass directions with the Bagua. All Feng Shui methods have their own unique approach and have proven their validity through the centuries. Process all the schools and techniques through your intuition to determine which works best for you.*

### Bring more wealth into your life

There are four different directions that relate to wealth: north for career and business success, east for fortune, south for prosperity, and southeast for wealth. Use a compass[5] to find those four directions in the space you are working on. Look around the room to see how you can move furnishings and accessories to enhance the energy of the area and to affect changes.

In the north part of your space, you could add *one* (the **Number** associated with north) object that was not there before, or something *black* (the **Color** associated with north); anything representing *water* (the **Element**); or a *tortoise* (the **Animal** symbol). Use what you have.[6] Rummage around your home or office and you will probably find what you need. It makes no sense to spend money when you are trying to increase wealth! This anecdote underlines the point:

> *A client told me that ever since she moved into her new, very expensive home, she was spending money at an alarming rate. Imagine my astonishment when she told me that a Feng Shui assessment had already been done on her home, and she had spent over $2,000 on wind chimes, crystals, and flutes. Although I have heard of spending money to make money, the amount was excessive and unnecessary.*

Now look at east on the chart to determine alternatives. Notice the **Color** is green, the **Animal** symbol is a dragon, the **Number** is three, and the **Element** is wood. Increasing your cure in the east could be to add three green plants. In the south, you might put a collection of nine red birds.[7]

---

5    Compass School Feng Shui was developed by the Northern Chinese to determine various directions in the part of their country which lacked distinguishing geographical and topographical features. A Western style camping or scout compass can be used here.

6    Syndicated columnist Jane Applegate once said, "Use what you have and you'll always have what you need."

7    The secondary compass points: NW, SE, NE, and SW do not have animal symbols or elements.

Try to select items that are symbolically meaningful for what you want to accomplish. In the southeast, consider wealth-enhancing purple satin pillows or four purple pencils in a wealthy looking brass pencil holder.

What can you place around your room in the appropriate spots? The answer is just about anything: flowers, plants, pottery, statues, stuffed animals, books, paintings, photographs, or pictures and other artwork.

*One client, a public relations professional for writers, had a wall-to-wall bookcase in the southeast area of her study. We found four books with purple covers and grouped them together on the same shelf.*

*Another client, a free lance writer, wanted to stimulate new income. We moved a large, potted indoor plant into the wealth corner of her office. The next day, she received four commissions.*

### Enhancing relationships

If you are interested in enhancing your relationships (including finding a life partner) or would like to have a child, you need to concentrate on the southwest area of the Bagua. The number related to this direction is two, the color is yellow, and the element is earth. If you desire parenthood, painting the master bedroom walls a light yellow and hanging a grouping of pictures of children on the southwestern wall are effective cures. A fertility icon would also be an ideal addition.

If you have marriage or a committed relationship in mind, add souvenirs and photographs of weddings, anniversaries, or a loving couple in the southwest area. Yellow flowers like irises, sunflowers, or roses are nice additions. Remove dried flowers, branches, or brooms from your bedroom as these are dead things and considered detrimental to both your love and sex life. The bedroom must be a cocoon, a sanctuary that nurtures, rejuvenates, and refreshes your mind, body and spirit, while reflecting the *inner you*.

As a general rule, caution must be taken when adding objects of unknown origin to your space. Avoid introducing antiques,[8] except from people you have known, loved, and respected. Remember that objects absorb the energies surrounding them, both positive and negative. These energies will emanate into their new environment, namely *your* home or office. Avoid: funeral masks, burial pieces, and jewelry from tombs, as they symbolize death, and your goal is to bring vitality into various aspects of your life.

Remember that you can apply Feng Shui to one or all of your rooms. You may wish to change everything around at once, or just one item, giving yourself time to become accustomed to the change. Use what you already have before going out to make new purchases. You have the power to create an environment that will give you control over your surroundings so you can proactively participate in your own destiny.

**Good Feng Shui suggests it is most important to tap into your own creativity, intuition, and common sense so that your home or office feels simply wonderful.**

Practical Feng Shui can ensure that your environment is always energized and harmonized, which is the way of nature and the universe. A simple activity like opening all the doors and windows and letting the wind and sunshine move through your space can bring a *dead* home back to life. Using Feng Shui will empower you and help you live a more natural, intuitive, and spiritual life. You too can ride the wind and harness the water of Feng Shui.

---

[8]   *Create your own ceremony to cleanse the ancestral history of antiques when including them in your Earth Design.*

# Classical Feng Shui

## Kathy Zimmerman

You have just found out that the dream house that you and your newly betrothed want to buy has been sold the last three times by couples who were divorcing. Would you still buy it? You are working on the great American novel but have been pacing in your office for a month, unable to write a word. Should you stick with it? If you know the principles of Feng Shui, the answer to both is yes![1] Feng Shui gives you the tools to change the energy in those spaces to make them support the life and work that you most desire.

Four key ingredients: environment, people, timing, and building make up traditional Feng Shui. They are used when analyzing and making the appropriate recommendations, changes, suggestions, and cures to improve the energetics of a space:

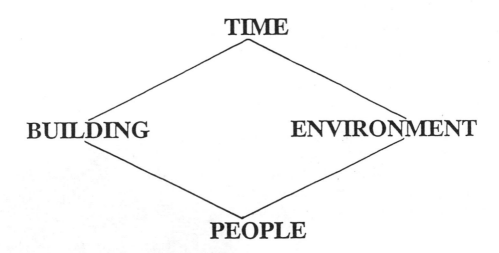

TIME

BUILDING          ENVIRONMENT

PEOPLE

---

[1] Traditional or classical Feng Shui is considered a natural science, a form of Chinese geomancy ("geo" meaning earth, "mancy" meaning knowledge.) It is based on a complicated set of theories and calculations derived from the I Ching, the Chinese Book of Changes.

## The Environment

The surrounding environment plays a critical role in Feng Shui. Although you may have the ideal Feng Shui interior, it means little if you are living next to a toxic waste dump. The harmony of the internal environment cannot compensate for the detrimental effects of the external environment. By examining some environmental factors, you can better appreciate how influential they are.

**Examples of environmental factors:**

If a house is built on stilts, there is a strong likelihood that the occupants will experience a lack of foundation and a lack of money. Look at this condition as a metaphor. If a house is not solidly planted on the earth, it is not grounded and neither are the occupants.

If there is an overgrowth of trees blocking light from coming into the house, the people living there could experience lethargy and depression.[2] The solution is easy; trim the trees to let the light in.

---

[2]  For example, the Scandinavian countries in winter, with scant hours of sunlight, have high rates of alcoholism, suicides, and depression.

If your home is on a busy street, the constant sound of traffic can cause anxiety. Planting trees or shrubbery as a buffer or installing double pane glass windows to help block the noise are options. Moving may be an even wiser one.

*Debbie bought a condo on a busy street in Los Angeles. The traffic was constant, twenty-four hours a day. Soon after moving in, she became very anxious and stressed. Finally, at the end of her rope, Debbie moved onto a very quiet street and within a month became calm, composed, and a dramatically different person.*

In a house where the back yard drops off into a hill or cliff, people in the house will have no *backing* and poor finances.

Electric power lines and especially high tension wires are unhealthy. <u>The Los Angeles Times</u> reported,

"A number of scientific studies suggest electromagnetic fields (EMF's),[3] which emanate from electrical currents that flow through power lines, and all electrical circuits might cause deadly diseases such as childhood leukemia, lymphoma, and brain cancer. Although the electric portion of those fields can be shielded, the magnetic fields penetrate concrete, soil, walls, and other solid objects without losing intensity."

*A family had just purchased a condominium near some huge high tension wires. I told them simply to move. Like the the toxic waste dump example, you cannot put a price on health. If they were unable to move, I suggested they put a big rock between the wires and them. Rock (earth)[4] grounds the effects of the high tension wires.*

This case is a poignant reminder of **how important it is to use Feng Shui principles** *before* **you purchase your home.** Remember, "an ounce of prevention..."

---

[3]    *Please refer to "Energy Fields, Fragrance and Feng Shui," p. 339, and "The Energetic Basis of Good Health," p. 293.*

[4]    *Please refer to "The Five Phases of Energy," p. 81, and "Energy Fields, Feng Shui, and Fragrance," p. 339.*

## People

It is important to understand the people who are living in a particular space.

Each person is unique, with a distinct energy blueprint and resonance. Just as you have a relationship with other humans, you also have a relationship with your house or office.

One method for understanding your personal relationship to your home is using East/West teaching. It uses the eight principle directions, or eight types of magnetic fields and their corresponding trigram, to determine which directions are favorable for you and which are not. Your year of birth determines which trigram is yours, and consequently, it determines your corresponding compass direction.

The trigrams have many specific symbolic qualities and meanings. By knowing your personal trigram or *Feng Shui personality type*, you can determine many things, including your best sleeping direction along with your highest energy direction. Determine your trigram by consulting your birth year and the appropriate column: male/female. (If you were born between January 1 and February 3 of any year, see the note for the Chinese calendar conversion.[5])

---

[5]   The Chinese use a lunar calendar. Anyone born January 1 to February 3 is considered born the year before. A person born on January 2, 1965, would look at 1964 as the birth year. A person born on February 4 or "bridge day" must consult a Chinese calendar. Depending on the year, it may or may not coincide with the Western calendar year.

# Birth Year & Trigram Chart [6]

| Year | Trigram | | Year | Trigram | |
|------|---------|--------|------|---------|--------|
|      | male    | female |      | male    | female |
| 1900 | K'an    | Ken    | 1950 | K'un    | K'an   |
| 1901 | Li      | Chien  | 1951 | Sun     | K'un   |
| 1902 | Ken     | Tui    | 1952 | Chen    | Chen   |
| 1903 | Tui     | Ken    | 1953 | K'un    | Sun    |
| 1904 | Chien   | Li     | 1954 | Kan     | Ken    |
| 1905 | K'un    | Kan    | 1955 | Li      | Chien  |
| 1906 | Sun     | K'un   | 1956 | Ken     | Tui    |
| 1907 | Chen    | Chen   | 1957 | Tui     | Ken    |
| 1908 | K'un    | Sun    | 1958 | Chien   | Li     |
| 1909 | K'an    | Ken    | 1959 | K'un    | K'an   |
| 1910 | Li      | Chien  | 1960 | Sun     | K'un   |
| 1911 | Ken     | Tui    | 1961 | Chen    | Chen   |
| 1912 | Tui     | Ken    | 1962 | K'un    | Sun    |
| 1913 | Chien   | Li     | 1963 | Kan     | Ken    |
| 1914 | K'un    | Kan    | 1964 | Li      | Chien  |
| 1915 | Sun     | K'un   | 1965 | Ken     | Tui    |
| 1916 | Chen    | Chen   | 1966 | Tui     | Ken    |
| 1917 | K'un    | Sun    | 1967 | Chien   | Li     |
| 1918 | K'an    | Ken    | 1968 | K'un    | K'an   |
| 1919 | Li      | Chien  | 1969 | Sun     | K'un   |
| 1920 | Ken     | Tui    | 1970 | Chen    | Chen   |
| 1921 | Tui     | Ken    | 1971 | K'un    | Sun    |
| 1922 | Chien   | Li     | 1972 | Kan     | Ken    |
| 1923 | K'un    | Kan    | 1973 | Li      | Chien  |
| 1924 | Sun     | K'un   | 1974 | Ken     | Tui    |
| 1925 | Chen    | Chen   | 1975 | Tui     | Ken    |
| 1926 | K'un    | Sun    | 1976 | Chien   | Li     |
| 1927 | K'an    | Ken    | 1977 | K'un    | K'an   |
| 1928 | Li      | Chien  | 1978 | Sun     | K'un   |
| 1929 | Ken     | Tui    | 1979 | Chen    | Chen   |
| 1930 | Tui     | Ken    | 1980 | K'un    | Sun    |
| 1931 | Chien   | Li     | 1981 | Kan     | Ken    |
| 1932 | K'un    | Kan    | 1982 | Li      | Chien  |
| 1933 | Sun     | K'un   | 1983 | Ken     | Tui    |
| 1934 | Chen    | Chen   | 1984 | Tui     | Ken    |
| 1935 | K'un    | Sun    | 1985 | Chien   | Li     |
| 1936 | K'an    | Ken    | 1986 | K'un    | K'an   |
| 1937 | Li      | Chien  | 1987 | Sun     | K'un   |
| 1938 | Ken     | Tui    | 1988 | Chen    | Chen   |
| 1939 | Tui     | Ken    | 1989 | K'un    | Sun    |
| 1940 | Chien   | Li     | 1990 | Kan     | Ken    |
| 1941 | K'un    | Kan    | 1991 | Li      | Chien  |
| 1942 | Sun     | K'un   | 1992 | Ken     | Tui    |
| 1943 | Chen    | Chen   | 1993 | Tui     | Ken    |
| 1944 | K'un    | Sun    | 1994 | Chien   | Li     |
| 1945 | K'an    | Ken    | 1995 | K'un    | K'an   |
| 1946 | Li      | Chien  | 1996 | Sun     | K'un   |
| 1947 | Ken     | Tui    | 1997 | Chen    | Chen   |
| 1948 | Tui     | Ken    | 1998 | K'un    | Sun    |
| 1949 | Chien   | Li     | 1999 | Kan     | Ken    |
|      |         |        | 2000 | Li      | Chien  |

---

[6]    Chart courtesy of American Institute of Feng Shui.

Note: February 5th begins each western year according to the Chinese calender.

## Sleeping Direction

The East/West School has peaceful sleeping directions for each trigram or personality type. The compass direction that corresponds to your personal trigram is the direction where the *top of your head* should point when you are lying down.

### PERSONAL TRIGRAM
### SLEEPING DIRECTION CHART
(top of head this direction when sleeping
in order of most restful to most active)

| | | | |
|---|---|---|---|
| **KUN** | SW, NW, W, NE | **SUN** | SE, E, S, N |
| **KEN** | NE, W, NW, (SW) | **CHEN** | E, SE, N, S |
| **CHIEN** | NW, SW NE, W | **LI** | S, N, SE, E |
| **TUI** | W, NE, SW, NW | **KAN** | N, S, E, SE |

Because each bedroom is different, you must also use your common sense. If your favorable sleeping position puts your bed in an awkward area of the room, do not move it. If your spouse is a different trigram, you may have to compromise by one or both of you sleeping in the second or third most favorable position.

*A couple tried everything to get their two year old to sleep well: warm milk, herbal remedies, even physically wearing the child out through playing with him. The child was "kun," so I suggested the parents move his bed so the top of his head was facing southwest, his most peaceful sleeping direction. Now everyone is sleeping soundly.*

## Highest Energy/Most Active Direction

When you know your personal trigram, you can determine your most active or highest energy direction. For example a *li* person would face east. When you face in this direction, meeting a deadline or exercising to your highest capacity is much easier.

**PERSONAL TRIGRAM
MOST ACTIVE
DIRECTION CHART**
(body facing this direction)

| KUN | NE | | SUN | N |
|-----|-----|---|------|---|
| KEN | SW | | CHEN | S |
| CHIEN | W | | LI | E |
| TUI | NW | | KAN | SE |

## Building

Environment and personal energy are both important factors in implementing Feng Shui cures; the building itself also holds specific energy that must be analyzed. Look at the magnetic energies of a building to determine its positive or negative energetic qualities. Begin by dividing the building into nine equal quadrants. Eight of the quadrants represent the eight directions around a compass, and the ninth represents the center.

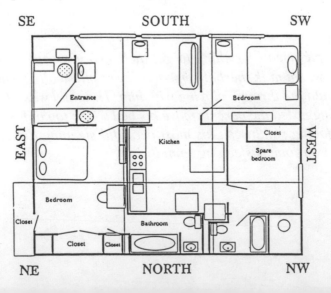

The compass[7] has been used in geomancy for hundreds if not thousands of years.

The use of a loupan, Chinese geomancer's compass, shows the electromagnetic energies of a structure.

This tells you the exact magnetic direction of the building. Within each of the eight compass directions are three sub-directions, for a total of 24 possible directions for a building.

If there is a row of identical houses on the same street, all built in the same year but one angled a mere five degrees differently from the others, not only would it have a different compass reading, it could have a totally different energetic quality or personality. For example, all these houses, except the one on the far right, could be great for making money. Because the home on the right has a different compass reading, which may be as little as a few degrees, the structure will have different potential. Once you know the building's magnetic direction and exact date of construction, there is a wealth of information that you can learn about it.

---

[7]  The ancient Greek geomancers used a compass; the Indians use the compass directions when practicing Vastu Shastra, the Vedas sacred geomantic architectural system; and of course, the Chinese use it.

## The Personality Type or Potential of the Building

Does your house have the potential for arguments and lawsuits, for making lots of money or. . . .?

*A colleague called to say, "Feng Shui is so incredible." By doing a compass reading on a house, she was able to calculate, by using the magnetic direction and exact construction date, that it had a potential for divorce and separation. The couple seemed quite happy. Not wanting to put any negative ideas into their heads, my friend simply asked if there was anything in particular they wanted to discuss before the reading. She almost fell off the chair when her clients told her that their new neighbors had commented that the last three couples who had lived in the house had gotten a divorce.*

Based on the magnetic direction and date of construction, the energy of your house or business can be inherently positive or negative, which does not mean if the energy is *negative* that you should move. It simply means you need to be aware and to implement corresponding Feng Shui cures to improve the energy of the space. The key lies in what you do with the information. This example shows how a *negative* space can be *made* positive or improved.

*One client owned a furniture store that had negative energy based on the magnetic reading and date of construction. At first glance, it would seem that the store would have major problems getting clients and making money, yet it was making a handsome profit. What mitigated this negative building personality were the additional factors that offset or softened it.*

*The most important factor for a building is the door people use. The door brings in Chi (energy) and profit for a business. This business had its door on the corner of two streets with high pedestrian traffic, in a wealthy neighborhood, with convenient parking. The cash register had also been placed in a very auspicious area of the building.*

> *To further enhance their business, I stationed the*
> *salespersons' desks in the most beneficial part of the*
> *building, in accordance with each of their personal trigrams,*
> *so they could prosper to their full potential.*

This store is a great example of how you must look at the whole picture and not just one individual detail.[8] It would have been misleading to abandon the reading after determining that the building had a negative energy personality.

## Time

Two elements must be factored in when considering time: twenty-year cycles and one-year cycles. Life is about cycles.[9] These cycles represent predictable trends that can impact people in a variety of ways. You can tap into the positive energies of a cycle and remedy and/or avoid the negative ones.

## Twenty-Year Cycle

The twenty-year cycle is based on a Saturn/Jupiter alignment or conjunction with the corresponding magnetic-energetic shift.[10] The twenty-year cycle has a profound effect on you and your surroundings. It is an important consideration in a Feng Shui reading. An earthquake in Southern California gives us an interesting example of how the twenty-year cycle plays out.

---

[8]    A good metaphor for life.

[9]    *In accordance with natural laws, everything is cyclical.*

[10]   History has proven how important these twenty-year cycles are. An article in the July, 1995, issue of <u>The Mountain Astrologer</u> revealed that every United States president who assumed office under this conjunction in the earth family died in office: Harrison, Lincoln, Garfield, McKinley, Harding, Roosevelt, and Kennedy.

Each house is identical, on exactly the same street facing exactly the same direction.

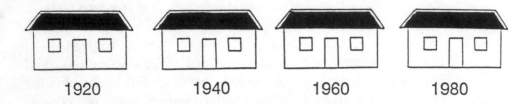

The only difference in the houses is that they are built in different twenty-year cycles. The house built in 1920 could have a potential for divorce and separation, the house built in 1940 could have a potential for illness, the house built in 1960 could have a potential for creativity, and the house built in 1980 could have a potential for making a lot of money.

*A client had a home built in 1942, long before many earthquake building standards were in effect. It was condemned after a recent earthquake, and a new one was built on the exact same site, facing the exact same direction.*

*The reading I did showed that the old house had a potential for illness, which the client confirmed. The new house, built during a different twenty-year cycle, showed a potential for making money. Six months after moving into the new house, in the same spot and the same direction, the owner got a promotion and a substantial raise.*

## Annual Cycle

Once a house is built, it has a certain energy and a certain personality. Annually, there is a distinct energy, whether positive or negative, that comes in and affects every part of the house.

*A colleague did a reading on a condominium. This place was like Fort Knox; he had to go through two security gates to enter. There was no way an intruder could have broken in. Yet, when he did a reading, he was able to pinpoint that a robbery had taken place in the bedroom in 1993. The shocked owner confirmed that during a party someone had stolen all her jewelry from the exact spot my colleague had pointed out to her.*

The most dramatic example of this annual energy cycle and its effects is a very personal story.

*My mom slept in a room that had terribly unbalanced energy. In 1974, the annual energies came in and intensified this negative energy; that is the same year she got cancer and had a mastectomy. Just think, if I had had Feng Shui knowledge then, I might have prevented or at least used a remedy to soften the effect of her illness.*

### Role of Feng Shui

Feng Shui is a tool to help you on your path. It is not a cure-all, but it is a powerful ally to help you make positive choices about how you live. The Chinese believe that destiny, luck, charity, effort, and work/study comprise the majority of who you are and that Feng Shui can help you mold these elements into life-transforming gifts. You are born with varying degrees of potential in each aspect of your life, but what you make of these gifts is based on the choices you make along the way.

Master Larry Sang, my master teacher, whom I thank for bringing much needed information on Feng Shui to the general public, has this for you to consider:

**Yesterday's mysteries are today's sciences
and today's mysteries are tomorrow's sciences.**

# The Mystical Meaning of Feng Shui

## Juan M. Alvarez

Mysticism is a refined stage of consciousness that connects our beings with the essence of all that manifests in the Universe through light, colors, forms, and life. Our physical and logical world is nurtured by energy particles that manifest from another dimension, not part of the visible and invisible nature of things. The Transcendental Method of Feng Shui, as taught by Professor Lin Yun, Spiritual Master of the Black Hat School, Tibetan Tantric Buddhism (BTB), works with this channel of pure and harmonious energy which radiates from the unmanifested source of the power of creation. This subtle and powerful energy is Chi or spirit.

Feng Shui provides a system for evaluating existing influences in your surrounding environment, both the visible, such as land, buildings, and furniture, and the invisible, such as electromagnetic fields. It then balances the flow of Chi with corresponding cures that can be made on the visible level with the nine basic cure items (crystals, chimes, mirrors, and so forth) or the invisible level with Bau-Biology. BTB Feng Shui goes a step further and uses transcendental methods, like the Three Secrets Reinforcement and Tracing the Nine Star Path.[1]

Intention is the connection that establishes and seals Feng Shui cures in order to manifest harmonious Chi in the environment. The combination of body, mind, and word, or the *Mystery of the Three Secrets*, is the means of manifesting this intention, sealed when honoring the tradition of the red envelope.[2] Through reverence (body: mudra), heart (word: mantra), and mind (visualization: sutra), you infuse the Feng Shui

---

[1]     *Please refer to "Spirituality and Feng Shui," p. 357.*

[2]     *Please refer to the Glossary, p. 427 for information on the red envelope.*

adjustments with your own divine nature and spirit. The result of the cure is then 120 percent.

BTB Feng Shui establishes a discipline for the study and application of the universal principles of creation as they are manifested throughout the symbols of the Bagua.[3] Feng Shui is based on the history and philosophy of yin and yang, Tao, the I Ching, the trigrams of Feng Shui, as well as the Theory of the Five Elements,[4] The Lines of Harmony of the Bagua,[5] Buddhist meditations, and Chinese Astrology to determine the best times to perform Feng Shui adjustments.

### The Three Schools of Colors

Other valuable tools of BTB Feng Shui that are less often talked about are the Three Schools of Colors. These are representative of the Law of the Triangle, also known as the Law of Creation. Each *creation* starts at the first point of the triangle, with the *idea* or yin. It follows with the second point of the triangle, with the *action* or yang, and it manifests at the third point of the triangle, as *creation* or Tao. The objective of Feng Shui is to create harmonious spaces, complementing the negative/yin aspects with the positive/yang aspects to create harmony, or the unity of Tao.

---

[3]  *Please refer to "The Bagua," p. 35.*

[4]  *Please refer to "The Five Phases of Energy," p. 81.*

[5]  The lines of harmony represent each of the eight lines connecting the Bagua to the forms or shapes of living spaces. These lines can also be visualized as the diameters of vibrating energy circles, providing a frame of reference for the creation of harmony between heaven and earth in its habitats.

Each of the Three Schools of Colors represents a point of the Law of the Triangle.

1.   The School of the Seven Colors of the Rainbow, or the psychic vibratory nature of colors, is used for creating internal harmony, personal Chi, or the yin aspect of the triangle and Feng Shui design.[6]

2.   The School of the Colors of the Five Chinese Elements, or the color association of the elements, is used to create harmony in the external environment, external Chi, or yang aspect.

3.   The School of the Colors of the Six True Words,[7] or the divine essence of the eminent nature of things, is used to create harmony between heaven and earth, spiritual Chi, or the Tao aspect.

## The Theory of the Elements, both East and West

The works of the Greek philosopher Aristotle speak about the theory of the elements. The elements proposed in Aristotle's works included: Water, Fire, Earth, and Air. The development of his theory later gave rise to a fifth element known as the fifth essence or spirit. Each of the metaphysical elements of the West has a corresponding Chinese element.

Each of the elements identifies a manifestation of energy that is reflected in many forms. For example, the energetic manifestation of the element *wood* can be seen not only in the many colors and species of the vegetable kingdom, but also as it is revealed in human personality traits.

---

[6]   *Please refer to "Color and the Chakra System," p. 311.*

[7]   *Please refer to "Spirituality and Feng Shui," p. 357, and "The Magic of Ritual and Feng Shui," p. 369.*

Eastern and Western philosophies are united through the symbols of the five elements as follows:

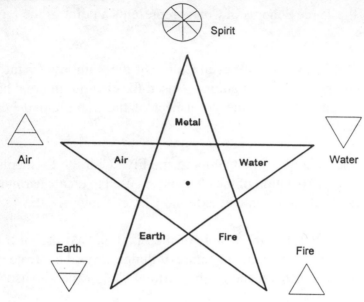

## The Bagua

The Bagua is one of the special tools used in the environmental art of Feng Shui. It is composed of eight symbols or Guas, each depicted by a trigram (a combination of yin and yang symbols, in groups of three.) Each of the Guas has a corresponding color, element, manifestation of nature, mundane activity, cardinal direction, and planet, among others. The nature of these manifestations is to connect the visible and the invisible universe with its unmanifested essence, to create harmonious environments.

One of the aspects connecting mystical philosophies can be related to space or the four cardinal points. The Bagua, Chinese and Western Astrology, and other ancient systems were aligned to the four cardinal points. For example, a study of the relationship of angels to cardinal directions is known as The Four Angels of the Wind. They were identified as: Mikhael (East Wind), Uriel (South Wind), Raphael (West Wind) and Gabriel (North Wind).

Relating the four cardinal points to the Bagua, Chinese and Western Astrologies, and the Kabballah Tree of Life, the following correspondences exist:

| CARDINAL DIRECTIONS | KING-WEN BA-GUA | CHINESE ASTROLOGY | WESTERN ASTROLOGY | TREE OF LIFE |
|---|---|---|---|---|
| EAST | WOOD | DRAGON | ARIES | MIKHAEL |
| SOUTH | FIRE | PHOENIX | CAPRICORN | URIEL |
| WEST | METAL | TIGER | LIBRA | RAPHAEL |
| NORTH | WATER | TORTOISE | CANCER | GABRIEL |
| CENTER | EARTH | SERPENT | GEOCENTER | ZAPHIEL |

The eight symbols of the Bagua are connected to hermetic, Rosicrucian, and other metaphysical teachings, including the philosophy of Kabballah.

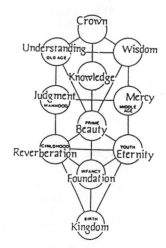

The Tree of Life of the Kabballah explains the creation of the Universe and holds the key to finding the connection between human life and its divine source.

**Sephirotic Tree of the Kabballah**

According to this philosophy, the Universe emanated from the Void, by the Will of a Supreme Force or God, which projected its essence through four realities and ten dimensions or sephirots.

Hebrew philosophers related and understood the sephirots through the use of an archetypal form known as the Tree of Life. The Tree of Life is divided into two types: The Small Tree of Life and the Large Tree of Life.

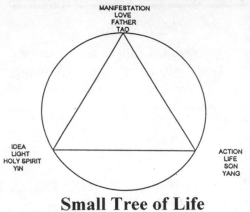

**Small Tree of Life**

The Small Tree of Life represents the unmanifested and consists of three symbols or spiritual forces: the Father (Kether), the Son (Chokmah) and the Holy Spirit (Binah). It also relates to the Tao triad philosophy: Tao (Father), Yang (Son), Yin (Holy Spirit).

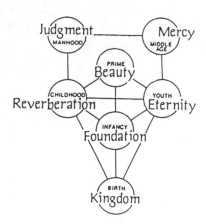

**Large Tree of Life**

The Large Tree of Life represents creation, including forms, colors, and substance. It emanates from the Small Tree of Life and consists of seven sephirots or symbols.

Each of the ten dimensions or sephirots represents an emanation from the universal essence/consciousness of God and corresponds with many manifestations. The law of correspondence is an aspect of the evolutionary process of the Universe.

One of the geometrical symbols describing spiritual and material evolution is the spiral. The process of evolution follows the geometry of the spiral, vibrating from the infinitesimal instant to the infinite and eternal Universe. At each turn, the vibratory energy aligns with the previous position, at a higher level. Each sephirot can be described as a harmonic manifestation of the emanation of God through the evolutionary process of the Universe. At a given dimensional point, it is given a name and correspondences as follows:

## The Essence, the Unmanifested

1.   Kether, Father, Crown, Metatron, Seraphims, Love of God, Tao.

2.   Chokmah, Son, Wisdom, Ratziel, Cherubims, Light of God, White, Zodiac, Yang.

3.   Binah, Holy Spirit, Understanding, Zafkiel, Thrones, Life of God, Black, Saturn, Yin.

## The World of Creation

4.   Chesed, Mercy, Zadkiel, Dominations, Expansion, Jupiter, Blue, Thursday, Yang.

5.   Geburah, Strength, Kamael, Powers, Will, Mars, Red, Tuesday, Yin.

6.   Tiphereth, Beauty, Mikhael, Virtues, Love, Sun, Yellow, Sunday, Tao.

## The World of Manifestation

7.   Netzach, Victory, Anael, Principalities, Creative, Venus, Green, Friday, Yang.

8.   Hod, Splendor, Raphael, Archangels, Healing, Mercury, Orange, Wednesday, Yin.

9.   Yesod, Foundation, Gabriel, Angels, Infinite Mind, Moon, Violet, Monday, Tao.

10.   Malkuth, Kingdom, Uriel, Elements, Experiences, Saturn as the planet of the Earth, Ying-Yang-Tao.

Ancient studies of the Kabballah related Angelical orders to each of the sephirot. Each of the orders is related to a power of God and can be used for protection, healing, and spiritual development. For example, if your house is showing a deficiency in the health area (a bathroom or kitchen in the middle of the house), a Feng Shui cure could consist of placing a figurine of the Archangel Raphael, representing the healing power of God, and then reinforcing it with the Three Secrets.

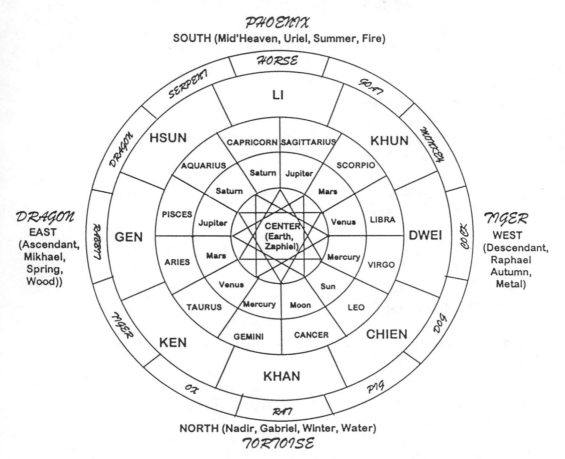

Feng Shui is a living experience which expresses the relationship of human life to shapes, substances, and environmental and technological forces. Construction patterns have been created throughout human evolution, manifesting the archetype of homes and buildings, expressed in the mysteries of the trigrams. The visualization of the lines of harmony of the Bagua in homes and work places expresses the transcendental relationship of space, time and energy that humanity has created in a dimension beyond reality.

# Architecture
# and Landscape

# feng Shui and Healing Architecture

### A.T. Mann

It is one thing to understand the theory of Feng Shui, but if we follow the advice of some practitioners, our houses are likely to end up looking like a Chinese restaurant, festooned with bamboo flutes, gaudily painted mirrors, and who knows what else. The challenge is to integrate Feng Shui principles into a vision of architecture, design, and interior design that reflects our personal taste and spiritual path.

The Chinese based the art and science of orienting and siting buildings upon the workings of mysterious earth forces which were known as Feng Shui, literally *wind and water*. The earth is criss-crossed with energy lines that affect and are affected by virtually all geographical and topographical phenomena. This means that we are affected by our environment, and we in turn modify our environment by what we do within it.

We can better understand this concept of Feng Shui by viewing the parallel system of Chinese medicine and healing. It is based upon interplay and balance between the twelve energy channels, the acupuncture meridians which travel through the physical body. Meridians carry vital energy and information along specific routes and distribute them by various loci and internal organs connected to external outlets. Hundreds of acupuncture points lie along the meridians. Similarly in Feng Shui, there are forces in the earth and those carried by the wind which are connected and can be modified.

Every earthly and bodily energy channel contains both yin/passive and yang/active components. For health and good fortune, it is essential to have a balance of the two; yin/yang energies are never separated because everything contains both in some proportion. The idea of the Chinese life philosophy, as manifested in the I Ching, is the interplay between these two dancing energies, and both architecture and healing are popular and necessary grounds for their interaction.

The cosmic currents are collectively called Chi, the same term which describes life energy pulsing through the body.

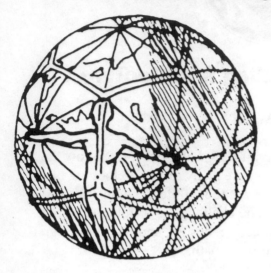

The earth currents or energies can be seen as the acupuncture meridians of the Great Mother, who in turn created the polarities.[1]

Feng Shui is a form of geomancy or geographical divination which utilizes principles such as astrology as well as psychic and physical phenomena to determine whether the location, form, and orientation of a building or monument is auspicious or inauspicious. Like Chinese medicine, it has both diagnostic and therapeutic forms. Buildings which utilize the natural elements of the land and tap into its energy are healthy, auspicious places to live, work, or bury the dead, while places that are antagonistic to these energies are unhealthy and inauspicious.

## Water and Mountains

In Feng Shui there are two primary natural forms which must be respected and utilized, water and mountains. In the analogy of the Tao, water carries the yang or active principle and mountains carry the passive or yin principle: water nourishes and hills separate.

**The interaction and intrinsic harmony of water and mountains are essential for the proper site selection of buildings.**

---

[1]    *Please refer to "Energy Systems and Feng Shui," p. 275.*

Water is the essence of life and is critical for its processes. The potency of the landscape is determined by the flow of the water. Its clarity shows the positive qualities of the Chi it carries through the land, like an abundance of pure blood circulating through a healthy body. If the water flow is too straight or excessive, the land is susceptible to flooding and should be subdued or avoided. The land could have a heart attack!

Flow, location, depth, purity, and strength of bodies of water are used in evaluating the correct location for a building. Water flows from above to below, and building orientation can go with or against this underground movement. Dowsers know that if houses or other buildings are sited above such watercourses, it is an indicator of ill health and disruptive energy for the location. The electromagnetic currents generated by running water can disrupt the human energy field. Because water originates in mountains or hills and flows down, buildings must respect their relationship with the mountains and hills within their view.

Mountains are intersections of earth and heaven, and as such, they dispense energy to the surrounding land. Early geomancers likened the mountains, which meandered across the spectacular landscape of China, to dragons which carried power and influence, for good or evil, over the wealth and happiness of inhabitants of the land. If the landscape dragons remained happy, then the people living with and around them prospered. If the dragons were aroused by ignorance, insensitivity, or maltreatment, they brought the inhabitants illness and poverty, if not outright destruction. While this description might seem superstitious and mythic, I believe it is an absolutely correct view, which we should regard highly indeed.

**The powerful dragons guarding the land need
plenty of clear water to drink.**

All natural shapes in the landscape have meaning to the Chinese and correspond to the animal qualities which they reflect; a particular pinnacle might be a tiger's ear, while a benign mountain might be a protective watch dog. The determination of direction and the site either utilize these forces or antagonize them. They not only affect the luck of the inhabitants, but they determine the prosperity and health of everyone living within their realm of influence. It is common sense to be sensitive to and respect the earth energies, but this is rarely the case.

The veins and meridians of the landscape run down hillsides and across valley sides, criss-crossing to create energetic nodes of activity. Certain places tap into beneficial Chi, while others are devoid of it and lead their inhabitants to stagnation. Proper siting taps the Chi at the points where it is closest to the surface. Such places can be easily identified by lush foliage, strong trees, rich soil, and healthy, and prosperous inhabitants. Flat valleys, areas without nearby flowing water, or places where the topography is too violent, which could signify a dragon's mouth or lashing tail, are to be avoided. They bring bad luck and ill health for inhabitants.

For most of us these principles ring true, but they are extremely difficult to apply to *real* situations. And it is quite rare for an architect knowing these principles to have the opportunity to utilize them in an entire site and in buildings on that site. I have been lucky to have had this chance.

## The Perfect Project

I started my architectural education expecting to be initiated into an ancient, magical tradition which utilized shape, volume, and movement through time to enhance the environment and humanity. It was quite surprising and disturbing to realize that such knowledge was not a part of modern architectural education. I discovered that architects tended to resist self-knowledge in favor of self assertion. The only magical quality they desired was to make money and achieve fame.

Thus I began a very long and frustrating journey in search of meaning, which has now lasted some thirty years. I have discovered that there are ancient traditions, which are still very much alive that carry the mystery, magic, and spirituality I sought. I have investigated the cathedral schools,

Egyptian religion and architecture, Indian thought and its manifestations in sacred architecture, Buddhist temples and Islamic mosques, megalithic monuments, memory theatres, and others. In every case, I looked for the underlying logic and feeling inherent in certain buildings and monuments which we all know and love: Stonehenge, the great cathedrals, the Taj Mahal, the stupas of the Indian subcontinent, and many others.

I became an amateur dowser, following energy channels through the landscape and also through the human body. I learned radionics, a healing technique which works with patterns for diagnosis and healing the *subtle body*. For 25 years, my primary occupation has been professional astrologer, working with patterns in both space and time.

Then, ten years ago, I began studying and using Feng Shui. Of all the arcane arts of the East, Feng Shui is the most universal. It ties together, like Ariadne's thread, astrology, orientation, healing, earth energies, the ancestors, geometry, pattern, colour, time, and their spiritual interactions. Throughout all the years and spiritual pursuits, I never lost track of my original love, the sacred in architecture; Feng Shui was a way for me to bring the sacred back into architecture.

In 1993, I was fortunate to be chosen to design a house for a lovely, spiritual couple in Denmark. It was a wonderful project that beautifully illustrates the universal appeal and application of Feng Shui.

This couple was extremely active and committed to co-housing, recycling, and alternative forms of energy. They wanted to implement a type of land use called *permaculture*, where the land is formed to attract animals, winds, the sun for warmth, natural water for irrigation, and many other obvious and sensible concepts. I realized that my work would entail enabling them to integrate their spiritual and ecological consciousness within a place to live. It was an inspiring project.

The land they had purchased in western Denmark had been called The World University since the 1960's; it was the place where Yoko and John Lennon learned meditation from the Marishi Mahesh Yogi. They wished to create an ecological co-housing project called Gaia Fjordvang (the earth goddess' place on the fjord), which would enable them "to live more lightly on the earth and in harmony with nature." In addition to a house for themselves, they wanted many co-housing units spread around the large piece of land, interspersed with permaculture farming projects, natural crafts, kitchen gardens, animal shelters, and so forth.

My friends had made a list, which they dowsed to see which of the designers or designs were ideally suited for the project. Unfortunately, the dowsing pendulum refused to select any of the projects or architects. In a sudden act of intuition, they included my name at the end of the list, and the pendulum automatically selected me. So even the selection process, about which I knew nothing, supported the ideas I had been working with for so many years.

Although brave and futuristic in concept, the property had seen its ups and downs; the previous Swedish owner had experienced many years of financial insecurity and bad health. Upon visiting the huge site (L-shaped, about 700 m x 400 m), I discovered it to be a natural for Feng Shui techniques for a number of important reasons.

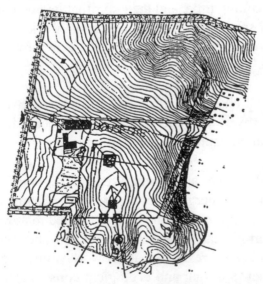

The existing building was a large classic Danish farmhouse composed of two wings (L-shaped like the land) that faced down a hill, sloping towards the fjord.

Because an L-shaped building[2] is irregular and shows incompleteness of some kind, I knew that the new house, which had by law to be quite close to the existing building, would have to remedy some of the existing problems. I realized that the financial and health problems experienced by the previous owner were inherent in the L- shaped building and site.

---

2    *Please refer to "Outdoor Feng Shui," p. 155.*

Denmark contains more megalithic earthworks than any other country in Europe, and my friends were fortunate to have a series of seven megalithic burial mounds, approximately five thousand years old, stepping across the property. As the Chinese revere their ancestors and particularly their burial places, this would immediately cast great seriousness and importance on the way the site was to be used.

The site contained much water already: a stream, the fjord below, a disused well, a pipe for municipal water supply, and the clients intended to recycle site water and to create some ponds on the land.

## The Feng Shui Analysis

In my early interactions with the clients, I spent some time investigating the site and not only dowsed on-site by walking around searching for earth energies, ley lines, and watercourses, but also rechecked my findings by map-dowsing the site. There was no doubt that the site was a powerful energy node and as such needed to be treated very carefully. To me, it was a bit like working with a large crystal, which contains powerful healing energies but is also a considerable force, which requires great understanding and skill on the part of its owners. My analysis of the site follows; some of the insights described here came through advice from my friend, astrologer, and Feng Shui practitioner Angel Thompson.[3]

The site has good Feng Shui, due to the land sloping towards the water to the southeast and because the buildings can face the south and its views. The site is shielded from the prevailing westerly winds by a line of trees. From the proposed house site the views are good and the existing building blocks the detrimental western setting sun.

Ponds near a house (which is a condition of the clients) are good in general, provided they are not too close. When ponds are close, there must be circuitous paths to them to disperse the Chi. The fjord below the property is in a wonderful position, being to the south and east, within

---

[3]    *Please see Angel Thompson's article "The Power of Chi," p. 49.*

view of the house, but not too close. The well is a serious problem. Blocked, disused, or poorly maintained wells may become *reservoirs of sorrow and bitterness* or sources of health problems or financial decline. This may explain why the previous owner experienced such financial and health problems. The well should be neutralized, either by making it operable again or by planting above and around it.

The neolithic burial mounds are aspects of a Venus Dragon and must be treated with extreme care and caution. Disturbing them would disperse negative energies to all those living on or near the site.

According to the School of Forms, the mounds represent the humps of the dragon living under the ground, with the head of the dragon, the largest mound, closest to the house site, and the tail leading away to the south.

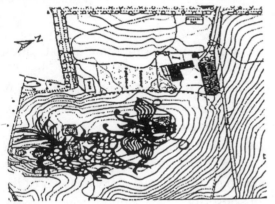 

The best approach may be to echo the form of the mounds in the house in some way, such as a curved or semi-circular end towards the east, a dome or curved roof in that direction, or some other such solution to befriend the powerful forces of the dead on the site.

According to the School of the Compass, there are two possible orientations for the front entrance, which will determine the overall character of the house. If the north entrance, through the line of trees is used, it would correspond to the water element *kan*,[4] the moon, and Winter.[5] If the entrance from the proposed private garden to the northwest is used, it will correspond to *tui*, the elements water and fire, the lake, and

---

[4]     *These directions and trigrams refer to the Bagua locations.*

[5]     *Please refer to "The Bagua," p. 35.*

Autumn. A main entrance through a line of trees is not good Feng Shui, and kan is more difficult and less benign than tui (wisdom and social interaction), which are qualities most valuable to the clients. The best solution is a formal entrance from the northwest garden, with a secondary or back entrance from the north through the row of trees.

The access road, which extends along the north side of the trees to the house, should have a curved, circular ending or a turnaround, as straight roads which end abruptly create difficult Chi.

## The Design

The preliminary design I submitted to the clients reflected their architectural needs and also satisfied as many of the Feng Shui conditions as I could within the limited scope of the house project itself.

The house was to blend into the environment by having structural walls made of stone found on the site. The site sloped some three meters from back to front so that there would be substantial walls facing the fjord. I felt the part of the house facing the *mouth of the dragon* should both echo the form of the mounds and also reflect and disperse their substantial energies from entering the house.

It was natural that the clients wanted to be able to see the beautiful mounds from the house. I therefore designed the bulk of the house with a pitched, thatched roof, which softened the roof line as seen from the rest of the site. In the corner of the house, towards the mouth of the dragon, I made a full height glass conservatory which functioned as a heat collection and retention space for the passive solar heating the building possessed. The corner towards the mouth was curved in a semicircle of glass. Above the curved windows, the glass met at an apex, creating a crystal form exactly facing the dragon's head. This would both reflect the dragon's form and also reflect the low light coming from the detrimental western setting sun, while allowing the clients to see both the mounds and the sunset. From a distance, this side of the house would look like a brilliant crystal embedded within the stonewalled, thatched-roofed farmhouse typical of the area.

## Epilogue

My clients were thrilled with the preliminary design I presented, yet there were complications. The site was in a rural conservation area of Denmark, and it was extremely difficult to get planning permission to build co-housing units on the property. My clients also had a teenage son who missed his friends and school from Copenhagen. The resistance of the planning authorities and their son's unsettled state convinced my clients to postpone building the house and move back to Copenhagen. As they intended to keep the property, I insisted that they open the well. I explained that as owners of the site, they were taking on the energies of the Venus dragons, which astrologically govern finances and health.

My clients owned an extremely successful international investment/currency trading firm whose fortunes had been decreasing during the time the project was being developed. After they moved back to Copenhagen, they had the well redug and reopened. Almost instantly, they received the planning permission, which had been a formidable barrier to further development, and the money markets took a signal upturn which has continued to this day. In addition, the relief of having the flow of their lives return by the combination of these decisions provided them with a new and fresh outlook, which they had been lacking for many months.

While one could say that these reversals would have happened anyway, they gave me a great and secure understanding of the mysterious ways in which Feng Shui works to balance our world.

# Contemporary Architectural Design

## Hank Reisen

Many people are interested in applying Feng Shui principles when they are designing a new house or an addition. They are curious about the process employed when first approaching a new site or when analyzing an existing structure to improve the Feng Shui. The thought of using seemingly foreign concepts may seem a bit daunting at first, but Feng Shui solutions are truly accessible to everyone.

There are several schools of Feng Shui, the most common being Form School and Compass School. A more recent practice is that of Black Sect taught by Professor Lin Yun. Although the various approaches draw upon the same theoretical foundation of Chinese philosophy, they are very different and do not always come to the same conclusions. People often ask which school is the most effective. In truth, each has merit; they complement one another and are useful for different things. Working with a knowledge of the various systems provides a greater understanding of the ways in which Chi behaves in any particular space.

The use of these different systems of Feng Shui is analogous to the way an architectural space must be analyzed from a number of viewpoints to arrive at a design that satisfies all the needs to be consolidated in one building. The designer must create a sound structure, rooms of dimensions appropriate to their projected use, and a proper circulation pattern. Plumbing, wiring, and venting must be routed to deliver water, electricity, and heat to their intended destinations. Any of these concerns could be the focus of a separate study, yet the real challenge lies in combining all of these systems into an aesthetically pleasing and supportive environment for people to live, study, or conduct their business.

Each school of Feng Shui focuses in a slightly different manner on the ways in which Chi effects the quality of human life.

Compass School uses a magnetic compass called the loupan to orient buildings, aligning the new structure with overarching geophysical forms and energetic patterns.

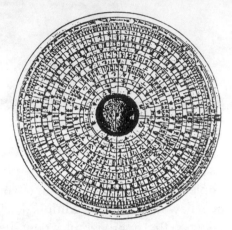

Form School looks more closely at the effect the placement, shape of land forms, and structures may have on the building or lot under consideration.

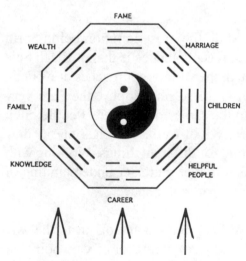

Black Sect Feng Shui incorporates many traditional Form School concepts. It also analyzes places by the application of the Bagua[1] diagram, which represents the essential energy patterns of life applied to where human activity enters.

If there is a door along this wall, at any of these three positions, the Bagua is applied over your floor plan as shown.

In architectural terms, it could be said that these different schools are all capable of operating at different levels. They can examine the patterns of an entire region, the larger context of a site, and the specific locale of a building, as well as the interior environment. By incorporating the techniques of more than one school, you can design for the optimum Feng Shui effect.

---

[1]    Please refer to "The Bagua," p. 153.

## The Big Picture

How do you choose a site, design a house, or adjust an existing building in order to create good Feng Shui? Professor Lin Yun provides a basic guideline by quoting the Chinese saying:

風 和, 日 麗, 水 清, 樹 茂

**"Feng he, ri li, shui qing, shu mao," which means**
**"Mild wind, warm sun, clear water, lush vegetation,**
**the essential ingredients for a site with good Feng Shui."**

In effect, look for a site and specific building location with Chi that will support and enhance life, where humans will thrive. Important first questions to ask are: What are the major land forms? Which direction does the site face? How does a person enter the site? What are the shapes of other land forms and buildings adjacent to the site?

Look to see if the site has the backing of a mountain or a large land form and flanking hills to either side. These elements will provide a sense of support, enclosure, and balance. It is also important that there is an open, relatively level area to the front such as a lawn, a field, or a pond that will allow the Chi to accumulate and benefit the dwelling. In traditional Feng Shui, this is called the Ming Tang or bright hall. Ideally there should also be a smaller hill, building, or landscape feature slightly beyond this area that will serve to contain good Chi in the Ming Tang. This will provide a good view and point of visual interest in the near distance.

Sites with the best Feng Shui are those where a beneficial armchair-shaped enclosure is created by mountains wrapping around the back of the site.[1]

---

[1] *Graphic: Earth Design: The Added Dimension*

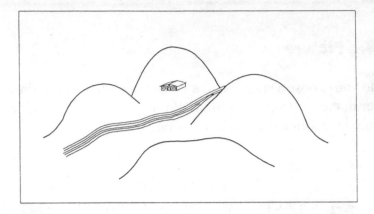

The direction this enclosure faces is also important. Traditionally, south was considered ideal. This is also consistent with the modern design placement for passive solar heating in temperate climates and for protection against the prevailing winter winds. When facing other directions, this *armchair* might not contribute the same climatic benefits, although it would still be considered auspicious as it provides a psychologically comforting sense of protection.

How people enter a site also impacts the Feng Shui. Approaching roads, driveways, and walkways that meander like a Chinese garden path allow for gentle Chi flow. Long, straight roads aimed directly at the site are considered inauspicious as Chi may become too sharp or injurious.

Places of power such as temples, churches, palaces, or political seats are the exception to this rule. Long, straight paths function as a way of concentrating Chi at the terminal point, which often houses the altar or the seat of the most important person. Care must still be taken to prevent fast moving Chi from negatively affecting its surroundings. Architectural elements or objects such as incense burners, statues, decorative screens, or fountains should be placed along the path so that Chi is forced to flow around them and become more manageable.

Shapes of other land forms or buildings seen from the site influence it by symbolic association with the energy their shape resembles. For example, the Chinese village of Canpo is thought to produce scholars because of the influence of a nearby mountain range shaped like a writing-brush stand. This beneficial influence has been reinforced by the villagers, who laid out a road in the town called Writing Brush Lane, which is aligned to appear as a brush resting in the crook of the mountain. To further augment this scholarly analogy, they lined the sides of the road with large stones in the shape of ink sticks.

## Adapting to a Smaller Scale

These same Feng Shui concepts can be applied with some adaptations to suit the smaller scale. A good example of this is the Ming Tang or the open area to the front of the building where good Chi can accumulate. In cities that were designed using Feng Shui, such as Beijing or Seoul, the Ming Tang is a large plane bounded by mountains. The Ming Tang for a temple complex or house would be proportionally smaller. Its purpose is to provide a pool or source of good Chi that will benefit the people occupying the city, sacred or governmental structure, corporate building, or home. Even on the scale of an office or a study, there should be a Ming Tang area in front of the desk.

For urban sites, apply nature's principles to man-made objects. Consider buildings as mountains and roads as rivers. In an ideal location, the building you want to buy or build would have a larger supportive structure or building to the back (mountains) with balanced buildings of a slightly smaller size to the right and left. A well proportioned Ming Tang or open area would have roads that curve to embrace the site at the front (rivers), and a tree in a park beyond.

Since not all sites have these ideal configurations, pay close attention to the way the land slopes in relation to the building. Where the land falls away from the back of a building, you will need to compensate for the lack of support that a mountain or taller building would have provided. A stand of large upright trees, vertical architectural elements, terracing, or fences in the back yard could provide this support and keep Chi as well as money and opportunity from slipping away. The Feng Shui principle, *mountain to the back and water to the front*, is a good guideline when examining the relationship of water, roads, and circulation pathways to the building.

Ask about the previous uses of the structure and fate of the former occupants. This offers insight to the predecessor's Chi, how the Feng Shui impacted them as well as what energies the site or building still contains from the past.[3]

Check for any *secret arrows* or lines of unseen negative energy aimed at the site. These can have a hidden yet strong influence. Secret arrows could be pointed shapes, sharp edges of neighboring buildings, like corners, ridges, and eaves, or landscape features.

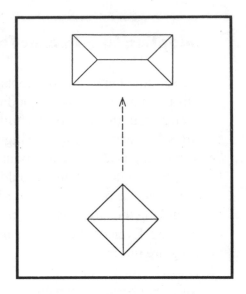

**Secret Arrow Created by Corner of Neighboring Building**

When building, if it is not possible to avoid these lines, care should be taken not to locate windows or doors in their path.

Face secret arrows with solid walls or deflecting forms, or place landscape features such as solid stone features in their path. This clearly illustrates the Taoist concept of *one ounce deflecting one thousand pounds*.

---

3    *For information on a clearing ritual, please refer to "The Bones of Your Home," p. 399.*

## Assessing the Body of a Space

The layout, shape, structure, and elements of a building create what can be called its *bones*.[4] Building elements are one area where there is general agreement between the various schools of Feng Shui and sensible design practice.

### Doors are the Mouths of a Building:

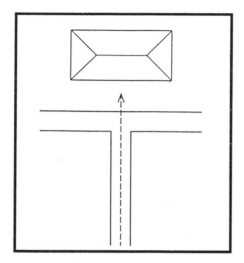

Avoid locating a door facing a secret arrow.

A secret arrow created by a straight road is also called a T-intersection.

Provide a welcoming open entrance.

---

[4]  *Please refer to "The Bones of Your Home," p. 399.*

Avoid elements that block, like trees or telephone poles.[5]

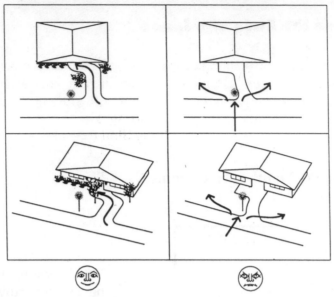

This allows for good Chi to flow in from the Ming Tang while keeping opportunities out in the world easily accessible to the occupants. Avoid a direct line between the front and back doors.

## Windows Are the Eyes of a Building:

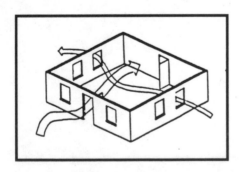

Windows should be located to provide good flow, natural light, and ventilation, and should be properly distributed so as to not create a glare or an imbalanced lighting situation.

 The windows should be located to take full advantage of beautiful views and scenes and to avoid any emphasis of views with negative connotations.[6]

---

5    *Graphic: Earth Design: The Added Dimension.*

6    *Graphic: Earth Design: The Added Dimension*

**Pathways Set up Movement Patterns and Chi Flow:**

The winding garden path is a good model. Long, straight, and narrow corridors create a poor quality Chi, causing problems at their termination point. They also divide a space into sides, preventing the desired interplay of yin and yang, one of the fundamental goals of good Feng Shui design.

**Stairs Create Strong Downward Flowing Patterns of Chi:**

Structures with stairs directly facing the exterior doors can lose Chi to the outside. It is best to locate the stairs so they send Chi to an area where an augmentation will benefit the occupants, such as a kitchen, living room, or study.

**Proportion and Dimensions Are Extremely Important:**

The dimensions of buildings, rooms, and elevation composition are critical from both a Feng Shui and an architectural perspective. Use proportional shapes and ratios such as the Golden Mean or Pi. Chinese geomancy rules of dimensions help establish the proper proportion of width to length to height and the proper composition of buildings, rooms, built-ins, doors, windows, and trim details.

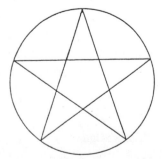

**Structural Elements Impact the Space:**

Beams, columns, floors, ceilings, and roofs can impact the Feng Shui of a space. As a general rule, avoid beams over important areas. Columns can be used to define a space, but their location should not block Chi flow. Sharp edges of columns and outside corners should be in areas that do not cause problems; otherwise, they should be rounded or modified to soften their effect.

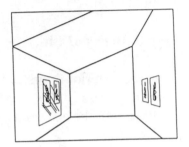

Avoid ceilings that slope in a single direction, or balance them with opposing forms.[7]

**Materials Provide Balance:**

Materials and colors[8] have qualities like hard and soft, warm and cool, rough and smooth. These polarities can be viewed in terms of yin and yang, which can be utilized to balance Chi in architectural spaces and should be chosen appropriately.

**Edges and Borders, Yin and Yang in Play:**

The transition between a building and the garden area[9] can be made with roof overhangs, decks, steps, or curbs to allow the most interplay of yin and yang: in and out, light and shade. Other conditions, such as a bathroom next to a kitchen, which are common because of practical plumbing considerations, would require a strong, definite separation. A solid, sound insulated wall with the door located away from the border area is one solution.

---

[7]    *Graphic: Earth Design: The Added Dimension*

[8]    *Please refer to Earth Design: The Added Dimension.*

[9]    *Please refer to "Turn Signals for the Unconscious," p. 171.*

This separates the energy of the kitchen and its life-absorbing principle from the energy of the bathroom and its energy-eliminating principle. In using the elements, keep the fire and earth of the kitchen away from the water of the bathroom.

The layout of rooms in a building can also be approached from a yin and yang perspective. The front of a building is considered yang: symbolically south, outer world, public. Toward the rear of a building, it becomes more yin: symbolically north, inner world, private. This concept is developed to an extremely high degree in the emperor's palace in the Forbidden City in Beijing, perhaps the most consciously Feng Shui designed space in the world.

The front of the building is more public, like the entry hall and living room. The rear of a building, or areas most remote from the front door, are more private and are a better location for bedrooms. There are always exceptions to these rules. Good design and Feng Shui principles consider other issues such as site, occupant Chi, and time factors.

Yin and yang also bestow energetic personalities to the sides of a building. Left is considered symbolically east or yang, and right is symbolically west and yin. The sides of a building should reflect a balance of yang and yin just as the ideal site has balancing land forms to the left and right. The center position of a building represents the *Tai Chi* position. Locating a kitchen or bathroom in this position is strongly discouraged as all good energy gets pulled down the center drain.

The Bagua associations[10] of Black Sect Feng Shui provides a useful framework for analyzing the energies of various areas of the building. Compass points[11] are helpful in determining the layout of the building. When the shadings of yin and yang through the building are derived from the true magnetic directions, they have an actual relationship to the sun and nature. An example of this orientation is to locate rooms that would most benefit from the energy of the rising sun to the east.

As with architecture, the highest practice of Feng Shui consists of much more than merely applying an amalgam of rules or of problem solving through just one discipline. Feng Shui transcends the practical solutions to problems to create a pleasing and harmonious blend of space and form and of light and shadow. The practice of Feng Shui and the deepest understanding of this complex system add up to the simplest division: Chi and the nature of yin and yang.

---

10    *Please refer to "The Bagua," p. 35.*

11    *Please refer to "The Seven Portents," p. 93.*

# Outdoor Feng Shui

## Terah Kathryn Collins

Why are most people so attracted to beautiful gardens and landscapes? One reason is because they generate a tremendous amount of Chi. They create harmonious rings of vital energy wherever they are, on our streets, homes, and workplaces. They inspire and relax us, even in the midst of a busy day. In Feng Shui, they also support and feed Chi adjustments and enhancements made indoors.

Whether you have a tiny condo, an industrial complex, or a tract home, you can introduce the principles of Feng Shui outdoors. Improvements made to outdoor areas will increase the supply of beneficial Chi that flows into your building and will enhance all aspects of your life.

Here are ways you can apply the dynamic principles of Feng Shui outdoors.

## Create Whole Shapes

Many Western structures are built in S, U, T, L, and other shapes that give them architectural interest. In Feng Shui, these structures are viewed as missing one or more pieces. They are not considered whole shapes, such as squares, circles, or rectangles, and therefore, they do not house enough vital Chi to support human health and happiness.

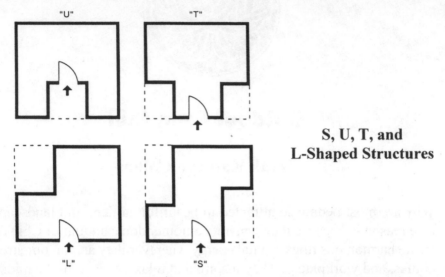

**S, U, T, and
L-Shaped Structures**

If you live or work in a building that is missing a section, your first order of business is to complete its shape in some way. If you do not want to add a new room to fill out the structural shape, you can create an outdoor area that looks and feels like it is a part of the building. To square off and complete the structure's shape, install any pleasing combination of patios, fencing, decks, arbors, porches, specialty gardens, lighting, boulders, statuary, sculptures, or water features.

*A client had purchased a building from a business that was having serious marketing and distribution problems as well as financial trouble. Using the Bagua,[1] we discovered the reasons for the lack of success. The areas related to wealth, love, and helpful people were all structurally missing from the building. In addition, there were plants and trees in those areas that were either unhealthy or dead.*

*Plans were immediately made to improve all three areas. In the wealth area, unhealthy plants were removed and giant Birds of Paradise were planted as guardians and energizers of the new company's wealth and prosperity. A dead tree was removed and a beautiful water feature was installed in the helpful people area to attract new*

---

[1]   *Please refer to "The Bagua," p. 35.*

*customers. Outdoor furniture and large pots of red flowers were added to the love area to enhance employee harmony and happiness.*

All of these improvements were purposefully introduced to fill in the building's missing areas and enhance the vital Chi for business success and employee happiness. The company is enjoying great success, the employees love to work there, and everyone is prospering.

Homes can also benefit from outdoor Feng Shui. A common house layout is the L-shape. The garage is usually built out toward the street as one leg of the L, with the rest of the house recessed behind it.

This condition is a Feng Shui challenge for three reasons:

The garage is given the most prominent placement and influences the residents to live at a *driving* pace.

The front entrance is recessed, diminishing its importance as the primary *mouth of Chi* and *gate of welcome*.

The L-shape leaves out areas of the Bagua that relate to important aspects of life.

The following is an example of how structural shape can affect people's lives.

*For several years, a client and her two daughters had lived in an L-shaped home with the career and knowledge areas missing. There had been a steady decline in the girls' study habits and grades, a situation often found where the knowledge area is missing. Additionally, my client was concerned that, with all her degrees, talents, and daily efforts, she was not getting good results in her business.*

*Together, we planned a patio edged with flowers and hedges for the front that would include a small waterfall flowing toward the house.*

*We also envisioned outdoor furnishings that would give the girls a comfortable place to sit and study. We then addressed the fact that the helpful people area, so crucial to good business relations, was in her crowded, chaotic garage. She needed to clear out all the old, unused possessions and symbolically make room for friendly, helpful people to enter her life.*

*Now, after a big garage sale, the installation of a waterfall, and a beautiful patio on its way, she is already experiencing an increase in business, and one of her daughters actually asked if she could go to summer school.*

To balance this home, outdoor Feng Shui was a perfect remedy. By filling in the missing areas mentioned above, the *gate of welcome* was drawn out flush with the garage. The missing areas became a beautiful outdoor lounge and Nature sanctuary with its own soothing water feature. These enhancements added tremendous support to this family, and they experienced their lives as being more balanced and fulfilling.

Whether the missing area is in the front, back, or along the sides of a building, do your best to complete the shape in a way you find appealing. When you do, you are inviting a whole new experience of balance and positive energy into your life.

## Create an Embrace

Humans are the "Goldilocks"[2] species, tolerating extremes only for short periods, if at all. A strong, cold wind can be invigorating and a humid, swamp interesting - for a time. Most people are quick to head for home where it is not too hot and not too cold, but ju-u-u-u-st right.

Ancient Feng Shui practitioners knew how important it was to honor people's preference for a balance between extremes. They located homes and villages in the *belly of the dragon*, where a nourishing balance of elements existed above the watery flood plains and below the windy mountaintops. In these locations, fed by a steady supply of friendly Chi, people had the best chance of experiencing long, happy, prosperous lives.

These days, it might be easier to think of an auspicious location as having an armchair configuration.[3] The seat of the chair represents the building site, while the back and the arms symbolize natural protective features rising in back and around the sides of the property, like mountains, hills, and forests. The front of the property, represented by the foot of the chair, drops down below the building site to a water source, such as a lake, river, stream, or pond. This places the building between the extreme forces of wind and water, in the embrace of natural features, and with a visual command of the front of the property.

Though most homes are not in such auspicious locations, there are many ways to landscape property to create the nurturing embrace of vital Chi. Hardy evergreen hedges and trees, as well as berms and fencing, can be combined to form natural protection as well as privacy in the back and sides of the yard. In the front, install water features - anything from a simple bird bath to an exotic waterfall and pond - to invite the flow of positive Chi toward the house.

**Beautiful views in your yard nurture you with color, fragrance, and vitality every day.**

---

[2]  *Look at the wealth of Feng Shui insight though nursery-rhyme mythology.*

[3]  *Please refer to "Contemporary Architectural Design," p. 143.*

The belly of the dragon, or the seat of an armchair, can be your model for bringing comfort, safety, and beauty to the land that surrounds you. Adapt the model to your liking and your circumstances, and watch for the balancing effects it will have in your life.

## Create Elemental Balance

After your building's shape is balanced and the property is embraced in natural beauty, look with an elemental eye at what you have created. Play with the *paints* of the elements, and fine tune your handiwork. All five elements reside within you, and bringing them into your environment can be extraordinarily soothing and nourishing.

# THE FIVE ELEMENTS
### Nourishing and Controlling Relationships

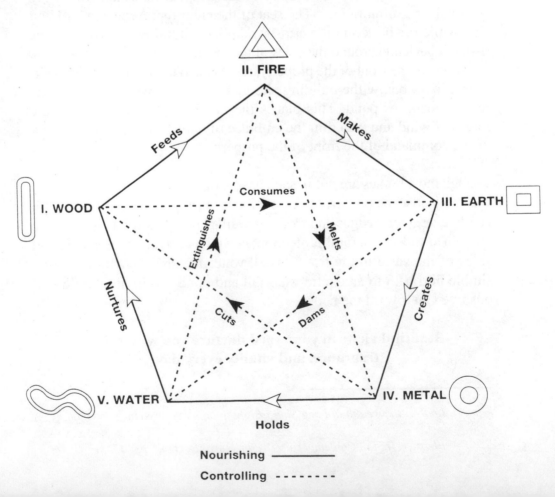

Use the following list[4] to determine the elemental make-up of an existing garden or one you are planning to create.

## The Wood Element

> All Plants
> Wooden Furniture, Decks, Fencing, and Pathways
> Rattan and Wicker
> Stripes and Floral Prints
> Columnar and Long, Thin Shapes
> Blues and Greens

## The Fire Element

> All Lighting, including Oil, Electrical, and Candles
> Fireplaces and Barbeques
> Pets and Wildlife
> Statuary and Garden Art depicting People and Animals
> Triangular and Conical Shapes
> Reds

## The Earth Element

> Brick, Tile, and Adobe
> Earthenware Pots and Garden Art
> Square and Rectangular Shapes
> Yellows and Earthtones
> Rocks, Stones, and Sand

4 *Please refer to "The Five Phases of Energy," p. 81.*

## The Metal Element

> Metal Furniture, Fencing, and Statuary
> Circular, Oval, and Arched Shapes
> White and Pastels

## The Water Element

> All Water Features
> Reflective Surfaces, Such as Glass, Crystal, and Mirrors
> Asymmetrical, Free Form Shapes
> Black and Dark Tones

Most gardens start with an abundance of the wood element represented by plants and trees. The other four elements often need to be introduced to complete the elemental picture. Gardens made up of green shrubs and trees with wooden decks and furniture are inherently *woody* and benefit from the presence of the other elements.

Many objects, through their shape, texture, material, and color, are a mix of elements: a red wooden chair mixes fire and wood; an earthenware pot of white flowers brings together earth, metal, and wood; a square glass table with a wrought iron base integrates earth, water, and metal. Imagine these three items placed together in an outdoor setting, and you have brought the five elements together.

**You can arrange the elements in infinite ways, creating a place of healing and rejuvenation just outside your door.**

Think of the many ways you can do this. You can plant red, yellow, white, blue, and dark purple flowers; create a sculpture garden that suggests fire, earth, metal, water, and wood; add lighting, tiles, boulders, water features, and trees. You are the artist, and the land around you is awaiting your personal touch.

## Other Possibilities

Landscaping can also help to balance extreme architectural features such as sharp corners, hard surfaces, and the common use of geometric shapes. Western culture builds using straight lines and angles. It is rare to see a round or asymmetrically shaped home or office. To balance the abundance of straight lines and sharp corners, introduce meandering, free form lines with pathways, patios, decks, and walls around which your gardens are planted. The straight lines and the curving lines compliment and balance each other, encouraging a healthy flow of Chi around your property.

Many people are buying homes in new subdivisions. If you are one of these people, you may be bewildered as you stand in your yard looking at the sea of other houses. Look at the bare dirt in front of your house as a blank canvas that will become your garden and landscape masterpiece. Then, start the planning.

Here are outdoor Feng Shui guidelines to begin the process:

When applicable, complete the shape of the house with artful landscaping or room additions.

Plant around the sides and back of the house to create a protective embrace and to assure privacy.

Create a beautiful view from every window and door.

Include a water feature in the front yard design, as well as a path designed to lead people to the front door.

Privatize the front yard, especially when it is on a busy street, cul-de-sac, or T-junction.

Bring the five elements into the landscape design.

When applicable, install gates in side yard fences to circulate Chi all the way around the house.

When the building is comprised of straight lines and angles, choose meandering lines for pathways, patios, and garden walls.

Outdoor junk stagnates vital Chi. Keep Chi healthy and flowing by selling, throwing, or giving away discarded or unused items.

Enjoy creating your own Personal Paradise. It will make life more magnificent for you, as well as for all the people fortunate enough to live or work nearby.[5]

---

[5]     This is an excerpt taken from Terah's next book, The Advanced Western Guide to Feng Shui, available in summer 1997. All rights reserved, copyright, 1996.

Graphics: Terah Kathryn Collins, The Western Guide to Feng Shui, Hay House Inc., 1996.

# Landscape Design According to Feng Shui

## Shelley Sparks

According to ancient Chinese tradition, the human character can be judged by the quality of its response to nature. A person who truly loves mountains and water more than worldly interests is seen as a person of deep spiritual cultivation. Gardens provide daily contact with nature that can bring you into closer union with its secrets. The principles of Feng Shui bring dimension and depth to garden and landscape designs so you can maximize nature's benefits in your yard.

The key to creating a beautiful landscape is to understand how land can be fostered as representative of nature. Much mental and physical disease can be attributed to humans' loss of connection to the earth. By creating a more natural setting within your garden and land, you are fostering an intimate and healing connection with the earth.

## Design Elements

**A more natural setting is created by imitating Nature's own curving lines, surprise turns, seasonal colors, fragrances, and enclosures.**

The line of demarcation between your private space and public land must be clearly identified. Chinese gardens are famous for their *moon gates*, beautifully shaped arbors or gates that mark the entry of their garden from the public part of the street. Where does your entry begin? How much public space is in your front yard? A sense of entry can be accomplished with arbors, gates, trees, and shrubs or simply with a change of pavement. A curved walkway to the front door is most desirable; it encourages the gentle flow of Chi into your home.

The materials and shapes used to construct the house should be utilized in the garden. For example, if your house has a Spanish tile roof, a rough form of this tile or brick can be used in the pathways or garden borders. Straight lines are generally not found in nature and should be softened. In the case of a rectangular patio, bordering it with curved flower beds filled with informally arranged plants can soften the hard edges.

In nature, plants of various sizes, shapes, and textures all grow together, and your garden and landscape should reflect this. Also, variations in light and shadow add richness and depth to your landscape. They bring alive the interplay and balance of the yin/shadow and yang/light. If your property is in complete sun, planting shade trees or building a shade structure will balance the yin energy and give you relief from the sun. If you have a very shady site, consider having an arborist thin out the trees to permit more yang energy to enter. Planting white flowering plants also lightens the space.

## Using the Senses

People are drawn to a garden by their emotions, memories, and five senses. The more these *triggers* are incorporated in the garden, the stronger your relationship is to it and the more effective your healing experience will be. Visualize the gardens you experienced as a child or those places that most captivated you in your travels. No matter the climate, the plants, or the spaces you have to work with, there are always methods of capturing elements of those special places and memories.

### Sight and Color

Vision is the most utilized sense. In designing a landscape with Feng Shui principles and the colors of the Bagua, incorporate plants which have the resident energy of each area of the lot. Not all plants in the *li* area need to be red, but adding red accent plants can definitely represent the energy of this area.

| Sun<br>purple | Li<br>red | K'un<br>pink |
|---|---|---|
| Chen<br>green | yellow<br>orange | Tui<br>white |
| Ken<br>blue | K'an<br>black | Chien<br>gray |

This Bagua is designed to be overlaid on your property with the ken, kan, and chien areas adjacent to the street.

You should also select a color-coordinated palette that pleases you, though it is still important to retain the yin-yang balance. If you are enthralled with the *hot* colors: red, orange and yellow, be sure to balance them with some *cool* colors: green, blue or purple. White always balances the color wheel, providing yin for the hot range and yang for the cool range. Change the energy in sunny areas by adding yin or cool-colored plants and lift the Chi of shade areas with yang colors in the hot range. When planning your garden, try to accommodate for seasonal interest with the colors to accentuate or de-emphasize the change of seasons.

## Smell and Fragrance

Our most primal sense is smell; memories are triggered most by the smells of our past. In addition to planting flowers with the fragrances you love, also plant with fragrances that create balance as suggested by aromatherapy. Fragrances are the essence of the plant that call forth the healing energy needed to bring you into equilibrium.[1]

One of my favorite fragrances is the gardenia. Place it close to your patio or walkway, and pick some of its fabulous flowers to perfume your home.

---

[1] *Please refer to "A Scentual Reminder of Feng Shui Remedies," p. 329.*

## Taste: Herbs and Food

Adding food and herb plants to your garden brings added dimension. Who has not experienced the miracle of watching a seed germinate and food ripen through the interplay of sun, water, air, and earth? Growing your own food in an organic garden is the only guarantee that you can get the freshest, purest food to nourish your body. Herbs are particularly powerful plants to include in your garden. Not only do they offer fragrance and taste but medicinal qualities as well.

They can be placed in the area of the Bagua that corresponds to the area of your body that may need healing or near the center of the property, which is the health area.

| Sun<br>thighs | Li<br>eyes<br>heart | K'un<br>abdomen |
|---|---|---|
| Chen<br>feet<br>throat | | Tui<br>chest<br>mouth |
| Ken<br>hands | K'an<br>feet<br>neck | Chien<br>head<br>lung |

## Sound

The use of water and sound in the front of the house is also highly pleasing. There is nothing like being greeted by the sound of running water. It is helpful in fostering harmonious relationships for the occupants. Wind chimes are beautiful positioned not only for the wind to animate them, but also so they can be rung by passers-by.

Other lyrical garden sounds belong to the birds and bees that visit your garden for the food, building material, and water that you share with them. A third method of creating sound in your garden is to use members of the grass family, like bamboo, which whisper beautiful music in the wind.

## Touch

Touch is experienced not only through your hands but also your eyes. Big, bold textured plants represent yang energies while finer, smaller plants represent yin. Balance is the choreography between the two. There are also many tactile plants that encourage a physical interaction and foster a connection with the plant kingdom.[2]

### Who can be cross when there are Lamb's Ears in your garden?

## Uses of Your Garden

How your garden takes shape will depend on how you intend to use it. If you want a garden or portion of it to be dedicated to spiritual practice or contemplation, there are a number of methods you can use. Zen gardens have long been used as contemplative spaces. Labyrinths and mazes using sacred shapes and numbers can be employed for walking or sitting meditations. In general, use cool, restful green plants of consistent texture that do not flower. This green backdrop emphasizes peace, calmness, and a quiet mind.

Any one of hundreds of mandalas can be created in a garden using plant materials, stones, and building or art material. Statues, gazing balls, and special stones or crystals can be strategically positioned as focal points for meditation. In Europe, secret gardens, enclosed green spaces, have often been used for quiet thought. Their placement would be most desirable in the chien (heaven and benefactors) or ken (knowledge) areas of the property or back yard.

| Sun<br>Wealth<br>Wood<br>4 | Li<br>Fame<br>Fire<br>9 | K'un<br>Partnership<br>Earth<br>2 |
|---|---|---|
| Chen<br>Family<br>Wood<br>3 | Health<br>Earth<br>5 | Tui<br>Creativity<br>Metal<br>7 |
| Ken<br>Knowledge<br>Earth<br>8 | K'an<br>Career<br>Water<br>1 | Chien<br>Benefactors<br>Metal<br>6 |

When placing objects in the garden, it is most beneficial to use the element that corresponds to each area.

---

[2]  *This is an important element for children's enjoyment of the garden where many times there is a "look but do not touch" policy.*

For example, a metal gazing ball or bronze statue would work best in the tui and chien areas; a stone statue, special rocks or crystals would work best in the kun, center, or ken areas; wood objects or topiary would be best in the sun or chen areas; fountains or garden pools are best in the kan area, and incense or flame would be best in the li area.

A standard guideline for designing with plants is to use an odd number, when creating a grouping of less than ten. Whenever appropriate, use the quantity (individual plants or number of groupings) indicated in the Bagua to further energize those areas.

**What is needed in all garden design is balance:
yin and yang in coordination.**

Honoring nature in your garden by including the elements and representations of earth will always produce nourishing energy for you and your home. A garden is a microcosm of nature, always changing as it grows.

As your garden grows and evolves, you are reminded of your
own growth and the work needed
to achieve and maintain balance
and harmony.

In your garden, there may come times when a color, texture, smell, taste or sound that once delighted you no longer feels right. You must be open to the change occurring within yourself and give it a voice and reflection in your garden. Your growth and health depend on reestablishing this awareness and your link to earth. Your garden will help you reconnect with nature and foster healing for both you and the planet.

# Turn Signals for the Unconscious

## Richard L. Phillips

The secret of good Feng Shui design is to be aware of *turn signals* to the unconscious. This clear and easily understandable principle can be applied to any space. Turn signals are positive, visual clues and subliminal messages that you can use to create a relaxed and nurturing environment.

Turn signals in a home work like those in a car. When you are driving, you use turn signals to advise other drivers, and you rely on them to do the same. If you do not receive these visual clues, your body responds with the appropriate physiological changes, such as increased adrenalin and erratic breathing. Your unconscious redirects your energy from its normal, natural, healing functions to keeping you safe from danger.

Turn signals in a house work in a similar manner. They tell you where to go and what to do, which room to use, and how to behave there. Positive turn signals in your home lower stress levels and give your body more energy for healing, growing, and being creative. Turn signals for the unconscious set the stage so you can empower yourself.

Before continuing with this chapter, inhale slowly and deeply. Now exhale and bring your shoulders back and down toward your waist. This is the *feeling* you want to create. This is the feeling of letting go and being relaxed.

## Outdoor Turn Signals

Unmarked landings and steps may add stress to your life. Often, contractors build steps, landings, and patios of white concrete, with no differentiation made between the elevation changes. If there is no visual demarcation between the landing that leads to steps, and the steps that lead to the patio, your unconscious is immediately put on guard. As you approach the steps, your thought pattern changes from what you are thinking to concentrating on not tripping and falling. This means that every time you go out to the patio, there is a behavioral change that may keep you from using the patio as much as you would like.

A good turn signal would be a clear transition to mark each separate elevation. Alternating colors, textures, and materials is a turn signal that says "landing ends, steps ahead, steps end, patio begins. Let's use this patio and enjoy the outside."

Appropriate changes may be:

Replacing concrete steps with flagstone or brick.

Covering the existing steps with brick pavers.

Staining the steps if they are made of wood.

Placing large pots of flowers or plants on both sides of the top and bottom step.

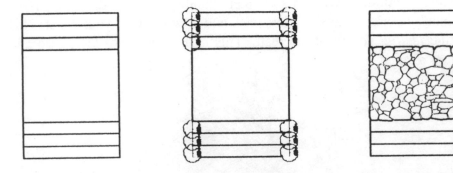

**Positive Turn Signal Solutions**

A good turn signal can be easy and inexpensive. If you are building a wooden deck with steps, instead of running the planks in the same direction, the solution is as simple as laying the wood on the deck in one direction and the wood on the steps in the opposite direction.

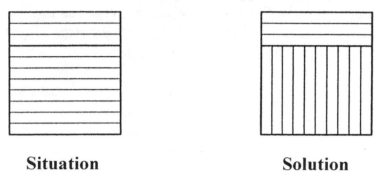

**Situation**                    **Solution**

Undifferentiated landings and steps in front of a house give the subliminal message that extra effort is required to get to the front door. Opportunities will evade the occupants. A house with well-defined walkways, landings, and steps will have increased opportunities.

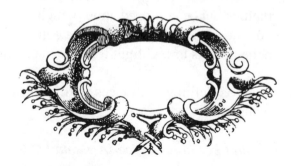

## Interior Turn Signals

The turn signals you use for elevation changes inside your house can affect how often you use a room. If there are stairs separating a hallway and a room, and they are all carpeted with the same floor covering, your unconscious might say, "Why use this room? It is awfully hard to get into; let's avoid it all together."

If it is the bathroom you avoid, your grooming habits may decline, and your organs of elimination may suffer. If it is the kitchen you are staying away from, you will probably not be nourishing the body or soul properly.

Provide clear turn signals by using contrasting carpets, rugs, and flooring patterns to highlight landings and stairs. Remember to put non-slip pads under area rugs. A sliding rug will send a message that this hallway or room is dangerous to use. Turn signals highlighting steps and stairs will make life easier and will improve the energetics of your house.

## Doors

Focusing attention on the main entrance to your house can help you take advantage of opportunities when they present themselves. The front door does not have to be the traditional Feng Shui red,[1] but it should be a color that contrasts with (but still compliments) the exterior color. The front latch or lock should function easily to let opportunities flow easily into your life.

If your house has a series of doors or similar multiple entrances, you may have many opportunities but be confused about which choices to make. To focus attention on the preferred door, paint it a contrasting color and install lights and potted plants to highlight it as the main entrance.

Simple changes, such as defining entrances with paint or plants, can profoundly affect your life.

> *One woman had her home office in a smaller building across the garden from her house. There were three sets of identically painted French doors leading from the house into the garden. Only one could easily be opened and used without hitting the interior furniture. Each time she approached her house, her unconscious asked, "Which door is it?"*

---

[1]    *Please refer to "Utilize All Your Resources," p. 189.*

*If I choose the wrong door, it will hit furniture. Can I squeeze past the furniture without bruising myself?" After painting the outside of the usable door in a vibrant color, she became calmer and found that she did not isolate herself in the office as much.*

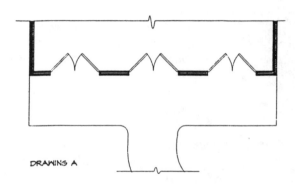

DRAWING A

## Situation

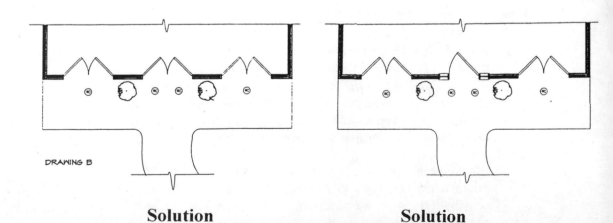

DRAWING B

## Solution          ## Solution

## Furniture

The placement of furniture also provides turn signals to the unconscious. If you do not have a comfortable place to sit and eat, you will not properly honor and nourish your body. If there is not an area for two or more people to sit and talk, then conversation will be limited in that room; thus, relationships and partnership may not be fulfilling in your life.

*A woman had several furniture groupings in her front room but only one chair. The main piece of art was a painting of weeping girls. It is little wonder why the woman felt lonely, isolated, and sad.*

*Her furniture placement and art choices sent a message to anyone entering the room, "It will be difficult for two people to talk in this room, and even if space is found, tears will flow."*

*Rearranging her existing to furniture to create an inviting conversation area and removing the melancholy art had a profound effect on the woman's life. Shortly after making the changes, she began dating a sensitive man, her friends began to drop by more frequently, and communication with her children was better than it had ever been before.*

Pay attention to the symbolism of art and objects you have in your home. Make sure your rooms and its furnishings are accessible and inviting.

*A single man seeking romance had his bed so close to a wall that he had to turn sideways to tuck in the sheets. He had only one reading light on the more accessible side. This arrangement sent a strong message to his unconscious and to anyone invited into his room, "This is a one-person bedroom. There are no provisions for another person to be comfortable."*

*After making the bed accessible from both sides and adding another light, he was able to find a steady partner. Additionally, with the new bed placement, Chi was able to circulate freely around the bed, so the man slept better and his health improved.*

## Lighting

Both exterior and interior lights should be bright enough to enhance a space but not to cause a glare.

> *A restaurant known for its excellent food and service recently relocated. The new building, chef, kitchen, dining room interiors, and location were considered superior to the original. Daytime business far exceeded expectations, but at night, the business was negligible. An examination of the parking lot showed why. The lighting fixtures in the lot shined directly into the eyes of automobile drivers approaching the restaurant. Potential customers were temporarily blinded while looking for a parking space. The customers received the message, "Entering the restaurant parking lot at night is painful and confusing. These lights blind me, and I might have an accident while parking the car. There are other places to go." Adjusting the lights sent the message that it was safe to park there, and night time business dramatically improved.*

Remember to pay attention to the details. Overhead lights that are too bright will make people in a room feel agitated and uncomfortable. Use table or free-standing lamps to improve the lighting and comfort in a room. Care should also be taken with the placement of ceiling fans. The bottom should always be higher than the trim above the nearest doorway, or at least 6'8" above the floor. In most houses, a ceiling-mounted fan should be the same color as the ceiling to make the fan feel less intrusive. Lights from most ceiling fans are usually too bright and should not be used.

> *The owner of a business could not understand why business was far below projections and customers rarely returned. Between the front door and the reception desk was a low-hanging ceiling fan with a light. Anyone approaching the reception area had to decide how to get from the front door to the reception desk without hitting the light.*
>
> *The low-hanging ceiling fan and light sent a very clear message, "There is a food processor-like blade whirling ahead. How tall am I in relation to the blades? Perhaps I should avoid this office." Even the receptionist, who knew the exact height of*

*the ceiling fan and also knew that it was securely installed, avoided walking under it. Taking the ceiling fan out removed the perceived danger from the reception area and dramatically improved the company's business.*

## Clutter

Seemingly innocuous garage clutter can give a powerful message to your unconscious.

*An admired, professional woman felt overwhelmed by little tasks in life. She had difficulty both leaving and returning to her house. The woman stayed away from home longer than she intended, and once home, she had difficulty leaving. She parked her car in the garage and used the garage door to enter. Paint cans and sprinklers were perched precariously on a shelf that was next to her car. She had to walk past sharp-edged tools, including the prongs of a pitchfork that pointed toward her face. Unfinished projects, boxes, and debris created an obstacle course between her car and the house. Her unconscious said, "This is a potentially dangerous and difficult situation. Do I really want to go from the car to the door?" Moreover, each time she saw unfinished projects, she got the stressful message, "Oh no, something else to do. When will I ever get it done?"*

Simply organizing her garage created a clear path between her car and her house. It suggested that she could manage her time both at home and away. This turn signal became symbolic of her career path and has had a profound effect on her life.

Giving turn signals to the unconscious will positively influence patterns of behavior in your home or office. Providing clear markers will remove stress from your environment and instruct your unconscious to relax. When your body is at ease, your breathing improves and your heart opens. New opportunities and energy can now enter your life.

# feng Shui and Real Estate Values

## Shera Gabriel

Real estate appraising views a home or property in monetary terms, and changes are made to improve its market value. Feng Shui, on the other hand, considers the home as a holistic environment. It searches for ways to enhance the flow of Chi and release energy blockages that may manifest in corresponding life areas.[1] Though seemingly very different disciplines, Feng Shui can help maintain the optimum value of a real estate holding or even increase its worth.

With Feng Shui, instead of viewing a home through only economic glasses, you experience your living spaces as an integral part of your life. Buildings are dynamic entities that can either nurture and transform your life or undermine and weaken it. When the life-enriching energy of Chi flows through your dwelling, you are supported in your quest for a prosperous and fulfilling life. This prosperity also flows into your pocketbook.

A house is much more than a physical structure of wood, concrete, shingles, and siding. It reflects who you are and who you hope to be.

Just as your identity may be linked to your children, work, or even your pets, you also personalize your living space and infuse it with your hopes, ideals, and ego identity.

---

[1] *Please refer to "The Bagua," p. 35*

Most people have a strong emotional response when allowing a real estate appraiser to inspect their property. Often, there is a sense of *showing off* the home just as one would show off a precocious child. Other times the owners display a certain shyness at having a stranger view their innermost sanctum.

> **People have an intuitive sense that their homes**
> **mirror who they are,**
> **reflecting both the loveliness of their spirits**
> **and the dysfunction of their egos.**

The real estate appraiser is an advocate for the home, looking for aspects that add or detract from its value. The Feng Shui consultant views it as a living space and uses cures for freeing blocked energy and enhancing the spirit. In Western society, property value is based on economics. Feng Shui takes you one step further; it helps maintain your home's economic value while increasing the blessings in your life.

## What is Value?

Economics defines market value as the most probable price a property will bring on the open market. On a practical level, you are concerned with protecting your home as an investment. You paint, repair, re-roof, and work hard to preserve its value.

When it comes time to sell, you want to receive the highest possible price.

But what really constitutes value in your property? Could it be the flow of Chi? A home with an abundance of positive flowing Chi attracts people and potential buyers like a magnet. This *vitality* is what constitutes the greatest value in real estate.

> *Viewing homes through the eyes of both a real estate appraiser and a Feng Shui practitioner, I have consistently seen a relationship between value and good Feng Shui. Homes that have good Chi are homes that often command the highest price in the neighborhood. Those with a certain stagnant, blocked energy are the homes that sit on the market the longest, often selling for less than the asking price and appraising for even lower.*

## The Relationship of Feng Shui and Value

Real estate guidelines and basic Feng Shui principles contribute to obtaining the highest property value estimate. These guidelines apply to current ownership as well as to buying and selling property.

### Explore the Neighborhood

Your property should be harmonious in style, design, and of comparable value to others in the area. The upkeep of your property should contribute to a sense of order and beauty with its surroundings and create harmonious relations with your neighbors. As everyone is interconnected, the relationships you foster with neighbors add to the vitality of the area.

There are some locations that are more auspicious than others, but no location is without hope. Some of the more challenging aspects can be put in balance with Feng Shui cures.[2] High tension wires nearby, environmental pollution, mixed zoning, and changing land use can affect not only the property value but the health and well-being of its occupants.

## First Impressions are Lasting

The first impression[3] is usually determined by the front door. It welcomes you or confuses you as to whether you are wanted in the home. All opportunity enters through the front door, so be sure it is inviting and welcoming to positive energies (and the real estate appraiser!) Front doors and exteriors should look fresh and clean, be in good repair, and exude a feeling of pride.

The exterior of your house is the face you present to the world. Winding pathways up to the front door allow Chi to meander slowly and flow smoothly into the home.

A well maintained landscape and exterior architectural features also contribute charm and grace to the property.

## Inside the Home, What Do You See?

How does it feel? How does it smell? Is it light and airy or dark and heavy? Upgrading windows can add value to your home. Clean windows add to the harmonious flow of Chi and allow nature to enter and become

---

2    *Please refer to "Using the Componets of Feng Shui Cures," p. 65.*

3    *Please refer to "The Room of First Impression," p. 207, and "The Entry: New Beginnings," p. 201.*

a part of the inside environment. Illuminating dark corners and hallways welcomes the light into your life and provides a sense of warmth.

Whether you are selling or maintaining your property's value, you will reap the benefits of putting your environment in order and keeping it in good repair. Clutter is stagnating energy. It clogs up outer and inner *arteries*. Lightening up and ordering will allow better Chi flow and is immediately evident to you and all who enter.

Some ways to add monetary value to your home:

Remodel the kitchen
Add a bathroom
Add a new room
Upgrade the basement

Feng Shui can guide you in the most auspicious design for these improvements, suggesting colors, room placement, or a layout that enhances life areas. With the help of the Bagua, additions and upgrades will enhance your home's value and provide blessings in your life.

## Buying Your Perfect Property

Following basic guidelines when searching for property will insure that your dream home, once purchased, does not turn into your worst nightmare!

### The External Environment

Consider what kind of neighborhood you want to live in. What is important to you: Friendly neighbors? Tranquil setting? Lots of trees? Slow, meandering traffic?

Avoid cul-de-sacs where Chi intensifies and has no outlet; neighbors get testy with one another here.

Property at the joining of a T-intersection should also be avoided. Chi zooms down a straight path right to your door. If you absolutely *must* buy that little house at the end of a T-intersection, there are cures to help deflect the rush of Chi like trees or a row of bushes between the street and the house.[4]

What about the name of the street? Is it Depression Lane or Happiness Court? Where would you rather live? In driving home from the office every day, what would you notice if you lived in this neighborhood? A cemetery? Prison? Junk yard? Are there high-tension wires on the same block? What about noise pollution?

What feelings would these sights evoke that might determine your mood for the day? Do the other houses in the neighborhood appear to be loved, the way you would love your house? Can you relax in this neighborhood and feel like this is your home?

**Good Feng Shui advises you to follow your intuition
rather than some abstract recipe that
may or may not be relevant to your needs.**

---

4   *Do not despair if you already own a property with one of these features. See
   <u>Earth Design: The Added Dimension</u> for additional cures.*

Check with the local zoning board to make sure there are no proposed land use changes that could be the source of stress in the future. Note if the street surface is smooth and even. Drive outward from the immediate neighborhood to outlying areas. What else do you find?

**Inspecting the Home (Enter at Your Own Risk)**

Stand outside the house awhile and look at it. Has this house been cared for? Does the shape of the house appeal to you?

Are there any broken or cracked windows?

How does the roof appear?

Does the house need painting?

Walk around the house and inspect the foundation. This will be the foundation of your life experience. You want it strong and solid with no cracks that could undermine its purpose. From a Feng Shui perspective, symmetrical shapes are best. A house with many offsets and angles could indicate fragmentation.

Is there a garage? A detached garage is best. If it is attached, it should be away from the front entrance so that it does not detract Chi in its path to the front door.

Once inside, check the ceiling for water marks that would indicate a leaking roof. Are there plenty of windows? Do they open smoothly, or are they painted shut? Are the floors solid and level? How does the traffic pattern feel? Walls that form many angles and slants give off negative Chi that is unbalanced and uncomfortable. Are there heavy beams overhead in any of the rooms? This downward energy can feel burdensome and may even contribute to headaches if you sit or sleep under them. A most troublesome feature is a stairway that faces the front door of the house. Chi comes rushing down the stairs and flies out the front door.

How is the house designed? Watch out for a bathroom or kitchen in the center of the house, Chi will flow down and out this *center drain*. A main bathroom that can only be reached by going through a bedroom is another negative feature. The bedrooms should be located at the back of the house away from the street. What is the first room seen upon entering the house? This will have an effect on all who enter. Is it a bathroom? Or a kitchen? A blank wall? Use your imagination to guess the effect each of these could have.

These guidelines are only a starting point in the creation of a harmonious living space. Purchasing property that has good Feng Shui helps the flow begin.

Combining the mundane aspects of real estate management and valuation with a spiritual understanding of Feng Shui can enhance your life on all levels.

You are caring for the earth and yourself when you bring harmony and balance into your environment. Profit then becomes simply a by-product of a higher objective, to aid in the unfolding of all of life's potential.

# Decorative Feng Shui

# Utilize All Your Resources

## Jami Lin

Because we live in the twenty-first century, our homes and offices do not look like traditional Chinese paintings. As an interior designer with over twenty years of experience, I have never hung a Chinese flute as a Feng Shui cure, and without reservation, I can say that I probably never will. While flutes are said to move Chi, in my opinion, they are neither decoratively attractive nor relevant to contemporary life. It would be a decorative anomaly to hang a flute near your Van Gogh reproduction or next to your contemporary stone sculpture.

It is important to use life experience and all your resources when designing your home or office according to Feng Shui. Just like the ancient and contemporary Earth Designers, you need to adapt the energy of the natural laws and the traditional rules to your personal needs. Traditional Feng Shui rules should not be used *just because* they are traditional. They must be evaluated by using your intuition, and they should be modified to produce real change in your current lifestyle.

**Only *you* know what feels right for you.**
**There are no absolutes!**

There are guidelines that can help you integrate traditional Feng Shui wisdom with the fountain of all truth, your own inner knowing, to create a balanced and harmonious life:

**Always Set the Intent.**
**Use Intuition and Common Sense as Your Guides.**
**Use Your Body as a Feng Shui Tool.**
**Combine Your Resources with the Rules of Feng Shui.**
**Be Aware and Re-evaluate.**

## Setting the Intent

Setting the intent is critical to making design changes that enhance life experiences.[1] To set the intent means to add the power of thought to all your Feng Shui adjustments. The strength of the mind to change physical reality has been the subject of scientific debate throughout time. Though the scientists may never agree, you can decide for yourself. Look at your own life experiences to see where intention has helped you manifest your desires and goals.

### Intention is Everything!

*While I was teaching a Feng Shui course for interior designers, the sponsor, Sue generously suggested I stay at her home. As she was respecting my off-duty time, we did not talk much about her home or her Feng Shui requirements. I did notice, however, that she had a pair of ceramic love birds in the marriage area of the living room.*

*During our private time, we got to know each other. She told me about the problems she was having with her boyfriend of over seven years. "A boyfriend of seven years!" I said to myself, "Why isn't she married, or why haven't they both moved on?" In class the next day, with Sue's permission, I mentioned where her love birds were located. Through giggles she said, "So why is my love life so messed up?"*

*I have found that people often intuitively place an accessory in the right place. Placing love birds in the marriage corner was the "right" thing to do. So why had seven years gone by and produced a stalemate? Because intention is everything! Unless conscious intent for change is attached to the Feng Shui placement, manifestation will not occur in acceptable time parameters or with the proper intensity.*

*A month later Sue called, "You won't believe what happened! I started talking to my love bird; I asked them to help bring love into my life in the same way that made them close and happy. Now, not only has Bob, my boyfriend of seven years, asked me to marry him, I've also met someone new. I have the opportunity to choose the love that is really right for me!"*

---

[1]   Please refer to "Setting the Intent" in my book <u>Earth Design: The Added Dimension</u>.

## Intuition and Common Sense

Both intuition and common sense are indispensable guides for making appropriate decorative Feng Shui changes and enhancing functional design. Traditional Feng Shui dictates that when a front door is painted red, it auspiciously welcomes good fortune. However, if your home is painted a color that would be unattractive or even clash with a red door, you just *know* that it would not be supportive of your goals in life. Common sense and intuition, along with the traditional Feng Shui color and five elements theory[2] will help you choose a more appropriate color that meets *your* needs.

**Knowing exactly what you want to accomplish will
help determine the best adjustment to make.**

Ask yourself, "What color will enhance my specific goals in life and look aesthetically attractive with my house?" Do you want more nurturing relationships, new business, and social opportunities to flow through your front door? What would common sense and intuition tell you is an appropriate color to welcome these specific goals? How about green, the color of spring's rebirth? What if you are looking to increase your financial riches? A faux metallic-finish would definitely invite financial riches into your life. The options are endless. Deep ocean blue can bring greater sensitivity and emotion, and black, the color of a purposefully empty mind, can give occupants clarity of thought and improved communication skills. Once you have defined your goals and chosen a color, remember to set the intent.

---

2    Please refer to "Color" and "The Elements" in my book, <u>Earth Design: The Added Dimension</u>, *and "The Five Phases of Energy," p. 81.*

## Function and Beauty

William Morris, a famous nineteenth-century English designer and artist, said, "Design should be part of normal daily life." In accordance with his advice, ask yourself, "Is my floor plan layout, this piece of furniture, that art or accessory useful and beautiful?" Common sense and basic design philosophy can help you answer this question. However, you must also listen honestly to what comes from your intuitive voice. The first step in any Feng Shui design is to evaluate what you already have. Be honest with yourself.

First ask yourself, "Is this piece of furniture, art, or accessory enhancing my home? Is it serving its true purpose?"

If you answer, "Yes it is! And I love it; it is perfect!" Go no further.

If you answer, "Yes it is functional, but I do not like it." Ask yourself if it can be decoratively modified with traditional or personal Feng Shui symbolism to enhance your life. Or can you wait for a sale to replace it with something that you do love?

If you answer, "No, this piece of furniture is not really functional." Get rid of it. It is blocking Chi flow in your home and creating unnecessary clutter.

Now ask yourself, "Do I find it beautiful and meaningful?"

If you answer, "Yes, I love it; it belonged to my grandmother; it makes me feel loved," or "Yes, I bought it on a fantastic vacation. What a great time I had." Then ask yourself where the piece can be moved to better enhance aspects of your life that are created from its symbolic memories.

If you answer, "No, I never liked it. It came from an old lover that never made me happy." How can that piece possibly make you happy now? Give it a send off!

Once you begin to use common sense while trusting your intuitive feelings, it is easy to follow the basics. If you like it and it is functional, keep it. If you do not like it and/or it serves no purpose, then this *stuff* has become old baggage and is keeping new opportunities from entering your life. By holding on to *things* that no longer serve you, you are holding on to *issues* or *ideals* that no longer serve you. Clean out the old. Now is the time to begin fresh; Isn't that why you are reading <u>Contemporary Earth Design</u>? [3]

## Fill those boxes and plastic bags: Have No Mercy!

Get rid of what is holding you back; welcome new opportunity! Recycle it.[4] Give it to a charity so it can go to someone in greater need who *will* find it functional or beautiful!

---

[3]  "When the student is ready, the teacher appears." When you are ready to make a change, coincidences in your life present themselves until you take notice and act.

[4]  It is not appropriate Earth Design to add to landfills.

## Combining Your Resources and the Rules of Feng Shui

Now that you are left with only functional furniture along with the art and accessories that you love, you can begin to experiment with what will support you. The life-situation Bagua[5] is a very important tool in Feng Shui. Because your life is an intricate web of archetypal experiences and energies, the major life areas represented in the Bagua are mirrored in your house and your life.[6] These energies should be combined to support one another for a balanced and complete *whole* life experience.

> **It is beneficial to use all of the Guas or life areas to energetically enhance the others.**

When you are using the Bagua on a floor plan, remember that there has been a great emphasis on the *wealth* and *marriage* areas while the *self-cultivation* and *helpful people* areas have not been used to their full capability. Self-cultivation and helpful people can greatly enhance opportunities in other areas. All the energies are mutually interdependent. They can and should be combined and used to enhance one another.

## Wealth

A Feng Shui wealth adjustment does not necessarily mean putting a symbol of monetary wealth in your wealth corner. To be a wealthy person, you need to know yourself (self-cultivation!) The most important wealth is being rich in spirit and enjoying life.

---

5    Please refer to "The Bagua" in my book, Earth Design: The Added Dimension, *and the article "The Bagua," p. 35.*

6    Going one step further, since everything is linked, one level of being is a mirror for the rest; the Bagua can also be overlaid on your body to give you similar information and solutions. *Please refer to "The Bagua." p. 35.*

**For Wealth of Spirit:**

In the wealth area of the major rooms of your home and office, place a symbolic piece of art or an accessory that reminds you to cultivate your greatest wealth, your spirituality and inner self. Let it remind you to take a breath and be glad you are alive.

Or hang a photo in a gold (wealth) frame of what gives you the most joy: your children, pets, or your favorite place. Do not forget to set the intent! *I am blessed for having such a wonderful life, may this photo always remind me of how rich I am.*

Use an empty gold box as the main accent on the table in the self-cultivation area. *I place this beautiful box here to be filled with the riches each new day will bring.*

**For Wealth in Business:**

For intuitive business acumen and to be financially rich, (No one said having money was not a good thing) put a clear crystal ball for clarity of vision on a gold metal stand for financial wealth in the career or wealth area of your office or on the wealth area of your desk. *I place this crystal ball in my career area to help me know myself clearly and to intuitively make good business decisions, which in turn will generate profitable results.*

**For Wealth of Relationships:**

For a loving marriage, you need to know *who you are* to be able to choose a partner that will make you happy. You need to have the clarity to recognize when a potential mate does appear. Put a carved rose quartz heart in the arms of a loving stuffed animal and place it in the self-cultivation area of your bedroom or in the self-cultivation area of your night stand. *May I know my own heart to accept love from my partner and to give it back in return.*

## Helpful People

They are part of everyday life. From the mailman to the dentist to the grocery store clerk and car repairman, helpful people are critical in your life. They are your children's teachers and baby sitters. They are your family, friends, and associates. How many times in conversation has a *helpful person* provided another perspective that helped you solve a problem?

### For Helpful People in Your Daily Life:

In your helpful people area, place a collection of personified creatures (Some people collect owls, angels, or dolls), of many different colors, materials and/or design. *May these helpful people be abundant and come from many different sources to support all aspects of my life. I ask that they also help me be of service to others.*

### For Helpful People in Business:

Helpful people for your business are your family and friends. They are clients, vendors, support staff, and employers. They are the phone company, the copier repairman, and the person that delivers lunch. They are the people that support your business and provide referrals.

In my office, located in the wealth corner of my home, I have a brass (metal for wealth) basket full of small gifts or *red envelope tokens*[7] given to me by students and clients. I have placed these tokens from my most *helpful people* in the *career* area of my office. These *helpful people* help generate financial *wealth* and *wealth* of being self-fulfilled.

### Notice how all the Guas and energies work together.

---

[7]    As in the Native American tradition, Feng Shui is "good medicine." I incorporate acceptance of a "medicine gift," which is symbolic of the work or has special significance to further solidify and set the intent of the traditional Feng Shui Red Envelope energetic exchange. *Please refer to "The Red Envelope," in the Glossary p. 427.*

One of these special gifts is a Guatemalan pin with six cloth people on it. I set it on the top of the basket and set the intent: *May I have many helpful people from all different arenas. I fill my wealth basket with the good medicine of those I have served in order that they support my Feng Shui work by sharing it with others.*

### For Helpful People for a Successful Marriage:

Your best helpful person is your soul mate. A helpful person may have introduced the two of you. Helpful people may include your spiritual counselor and friends that share in your partnership happiness.

If you have a mate, put a photo of your love in a nurturing wood frame or perhaps a memento of your relationship in the helpful people area. *May this symbol of our unity set the intent to help us take care of each other.*

If you are looking for partnership, put a pair of something in the marriage corner. *May this set of romantic pink[8] candles bring the light of love into my heart and life.* Also place a symbolic accessory in your helpful people area to bring in potential introductions from your friends and associates.

## Use Your Body as a Feng Shui Tool

Learn to listen to your body and the signals that it gives you. How does a room make you *feel*? Agitated, peaceful, uncomfortable, sleepy? Once you hear what your body is telling you, you can begin receiving intuitive insights.

---

[8]  While red is a traditional color of marriage and romance, experience has shown me that red may be *too hot to handle* and those relationships tend to burn out.

*At the end of a long and exhaustive day of travel, you finally reach your hotel. With your twelve pieces of luggage and very cranky family, you walk into a crowded lobby with people darting everywhere. What is the first thing you really see? Isn't it the flower arrangement on the main entry table?[9] For one brief moment, your focus shifts, and what happens to your body? You take a breath, which alters Chi, and you relax.*

## Feel the energy in your body by watching it respond to a space, and you will receive great feng shui insight!

When you walk into a room with a very low ceiling, notice how you *feel* like crouching. What common sense and decorative measures will give the illusion that the ceiling is higher? How does your chest *feel* when you walk into a musty room? What intuitive solution can you find to bring life back to the space? How do you *feel* when your home is at the end of a T-intersection and there is the ever present threat of oncoming cars? What can you do to creatively put up a protective shield? Trust yourself. *Feel the Force*[10] of your experience and intuition.

## Be Aware and Re-evaluate

Evolution takes time, millions of years. Like evolution, your life is always changing. You are not the same person you were ten years ago, last year, or even yesterday. So how can a Feng Shui evaluation be the same for you today as it was a year ago? When you re-evaluate, you will see how your priorities have changed and how your Feng Shui adjustments have worked to help you on your path. You now have to readjust your Feng Shui cures to reflect, project, and balance the new you. These do not have to be expensive or major changes. For example:

---

[9]  Though they may be plastic and full of dust, even the most moderate hotel has flowers.

[10]  *Please refer to mythology and Feng Shui in "Earth Design: The Roots of Our Nature," p. 25.*

You invited your love partner into your life by placing an empty heart-shaped box in the marriage area; now replace it with a romantic picture of the two of you in a nurturing wood or stable earth frame.

Your career has taken off and you are on the cover of <u>Newsweek</u>; if you have forgotten how to play with your children, place a stuffed animal on your bed or put your softball trophy in the children area of your nightstand.

Now that you have won the lottery and realize that money cannot really buy love,[11] paint your self-cultivation room purple, and hang pictures of nature in all its beauty to expand the abundance of self-understanding and your ability to love others.

With the awareness that you are evolving, make subtle decorative Feng Shui adjustments to augment the changes in your life. While you can usually see these energetic shifts from the adjustments within a moon cycle, learn to be patient with yourself.

## Evaluate Mind, Body, and Spirit

Sometimes the energetic shift needed to create change is greater than just a physical manifestation *of the body*. Be aware, try alternative solutions and be open to the possibility that the problem may lie deeper within you.

> *I am in the effect of the six curses energy, using Compass School.*[12] *It means that I have a lesson to learn, and it will be repeated until I get it right. Give me a brand new computer and in six months it will have problems that not even the smartest techno-heads can solve. Two laptop*

---

[11]   The contemporary mythology of John, Paul, George, and Ringo.

[12]   This is an extremely revealing Feng Shui modality that goes beyond the scope of this article. It is based on energetic directions and their corresponding influences. *Please refer to "The Energy of the Eight Directions" in <u>Earth Design: The Added Dimension</u>, and "The Seven Portents," p. 93.*

*computers have crashed wherever they were located. I have figured out that it is not an energetic location problem, which could easily be remedied by moving the computer to a more beneficial area.*

If the problem can not be resolved on the physical plane, you may need to assess your *mind* or mental process and make honest adjustments there. Watch all your life experiences. What lessons can they teach you that can be applied to your persistent problems?

*Back to my computer mayhem...The more stressed out I get, the more it is crash-city. It appears to be a mental problem! Using common sense and intuition, it is painfully obvious that I need to enlighten-up, relax, and perhaps pull some weeds in the garden. This level of resolution takes longer and requires more disciplined work since it is an issue of perceptions, habits, and the entire mental process.*

When therapy does not solve your computer problems and there is still no energetic shift, the deepest *spirit*, or karmic level, needs be evaluated. This evaluation requires the most time, perhaps lifetimes. Not daring to speculate that my techno-cure is located on the karmic level, I can only suggest for myself and others that we be the best people possible and continue to cultivate ourselves spiritually.

Become the reality of all you can be. Learn to live within the perfection of your perfect vessel. Combine all your resources: set the intent, use your intuition while observing your life experiences. Hold nothing back.

### This is your life! Enjoy it!

# The Entry: New Beginnings

## Kathy Mann

Feng Shui explains how energy or Chi flows into your life, through your environment, and how it can be altered to produce positive changes. A significant transition space for influencing the flow of Chi is where the external meets the internal, the entryway. The entry of a home or business is like a foreword to a book; it sets the tone for what is to come. Feng Shui gives you the tools to capture positive flowing Chi and deflect any negative Chi in a loving, compassionate way.

Feng Shui works on the eight areas of your life: career, knowledge, family, wealth, reputation, partnership, children, and helpful people, as they are seen and felt through your environment. The energy you need for making changes in these areas of your life can be found right on your doorstep. Making your entryway inviting will let positive Chi flow into your home and life.

**Feng Shui can teach you to interpret Chi, harness it,
and let it flow vibrantly into your life.**

## The Environment

When working with Feng Shui and Chi flow for your entrance, you must consider the larger environment where your home or business is located. If the Chi is not flowing in the surrounding space, it will not find its way to your door.

If your neighborhood has trees, parks, and abundant, beautiful scenery, it will bring a peaceful, clear, and clean energy to your home.

If your neighborhood is near a power plant, high tension wires, or a city dump, the energy that flows toward the home will be negative and harmful. Using a transcendental cure with mirrors is one suggestion for altering this negative influence. Place them with loving intent[1] to deflect and push that energy away from your home.[2]

Traffic and roads also play a crucial role in the movement of Chi toward a home or space. One-way streets channel Chi in a fast and direct manner that can blast a house. Plants, a water fountain, stones, or a statue placed with intent in the path of oncoming, rushing Chi can slow it down and transform it into positive energy. A business may use this fast-moving Chi to increase customers and profits by placing such items as flags, balloons, neon lights, wind chimes, windsocks, or banners to slowly invite it in.

> *A client with a business on a highway placed a windsock on the front door to attract fast moving Chi. She quickly saw an increase in business, more new customers started coming, and her regular customers began purchasing in higher volumes.*

Typical suburban streets with two-way traffic flow are ideal, particularly if they meander slightly. Trees on a straight street give it a meandering feel since the Chi interacts smoothly with the strong life force of the trees. T-intersections, dead-end streets, and cul-de-sacs have a one way pattern of Chi flow.[3]

**Cul-De-Sac**

**Dead-End Street**

---

[1]    *Please refer to "Setting the Intent" in <u>Earth Design: The Added Dimension</u>.*

[2]    Inside the home you may place a large crystal or a round cut glass; a 60 mm crystal is recommended.

[3]    *Graphics: <u>Earth Design: The Added Dimension.</u>*

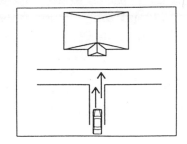

**T-Intersection**

This can cause a stagnant flow of energy and lead to a one-way mentality for the people who live there. Plants, trees, bushes, and flowers can be used to get Chi moving. Water fountains, whirligigs, windmills, flags, and wind chimes may also be strategically placed to keep the flow of Chi healthy.

## The Entryway

Every entrance has its own individual *feel*. A message about who lives in a home or works in a business is conveyed by what is at the entrance. The first impression is vital.

> *I arrived at a client's business to find two industrial-sized garbage dumpsters, one on each corner of the front of the lot. What do two garbage monuments say about this business? We moved the owner's dumpster out of view to the side of the building, and the neighboring business did the same. On the next visit, the lot had a new look and a welcoming energy.*

**Whatever is placed around the front door
is symbolic of the occupants.**

Be mindful of what is placed in this key location. The first step to achieve a positive transition space is to step back and observe your entrance. Does the landscaping and architecture flow together? How is the yard maintained? Is there clutter?

Enter your driveway or walkway and study it as if you were a stranger. Pay attention to the details. Are there any cracks in the sidewalk? Is the pathway wide or narrow? Is it straight, angled, curved? How does it feel to you?

Ideal pathways meander and curve slightly to keep Chi moving in a healthy pattern. Avoid sharp lines and ninety-degree turns whenever possible. Flowering and leafy plants that border the pathway will help to create the feeling of curves. Color influences energy, so when choosing flowering plants, consider red for Chi activation or yellow for strength and wisdom.

The pathway is a symbol of career and opportunity. How it is shaped and maintained is an indicator of your career.

> *A client was juggling three separate businesses. She had been trying for some time to sell one of them, as she no longer had time to run it successfully. Her career was mirrored in her entry; she had three clear pathways to the front door from the road she lived on. Closing one off stopped the energy flow to one of her career paths, and the business sold quickly.*

Lush and well-maintained landscaping is essential to good Feng Shui; it brings prosperity, harmony and health. Dry spots should be taken care of as soon as possible as they indicate dulled Chi and dried up opportunities. Keep trees and shrubs trimmed back and free of any dead leaves or branches. Remember to pull the weeds which choke your plants and your opportunities.

Overgrowth around the entrance also makes it difficult for Chi to flow and for new opportunities and wealth to enter. It gives the same feeling as cluttered closets and drawers inside the home or business. Avoid planting too close to the building or in the path of Chi.

**Any environment fed by a beautiful entrance will have good fortune and abundant opportunities.**

*A woman was seeking help with her career. Her home was lovely, and the landscaping was lush and beautiful. There were two potted plants on each side of the walkway, but they were so large they spilled over on the path and crowded the front door. I recommended she put these beautiful plants in a more spacious location since they were hindering her career movement. Soon after moving them, she was offered a chance to go into private practice after years of government service. She had done the career changing groundwork, and all she needed was to open up a space for the opportunity to come in.*

## The Front Door

The front door requires a careful range of Feng Shui analysis. Even if it is not used as the primary entrance, it still represents the main pathway of Chi and your career. The area around the door should be free of clutter. Check for any type of Chi restriction that blocks the front door. Unpruned trees and those planted too close to the house can block the view of the front door, and a clear view is a good indication of a solid career path.

Suggestions for beautification and Chi enhancement around the door are silk flags, wind chimes, brass bells, lions or foo dogs, flower boxes, welcome mats, hanging plants, or Bagua mirrors.[4]

A red flowering plant in a terra-cotta planter placed outside the front door will enhance a solid and stimulating career path. In the Bagua,[5] the element that corresponds to career is water, so a carefully placed water

---

[4]   It is best to consider the whole environment and elemental balance before suggesting any one enhancement. There may be influences from neighboring homes or businesses, which need to be considered when making the appropriate selection.

[5]   *Please refer to "The Bagua," p. 35.*

object near your front door can bring career success and prosperity. A man-made pond with fish, an electrically powered fountain, a bird bath, or water rock garden are also ideas to bring water and good fortune to your front door.

> *There is a very elegant hotel that is surrounded by a gently flowing, man-made river. It is abundant with ducks, geese, and vibrantly colored fish. The landscaping is full of palm trees, bushes, flowers, and nesting birds. Arriving at such a setting, you feel an immediate sense of peace. Who would ever want to leave? Not surprisingly, it is one of the most prosperous hotels in the area.*

Avoid square columns as an architectural feature near your front door. If you already have them, soften them with ivy, or use plants and crystals to deflect the negative influence of the secret arrow[6] Chi they project from their sharp angles.

Looking from your walkway, the area to the left of the front door is the knowledge area of the Bagua. Knowledge means more than intellectual book knowledge, it can mean cultivation of *inner knowing* received from your higher source. This life area is activated with the color blue. Blue accents can be added with flowers, a blue mailbox, a bird feeder, or blue letters for the address.

To the right of your door is the benefactors or helpful people area. The colors to enhance it are gray, black, and white. You might consider using a collection of stone statues, like personified garden frogs or your rose collection to bring helpful people into your life from many sources.

### What is on the outside of your environment reflects what is on the inside, in your heart.

Creating the passageway between you and the world is an intensely personal process. It should reflect your journey and the image you want to project. Balancing Chi energy at your entryway brings harmony, prosperity, health, abundance, and good fortune for all those who enter your home.

---

6  *Please refer to "Contemporary Architectural Design," p. 143*

# The Room of First Impression

## Bob Longacre

When you enter one of Europe's great Gothic cathedrals, you learn all you need to know about first impressions. All over the world, great structures were built based on the mathematics of the human body.[1] The ancient architectural masters knew full well that this initial impression of scale would act to harmonize people with the cosmic symmetry of the Earth and heavens. By studying this great architecture and scaling its ideas to size, you can achieve the same effects in your home and life.

When you realize that the Earth and cosmos are a single living entity, it becomes apparent that humans are not just insignificant specks in a vast unknowable universe. In fact, your body is a miniature hologram of the cosmos. Each person is like a pebble dropped in a pond causing ripples with their thoughts and actions that eventually touch the whole pond or universe. The life force that makes this all possible is Chi.

**Chi is the singular thread that animates and weaves everything into a living universal tapestry.**

---

[1] *Please refer to <u>Earth Design: The Added Dimension</u> for Leonardo da Vinci's theories on this topic. There is also a discussion of ergonomics which is pertinent to the mathematics of the human body.*

Chi is the force of life-consciousness that permeates all humans. It is part of your aura, that personal living template or hologram that makes you unique. Your individual Chi field interacts with everyone around you as you share air, affect other's thoughts, and manipulate matter in constructive and destructive ways.

Chi motivates galactic births, the wind, tides, and volcanoes. Like a stream flowing through a field, it percolates through and nourishes everything. Your role is to be a catalyst for Chi, ensuring its continued healthy flow through your life and the universe. You can do this by using the principles of Feng Shui in your home, office, and life. This subtle art awakens your innate abilities to *read* and *see* how best to conduct Chi throughout your spaces. The result is health, happiness, and success on all levels which gradually illuminates and eliminates loneliness, fear, and illness. Your home becomes an extension of yourself, needing your love, guidance, and sometimes a helping hand. This is Feng Shui!

### Moving Energy

Energy moves through your home like it moves through your body. Studying Chi's movement through the body can help you understand its movement on the macro scale of your house and environment.[2] And as everything is related, how Chi flows through your home can positively or negatively effect your health.

Chi is *breathed* into the interior through the front door. It circulates, ideally nourishing the entire home before flowing to the back door where it is *exhaled*. Like your eyes, ears, and skin, doors and windows are the house's apertures for inhaling Chi, air, light, and sound. The flow of Chi is a continuous process.

Your body's aura, that mostly invisible *energy glove* that surrounds the body, is the living circuitry that connects you to and also separates you from the cosmos. The equivalent circuitry surrounding your home is the web of the neighbors, trees, water and air quality, animals, and power lines. These define

---

2    *Please refer to "Energy Systems and Feng Shui," p. 275.*

the quality of the life force of the home; they can be a loving buffer or a chronic toxin. Your neighbors, their structures and environmental manipulations, are literally part of your energy field. This definitely gives new meaning to community!

## The Initial Impression

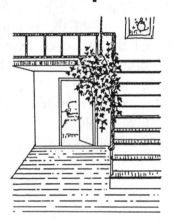

The initial impression of the property should be conducive to a healthy Chi flow with a large, well-maintained pathway.

It is vitally important that the area outside and inside the front door, or the *mouth of Chi,* be safe, well lit, and uncluttered. It should be proportionally sized to breathe in enough quality Chi to sustain a healthy home or apartment. Any entry room or mud room should also be large enough to handle the initial breath of Chi and conduct it harmoniously through to the inner organs of the home.

A mirror or artwork with depth, added to the back wall of an undersized entryway, will create space.

It is a law of physics that a mirror creates the depth equal to the observer's distance from it. Thus, a six-foot deep, cramped room can become twelve feet deep with a large mirror on the back wall. Any doorways or continuous combinations of doors should also be large enough and aligned on the same axis as the front door.

### Front and Back Door Alignment

A cramped entry can strangle Chi, but just as disabling is a direct view of the back door from the front door.

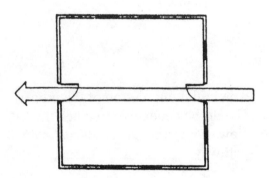

Chi will over accelerate and fly right out of the building through the back door, leaving the home gasping for air. This can create illness along the body's central meridians,[3] and intestinal problems, along with strained interpersonal relationships.

To remedy this condition, hang a multi-faceted crystal, wind chimes, or Chinese flutes just inside of the front and back doors as well as at any major intersecting doors along this axis. These act to slow down and circulate Chi throughout the home.

Hallways and doorways represent arterial breathing passages and valves for Chi and collectively must foster a meandering path for healthy Chi flow. The halls need to be wide enough to handle a healthy quantity of Chi. The doors also need to be wide enough and function smoothly on their hinges, handles, and locks. Carefully chosen artwork and mirrors can create depth. Certain colors and textures can visually enlarge these Chi pathways in the home and prevent choking and clogging as well as bickering types of disease patterns from manifesting in the occupants' health.[4]

---

[3]  *Please refer to "Energy Systems and Feng Shui," p. 275.*
*Graphic: <u>Earth Design: The Added Dimension</u>.*

[4]  *Please refer to the section of this book: "Feng Shui for the Health Body," p. 273.*

### Stairs

Many homes have front doors that open onto a set of stairs going to the second floor. Chi that is already inside the home as well as financial opportunities can roll back out the front door. Having stairs too close to the front door can also adversely affect the heart and divide the consciousness.

As a remedy, add a table with plants, a hanging plant, or artwork to pull the focal point away from the stairs. Placing a basket on one of the lower stairs acts to catch Chi and keep it from flowing back out the front door. A hanging crystal or wind chimes also helps circulate Chi.

Homes with an entry way that opens to stairs going down is even worse; it creates a feeling of insecurity, danger, or even of falling that can lead to fear and tentativeness in life. Fortunately, closing a door or adding a door can easily fix this. Otherwise, use objects chosen intuitively to change the focal point away from the stairs.

### Lighting

Interior lighting creates an encompassing overtone. Underlit and gloomy lighting is obvious in its effect, but excessive light also poisons the atmosphere. Glare from the outside poisons Chi. Caution should be used in adding large windows, greenhouses, or whole walls of windows. Avoid placing major sitting/conversation areas of chairs and sofas in the glare of a window or in a natural path of the Chi and traffic flow.

Natural light from northern facing windows is unique. It produces no glare, no fading of carpets and furniture, and no rapid temperature fluctuations. In southern exposures, pounding sunlight creates a tone of passivity and avoidance as well as too much energy.

## The Room that Sets the Home's Tone

The ideal first impression of a room is one of wide open space that is well lit and ventilated. This will set a tone of creativity, joy, openness, and a healthy expansion of emotion in both residents and guests. This room expresses the occupants' lifestyle. It is the initial *vessel*[5] or *organ* accepting Chi into the home. The contents of this space should be chosen and arranged as carefully as a symphony.

**A crucial juncture of Chi is the impression created by the first room[6] seen beyond the front door. This room sets the tone for the entire home.**

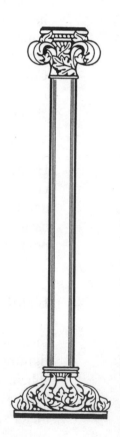

### The Living Room

The living room, the family room, or the study are the best first impression rooms because they promote relaxation, thinking, and hospitality. Carefully choose and place an initial symbol in this room. It may be a piece of sculpture or art work that will draw the eye to it and set the tone of the room. Let the symbol speak to the visitor (and the occupants!) of who you are or what your ideals are: a sculpture of the Buddha, a painting that inspires you, or a photograph of a whale breaching. Notice the different first impressions you get upon seeing a Monet print on the wall versus a poster of Mötley Crüe in concert. A properly chosen symbol balances the right and left brain and bathes the viewer in its beauty.

---

5    *Accept Feng Shui and Earth Design into your vessels: your home and your spirit. Please refer to the explanation of this book's cover in the opening pages.*

6    *The entry vestibule is also an important consideration. It should be well lit and inviting, with a noticeable feeling of demarcation and transition from the outside world into your home. Even in a small apartment, the feeling of an entryway can be created with an area rug or a change in flooring.*

### The Bathroom

Bathrooms should be avoided as the first impression. No one wants to set the tone of the house with elimination. Water represents wealth, and the home's Chi, opportunity, and success go straight down the drain with the water. The bathroom in the first room location will also create ill health, especially with such internal plumbing as the bladder.

Keep the door closed or use the trusted methods of art and texture to divert attention away from the bathroom. A plant outside the door will do the trick. In the Chinese harmonic flow of elements, the plant-vegetative forces of growth (wood) are nourished by water (bathroom) and in turn feeds consciousness (fire), preventing it from being doused by the bathroom (water).[7]

### The Kitchen

A first room view of the kitchen is not good either. The first impression becomes food, which could promote overeating, thus diminishing self worth in the residents. Children are especially vulnerable to this, and the propensity in modern architecture to enter a home through a kitchen-dinette area has contributed its fair share to overweight westerners. It also leads to excessive family dynamics, and bickering over kitchen issues: who gets what to eat when, who cleans up, and who does the shopping. This configuration attracts guests whose main reason for visiting is to eat.

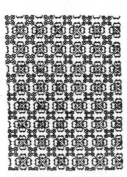

The solution is to shield the kitchen with a Chinese-type screen, a tall plant, or wind chimes to divert attention or to use any other means of creating separation.

---

[7]    *To learn more about the five element theory and the creative and destructive cycles of the elements, please refer to "The Five Phases of Energy," p. 81.*

### The Bedroom

The bedroom as a first impression promotes laziness. Residents will always be tired, yawning as soon as they walk in the door. Keep the door closed, put a mirror outside the room, or use anything that diverts attention. The master bedroom should also be off the main pathway or meridian of the home and away from the main entrance. This insures the residents control over their own destiny and a more peaceful life. A mirror hung beyond the central meridian can *move* the bedroom off of this unfavorable position.[8]

LIVING ROOM
Best of all.
Hospitality
Geniality

VESTIBULE
Hospitality
Good, if neat
and large
enough

SUNROOM
Enlivens ch'i
& success
unless over-
heated + glarey.

OFFICE-STUDY
Implies intel-
ligence, but
also nerdy &
workaholic

PLAYROOM
Life's a game.
I'm broke &
don't get
much done

BEDROOM
I'm always
tired & don't
get much
done

BATHROOM
I pee & do my
hair a lot.
I'm always
sick & broke

KITCHEN
I'm hungry,
overweight &
have mooch-
ing guests.

KEYNOTES SET BY DIFFERENT ROOMS OF FIRST IMPRESSION

---

8     Carefully placed mirrors can solve many location problems. Please use only one mirror solution at a time. This will allow you to monitor its effects exclusively and fine tune or abandon it when necessary.

Here are additional things to avoid and to seek when you are evaluating the room of first impression.

**Remember to trust your intuition when evaluating
your space and the changes you make.**

**Correct, change:**

Correct dangerous conditions: loose floorboards or tiles, psychically intrusive or sharp wall or ceiling objects

Secure fragile or tipsy objects.

Clean clutter, garbage, and dirty laundry.

Avoid using synthetic materials whenever possible.

Fix unmaintained conditions: peeling paint, broken windows, and blown light bulbs.

**Do:**

Seek spaciousness and the best maintained conditions possible.

Use pure uplifting colors, inspirational art work, natural materials, and whenever possible, soothing music.

Use live plants and real flowers; they attract success, maintain health, represent growth and potential, and their colors/aromas act as air fresheners and pure soul food.

Strive for synergy. Have hospitable, touchable objects, friendly colors and decor, and comfortable furniture. The decor and contents should inter-relate with who you are, your vision, and each other.

The first room in the home is the decompression chamber between the outside world and your nest. Great architecture and structures sweep you off your feet upon approach, and once entered, they evoke inspiration and awe. You can create the same feeling within your private space.

With intuition, imagery techniques, experimentation, and plain old asking, you can co-create with this *living being*: your home, apartment, or work space. Lovingly done and evolving over time, your spaces can grow to create an initial impression that uplifts, inspires, and above all, welcomes everyone involved in the loving arms of a spiritual oasis.

# Inspiring Arrangements

## Toni A. Lefler

The dance between the physical and energetic dynamics of an environment and its occupant is a fascinating aspect of Feng Shui. From a subtle adjustment to an entire make over, changes in your space can have a profound impact on you. Life enriching results can manifest when you flow with, rather than against, the powerful forces of nature.

The simple tasks of cleaning, organizing, and rearranging with heartfelt intention, communicate care for the soul, the space, and yourself. Like all living things, your surroundings respond to your actions. As furniture and accessories are brought to order in supporting you in your lifestyle or work habits, you gain a new appreciation for your possessions. Simultaneously, the related areas of your life are enhanced and healed.

**Your house is your larger body.**
Kahlil Gibran

How and where you spend your time is a reflection of your inner feelings and the circumstances in your life, both on the physical plane and in unseen energetic ways. As you become aware of your environment, you awaken to yourself. Everything is interconnected!

*One client with a home-based business had difficulty focusing. Projects were scattered throughout the living and dining areas. Her assistant sat at a desk in the laundry room with her back to the entry. This less-than-favorable arrangement caused major challenges in the business and took its toll on their working relationship. After we relocated the office to the wealth area, the results were dramatic. Not only did the business experience tremendous financial growth, the discord in the relationship was replaced with harmony, all within the first thirty days.*

Life is constantly changing, expanding and contracting with experiences. Marriage, divorce, birth, death, buying or selling a home, financial difficulties, and health problems are some of the changes you may encounter. To honor yourself, especially during transitional times,[1] you may need to adjust your surroundings to accommodate the new energy. That does not necessarily mean relocating, but simply realigning your present environment to a new, more expanded perspective. By applying the proven principles of Feng Shui, you can achieve and maintain a peaceful, centered feeling regardless of obstacles you encounter.

## How to Begin the Process

To begin the physical process of changing the energy in your space, take stock of what you have in and around your home. *One man's junk is another man's treasure* still rings true! Recognize the contributions you make to another when you release items you no longer want or need.

> *One man started this process in his home office and was delighted with the results. While working on other rooms, he would reward himself by revisiting the previously cleaned spaces because they felt so good.*

**Have nothing in your home that you do not know to be useful or believe to be beautiful.**
William Morris

---

[1]  *Like the wisdom of the I Ching (The Book of Changes), always reassess your life conditions to reevaluate your Feng Shui conditions. Please also refer to "Utilize All Your Resources," p. 189.*

Review your possessions and discard items that no longer hold value for you with the clear intention of releasing the old thoughts, beliefs, and emotions attached to them. By clearing out items, you open the path for new energy to enter your life. It can be a very liberating and powerful experience.

Streamlining your belongings can also be a profitable enterprise, especially when you are preparing a home for sale.[2] Most buyers visualize their possessions in a prospective home. To neutralize a space, begin packing personal, political, and religious items. The intention of selling your home will be empowered by your willingness to begin shifting your energy.

> *One family had their home on the market for 18 months with no possibilities on the horizon. After they stream-lined and rearranged their belongings, the realtor was able to raise the price. A cash offer materialized within 60 days at the higher price, and the sale closed quickly.*

Once you have determined what items to keep, you can go on a *treasure hunt*! Search closets, drawers, garage, attic, basement, and other rooms for cherished pieces that may enhance the room being rearranged. Consider symbols[3] for corresponding areas of the Bagua,[4] like a pair of angels for the partnership area or a rich forest painting for the family area. Once your awareness is expanded, you will view your belongings with renewed appreciation.

---

[2]   *Please refer to "Feng Shui and Real Estate Values," p. 179.*

[3]   *Please refer to "Art and Design Solutions," p. 225.*

[4]   *Please refer to "The Bagua," p. 35.*

*One client had a large living room that she never used. After rearranging it, she added newly rediscovered items from her treasure hunt that enhanced the space. Guests found the room inviting and gravitated there when previously they had only used it as a pass-through. The changes enhanced the architectural features while complementing the belongings, which resulted in an inviting and peaceful space.*

Only items you love and that serve you should remain. If you feel you need to add things, wait until after you have arranged what is on hand. Consider that even a simple environment can be surprisingly comfortable, restful, and refreshing.

**Do what you can, with what you have, with where you are.**
Theodore Roosevelt

Like working with a large three-dimensional puzzle, everything has a place where it will fit just right. Adjusting and fine tuning may be required to get the flow just the way you want it, but that is part of the fun.

Begin to view your surroundings as though it is the first time you are entering the space. *Feel the room.* As you walk around, experience the space from varied perspectives. How would it feel to place the sofa in a *commanding* position?[5]

---

[5]  *Please refer to "Feng Shui and Children," p. 349, and "Family and Space Relationships," p. 249.*

Consider angling or floating the furniture towards the middle of the room and away from the walls. Keep in mind how the areas of the Bagua relate to each room, including the complimentary colors and elements.

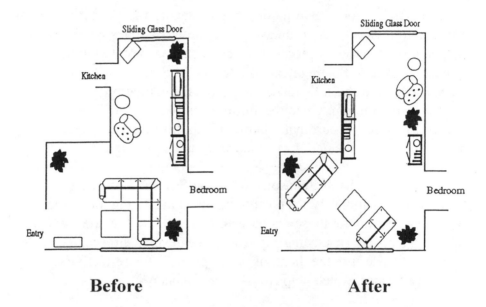

**Before**                              **After**

## The Bagua

| Wealth/ Blessings Purple | Fame Fire Red | Relationships Pink |
|---|---|---|
| Family Wood Green | Health Earth Yellow | Children Metal White |
| Knowledge Blue | Career Water Black | Benefactors/ Travel Gray |

**We shape our dwellings, and afterwards our dwellings shape us.**
Sir Winston Churchill

Using the living room as a model, begin placing the largest pieces of furniture to create a new foundation. Make the changes *work* with the architecture. Place heavy pieces: sofa, book shelves or entertainment unit on, near, angled, or floating next to large walls. Smaller walls or corners can be used to create a little niche away from the main grouping to use for reading or meditation. Once the furniture is placed, hang artwork and mirrors. Be sure to coordinate them with the furniture arrangement by size, shape, color, theme, or to enhance an area of the Bagua.

Mirrors are considered the aspirin of Feng Shui and can be used in a multitude of situations. When positioning them in a living room, they can reflect an entryway for those seated with their back to the door, which is a Feng Shui no-no. By placing a mirror above the mantelpiece, it can also energetically defuse the heat of a fireplace. The reflective quality symbolizes water, which helps to balance the energy.

The finishing touch is placing the accessories, or the jewelry of a room. Like artwork, smaller items should be positioned to harmonize with the grouping they are in and complement the room arrangement. Below are other guidelines for placement and how they relate to Feng Shui.

| *Design Placement Tips* | *Good Feng Shui* |
| --- | --- |
| **Place** the main seating in a commanding position, with full view of the entry. If you have an architectural focal point, (fireplace, expansive view) angle the furniture to capture both views. | The commanding position of a room is diagonal to the door, facing into the room. Facing a doorway is a powerful position which enhances control, concentration, and authority. |
| **Create** weaving traffic patterns and intimate conversation niches to slow the Chi down. Avoid straight pathways. | A front to back door alignment can symbolize energy and money rushing through your home and your life. |
| **Separate** modular wall unit pieces by placing two pieces on a large wall and the third on an opposite wall diagonal across the room. This balances the height and weight of the room. | Too much weight on one side of a room gives the illusion of *leaning* in that direction and of being *weighed down*, or even of being overwhelmed. |
| **Balance** lighting in a room by placing it either diagonally or in a triangle, rather than to one side of the room. | Leaving areas *in the dark* could symbolize corresponding life situations that one is in denial about or is ignoring. |
| **Add** plants and fresh flowers to a room to soften angles and fill in empty spaces. Live is best, silk is acceptable. | Live healthy plants and flowers contribute to the life energy of occupants and are a natural cure in many situations. |
| **Group** collections like crystals or animal figures in one or two areas rather than scattered throughout the room or house. | When items are scattered, it could represent being scattered in some area of life. |

**There's no place like home.**
Dorothy in "The Wizard of Oz"

Your home mirrors your personality, interests, experiences, beliefs, and uniqueness. By creating surroundings with harmony, beauty, and order, you honor yourself, your life, and your Creator.

"A house is simply a shell or a shelter from the elements, and the difference between a house and a home is how it is personalized and how people's personalities shape the environment to make it compatible with them."[6]

You have the ability to shape your life in a magical place called home. Let it begin in your heart. By bringing harmony to your surroundings, you can indeed bring peace to the world.

---

[6]  <u>Where the Heart Is: A Celebration of Home</u>, edited by Julienne Bennett and Mimi Luebbermann, Wildcat Canyon Press, 1995.

# Art and Design Solutions

## Pamela Laurence

Traditional Feng Shui cures such as crystals, mirrors, wind chimes, bamboo flutes, and beaded curtains have been used for centuries to activate energy flow. Though these are valuable Feng Shui tools, they may not be appropriate for your lifestyle or needs. Contemporary art, crafts, and design can also be used as Feng Shui solutions. Incorporating art and designs that have true meaning for you is always the most effective Feng Shui cure.

**Objects that you truly love and that symbolize
what you want to create in your life
will bring positive energy to the space and to you.**

The significance and symbolism of an object or piece of art is simply what you choose it to be. There are no rules or textbooks to tell you right from wrong about what an object means. You create your own symbolism and meaning by choosing art and objects with your intuition and feeling. Use color, pattern, texture, images, and themes as a means of creating your own Feng Shui cure.

For example, if you would like to incorporate the symbolism of the Earth into a Feng Shui adjustment, how would you start? Ask yourself what reflects the *feeling* of the Earth. Think of what the Earth means to you. What images and ideas come to mind? Protection? Mother? Roundness? Earth colors? What can you create or find to symbolize these qualities?

A large, round basket of fruit would give you the feeling of Earth by its roundness, natural texture, and the fruit of the Earth.

A painting of a mother and child may give you the symbolism of Mother Earth protecting her child. Look for objects that convey the *feeling* of the moods or the ideals you want to reflect.

What if you would like to create expansion and upward mobility in your career? What would reflect this *feeling* of moving upward and outward?

How about a painting of the sky or a large expansive plant?

Remember, how an object makes you *feel* determines if you should use it as a Feng Shui design solution.

Play and have fun exploring the possibilities. Collect information and knowledge about art and Feng Shui, but let your own intuition be your guide. Many people are afraid of making mistakes. They feel that they do not know enough to begin to make changes, but there is a big difference between knowledge and knowing. Let your knowing or intuition give you the answers; it is never wrong. Learn to trust yourself; what was right for Buddha may not be right for you.

**If you like something and you resonate with it,
use it as part of your interior design and Feng Shui solution.**

As a guide to help you create your own Feng Shui design cures, you can use the eight energies of the Bagua.[1] Bring art and symbolism into the life areas represented by the Bagua, and you will generate the flow of energy toward your goal.

---

1      *Please refer to "The Bagua," p. 35.*

**Fame**

Fame is who you are, your essence, what makes you unique. How strongly do you have a sense of yourself? What images come to mind when you think about who you really are? Can you be playful, serious, expressive, loving, wise, and compassionate? How can you reflect this in your space? Here are some suggestions for activating the fame area and its energy:

Hang a large painting or poster of a person you admire; place it in a gold frame to reflect your inner richness.

A ceramic vase in deep red in the fame area will show your passion; fill it with flowers that reflect your inner beauty.

Put a statue of a beautiful animal to symbolize your inner strength.

Hanging a round mirror will reflect your beauty and balance.

Make sure your selection has a special meaning for you. If your mother wants you to be a doctor but you would like to be a painter, hanging a portrait of a medical scene will not enhance *your* fame. This is your space; get rid of the back seat drivers in your life.

### Marriage

This is the area of relationships. What kind of relationship would you like to bring into your life or to nurture? Friendship? Intimacy? A business partnership? Let the design solution you choose reflect that. Here are some suggestions for fostering relationships:

Get a love seat for two with a beautiful, silky fabric for a loving touch.

A bronze sculpture of two hands touching can symbolize a strong, loving connection.

A porcelain figurine of a dancer shows freedom and lightness.

Hang an artistic photograph of a couple walking on the beach.

A painting of two friends fishing in peace and harmony reflects relationship in action.

Find a unique pair of metal or ceramic candlesticks to show two lights sharing a similar space.

Be mindful that some contemporary art may use odd-shaped faces and body features. Using this type of art, even though it may be a painting of two lovers, may undermine your cure if it is *far from reality*. What is considered good art may not be good Feng Shui.

## Children

This area represents not only children, but all your creative endeavors. What do you create: music, poetry, art, and/or business? Put something here of your own creation and expression. Suggestions for the children area:

Put a small fountain to reflect the deep waters of your soul and to allow your creativity to flow; incorporate crystals and stones that you have found on your own.

Hang a portrait of someone whose work you admire; use a white frame since white reflects all the colors of the spectrum.

Try a stuffed animal or something silly that will remind you to loosen up and play; creativity comes when you are playful and open.

If you have children, put their work in a *fun* frame to display.

Put a desk and chair in this area so you can sit, relax, and be creative.

Use a wall hanging of the sun to reflect your glowing, growing creativity.

Place your stereo here, and play inspirational music to spark your creative urge.

When you let yourself go with the flow, you open yourself up to the creative force. This is the area where you can be as playful as you want to be. Use whatever inspires you.

## Helpful People

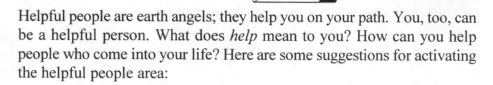

Helpful people are earth angels; they help you on your path. You, too, can be a helpful person. What does *help* mean to you? How can you help people who come into your life? Here are some suggestions for activating the helpful people area:

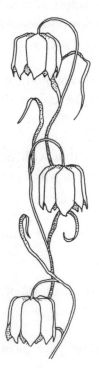

Angels are fun here. They keep you safe and protected.

Use a photograph of someone who has special meaning in your life.

Put up a painting of a heavenly scene in a white or grey frame.

A crystal lamp in this area will shine the light of protection.

This is a good place for a statue of Buddha or another figure that will make you feel safe.

Place some earth stones here to ground and nurture the energy from the heavens above.

I use a collection of clay characterizations of people in the helpful people area. They are fun and have great significance for me; I feel connected to the people they represent in a playful, loving way. Whatever you place here should make you feel safe, protected, and supported.

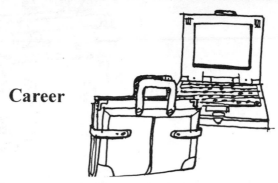

## Career

Your career takes you along your life's path. You do not want to be doing something you dislike as a career. What do you really want to do? What is important to you? Make your design cures reflect the career changes you want to make or support. Here are some suggestions to help you on your career path:

Hang a mirror to reflect your personal path.

A drum of any type in this area will remind you to step to the beat of your own drum.

A framed, artistic saying will keep you mindful of your true path.

A painting of a lovely river or a ship sailing on safe seas will symbolize that you are going in the right direction.

I use copper fountains here. The water element is a wonderful reminder that your path in life should always flow smoothly, and the metal element supports an abundance of career opportunity. What you place here should make you feel that you are on course and in alignment with yourself.

## Knowledge/Spirituality

Spirituality and knowledge is what you carry and cultivate inside yourself. Here are some suggestions to enhance your spirituality and self knowledge:

Place an empty crystal bowl to reflect your receptiveness to truth.

A rock, shell, or feather sculpture will connect you to nature.

Hang a scene of mountains and the sky to reflect your vastness and strength.

A musical instrument placed here will connect your chakras[2] with the musical tones.

A bookcase filled with books will reflect your knowledge.

Make your symbol and Feng Shui adjustment for this area reflect your true inner self and your connection to the earth and the heavens.

**Family**

Family includes friends as well as biological relatives. This area also relates to your ancestors and teachers. Here are some suggestions for the family area:

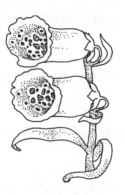

Hang your family photos in nurturing, wood frames.

This is a good place to put inherited art or furniture.

Antiques used in this area can reflect a sense of heritage.

I use baskets and vine sculptures in the family area. They bring the upward force and strength of trees along with the oneness of all things. Be sure that if you use inherited objects in this area that you truly love them. Do not keep them because you will feel guilty about giving them away. It is not good Feng Shui to keep anything that gives you unpleasant or negative feelings. Let go of the guilt; it is only someone else directing your life.

## Wealth

Wealth comes in many forms, not just money. In what ways is your life rich? What is wealth to you? Health? Luck? Strong friendships? Make your Feng Shui changes reflect the wealth you would like in your life. Here are some suggestions for activating the wealth area:

Put out your silver tea service to reflect old world wealth and the loving wealth of sharing over a cup of tea.

Place a collection of your choice in this area to symbolize bounty.

A purple vase of fresh flowers will show your wealth blooming.

Use silk or satin pillows so you can feel richness.

A fountain here will keep your wealth and abundance flowing.

I use a rock sculpture here with a feather accent: the rocks symbolize a grounding force, and the feather symbolizes the lightness of the wind. Together they represent the power of wealth and the grace of sharing it. Your symbol in the wealth area should reflect bounty and sharing.

## Tai Chi or Center

This is the center of your space. It contains all eight energies of the Bagua and none of them at the same time.[3] It reflects your health, for if everything is in balance, so is Tai Chi. Because it is in the center of the room, working with the ceiling and the floor are the best solutions. Here are some suggestions for the Tai Chi:

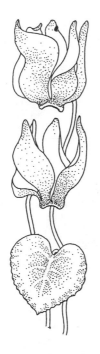

A ceiling fan will keep Chi flowing.

Paint the ceiling with light fluffy clouds or with accents of angels, birds, or faeries.

Put up a wonderful light fixture to illuminate your space with beauty.

Use a beautiful area rug to ground and balance energy.

---

3    *For an in depth look at the all/nothingness concept of the Tai Chi, please refer to "The Bagua," p. 35.*

Keep the five element theory[4] of Feng Shui in mind as you choose your design solutions. A balance of the five elements in your environment will bring harmony to your space.

| | |
|---|---|
| **Wood:** | Baskets Made of Rattan or Oak, Paper Boxes, and Frames Made of Wood |
| **Metal:** | Wind Chimes, Metal Sculptures, and Chairs |
| **Water:** | A Water Fountain and Glass Bowls or Boxes |
| **Earth:** | Clay or Terra-cotta Pots, Planters, Bowls, and Sculptures |
| **Fire:** | Candle Sticks and Incense Holders |

Go to local craft shows and art galleries to find new and unique Feng Shui solutions. Have fun and be creative in exploring arts, crafts, and designs. When you find that red clay dish with the silly feet, perhaps you can place it in the children/creativity area of your living space so you can discover other Feng Shui solutions by using lightness and humor.

Graphics: Ardis Heiman

---

4    *Please refer to "The Five Phases of Energy," p. 81.*

# Big Results for Small Spaces

## Linda M. Johnson

Feng Shui holds the key to the magical kingdom of peace and prosperity. How can simple concepts like rearranging furnishings or adding a plant, a mirror, or a touch of color have such a profound influence on people? Sometimes the littlest things create the greatest magic.

You may think you have to Feng Shui the entire house to see results. If you inhabit a small personal space such as an apartment, college dormitory, or mobile home, you might feel that you have to wait to do a Feng Shui cure until you own your own home. Destroy that myth right now!

**By taking control of your space, regardless of its size, you can positively affect your environment.**

## Tools to Use in Feng Shui

Feng Shui may seem overwhelming at first, with its use of unusual terms and concepts such as empowerment area, Chi, and cures. But once you understand and know how to use basic Feng Shui tools, you will be able to easily apply them to your living space.

## The Bagua

A working tool called the Bagua can be overlaid on any room to determine the different energies that are inherent to each space.

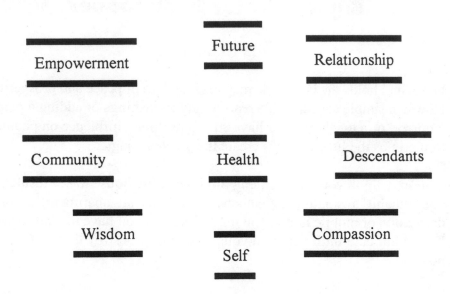

These Bagua descriptions[1] have been expanded and modernized. The traditional labeling of the Bagua fulfilled the needs of the adult, Chinese male. The new labels are designed to be suitable for both sexes and all ages:

**Self:**          (*Career*): By modifying this area's name to self, it becomes a more inclusive term. The term "career" can be misleading, especially with rapidly changing workplaces and family lifestyles. The term "self" connotes self-actualization and development of the inner person, something people of all ages can relate to.

**Compassion:** (*Helpful People*): Compassion is caring for your fellow humans.  How can you help others? It may be as simple as offering a hand to someone.

---

[1]    *This Feng Shui lineage describes the Bagua differently from the article "The Bagua," p. 35. It suggests a modern alternative to the traditional labels.*

**Descendants:** (*Children*): Not everyone has children, but many have nieces, nephews, and children of close friends. Descendants refers to the children you influence or the child within yourself. Your legacy could be your writing, speaking, or actions.

**Relationship:** (*Marriage*): A relationship may consist of a mate, a congregation, an organization, or a business partnership. It is not always marriage in the traditional sense.

**Future:** (*Fame*): Fame does not drive every person. What do you want to create in your future? How do you want to be recognized and remembered?

**Empowerment:**
(*Wealth*): The word *wealth* suggests money to most people. When you are empowered, money is just one element. Empowerment includes the ability to gain control of your life.

**Community:** (*Family*): In such a mobile society, you are sure to be involved in the community at large. In the past, families worked together on farms and in the family business; that is not done as much nowadays. Extended families are groups with whom you work and socialize. They are becoming increasingly important as children move away from their parents' cities and neighborhoods.

**Wisdom:** (*Knowledge*): You can read a book to gain knowledge; however, by experiencing life, understanding, and questioning, you gain wisdom.

**Health:** (*Center/Tai Chi*): When the exterior edges of the Bagua are set, you are centered in the Tao,[2] and health is created and sustained.

---

[2]  *Tao may be defined as the center of all things.*

Putting the Bagua into action and seeing results is easier than it appears, as this example shows:

> *One client, who lived in a mobile home, had difficulty with people keeping timely appointments with her. A certain repair man had failed to show up on several occasions, and her doctor had left her waiting, already undressed, for over an hour. It was time to check her compassion area.*
>
> *The doorway to her bedroom was in the compassion, (helpful people) corner of her home. I moved her free-standing mirror into the space opposite the doorway, creating a reflection of the missing corner to create a cure.*

> *The next morning, the repair man called, apologized, and set up a firm appointment. Then, the doctor himself (!) called, apologized, and sent flowers.*
>
> *A little cure, a big result!*

Can these things happen to anyone? You bet! What do you want changed or enhanced in your life? Start now and you will be surprised at what simple changes can do. It is not necessary to spend a lot of money; the adjustments can often be made with items you already own or that are inexpensive and readily available.

## The Five Elements:

Another effective Feng Shui tool is the use of the five elements: **fire, earth, metal, water, and wood.** They can be used to analyze and help make the necessary energy enhancing changes in your space. Each element has an identifying color, direction, shape, and meaning. A room or space is in balance when each of the elements is physically or symbolically represented and none of them dominates.

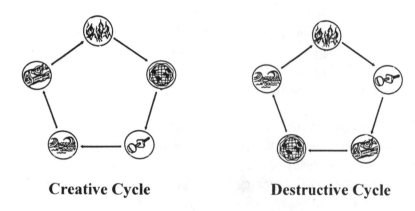

**Creative Cycle**          **Destructive Cycle**

If a room has an overabundance of an element, changing the progression or the cycle of creation/destruction[3] can be a cure.

**If there is too much:**

> **Fire:** Add water (puts out fire) or earth (dirt smothers fire).

> **Earth:** Add water (causes erosion) or wood (trees drain earth).

> **Metal**: Add fire (melts metal).

> **Water:** Add earth (fills water in) or fire (evaporates water).

> **Wood:** Add metal (chops wood) or fire (burns wood).

---

3   *Graphic: Earth Design: The Added Dimension*

Using the elements in analyzing a space can be revealing:

*One couple's apartment was dominated by the wood element. It had green carpeting, an abundance of photographs of forests and landscape paintings. Because wood symbolizes growth, they could never seem to settle down. New projects kept them so occupied they did not have time for each other.*

*We replaced the photographs with pictures of sunsets, placed a red pillow on the sofa (fire burns wood), and then added a metal candelabra (metal chops wood). A favorite picture of themselves was placed in the relationship/marriage corner. A small box with the yin/yang, the Chinese interlocking male/female symbol was also added. The box would remind them to cuddle and love each other.*

*To encourage the Tao, or centeredness, the central light in the overhead track lighting was pointed toward the middle of the room. This illuminated a medallion, or mandala, and centralized the focus of the room. They were able to make low cost adjustments; the room was balanced and the problem corrected. Voila! Inexpensive and simple cures enhanced their relationship.*

## Evaluate and Change Your Space

Beginning is simple; look around you. What is on the floor in your rooms? Are there things hidden under the bed? Are there boxes stacked in the corner? Do you have objects you have not touched in years sitting on your dresser?

### Eliminate:

One of the easiest cures is getting rid of *everything* you have not seen or used in the last year. Eliminating anything unnecessary will do a number of things:

> It will clear out needless items that impact your subconscious and upset your balance.

> The items will benefit a new recipient: Goodwill, the Salvation Army or a garage sale attendee.

> You will open up space for new opportunities to come into your life.

### Clean:

Clean everything! including the closets and drawers. (Okay, I sound like your mother...) The reason is simple. The subconscious is like a giant computer with unlimited memory. Everything is recorded and stored there, including annoying dirt and clutter. If it is not corrected, it gets imprinted again and again and blocks your subconscious. When you clear it away, your subconscious sighs with relief. As a result, your whole body relaxes, you sleep and function better, and your health and outlook improve. A pretty powerful reason to clean that room, isn't it?

### Evaluate:

Get to know yourself better! Look closely at your environment and how it impacts you. To help identify areas of your life that you would like to start working on, do the following exercise. Take a piece of paper and make two columns. In one column, write down all the areas in your life that you like and are satisfied with. In the other, put those areas that need improvement. **Do not rush this process.** It can be surprisingly enlightening and will help clarify your focus for beginning the necessary changes.

*The local library asked me for assistance. While doing the two-column exercise, several of the staff mentioned a problem with the weekly storytelling sessions. The storyteller could not maintain the preschoolers' attention.*

*At story time, the children sat facing a wall filled with many bright yellow and red phone books. The colors were distracting for anyone, let alone three and four year-olds. The library had a fireplace in a back corner. I suggested the storyteller sit on the hearth and have the children sit at her feet; the children's focus would be on her and grounded by the earth element of the fireplace.*

*The next week, several staff members commented on how much better the storytelling session had gone. After being identified in the two-column list, this little-big problem had been easily solved.*

**Diagram:**

Take a pad of paper, pencil, and ruler and go to the room where you spend the most time. Stand in the doorway and view the room as if for the first time. On your pad, draw the shape of the room; mark all doorways, windows, and architectural features, and locate all the furniture and lighting sources.

Next, use the diagram of the Bagua. You can chart where the specific energies of this octagon lie within your space. It works best if you sketch it as an overlay using a different color pen. The bottom of the Bagua is always where you are standing. The doorway will be in only three possible positions: the wisdom, self, or compassion area. Independent of your doorway's position, the empowerment corner will always be the farthest, upper left hand corner. The relationship corner will be in the upper right hand corner. From there, the other energies can be determined.

**Catalog Contents:**

Now you are ready to analyze the contents of the room. On a separate sheet, write in capital letters the first thing you see when you look into the room from the doorway. Starting on your right, walk around the room and list everything you see. **Be very specific!** Do not rush through the room. If there are posters or pictures on the wall, describe their colors, shapes, and subject matter. Is the furniture in the metal or wood element? Is there an abundance of red? Are there more light things than dark things?

You are looking for furniture, accessories and symbols represented by:

    &#10033; The Bagua energies  &#10033;  Chi: positive, life force energy
    &#10033; The five elements: fire, metal, water, wood, and earth
    &#10033;Yin: female, round, soft, dark, Yang: male, straight, hard, light
    &#10033; The Tao: centerness or what keeps you connected and grounded

When evaluating the bedroom, do this additional exercise. When you wake up in the morning, what is the first thing you see?

If it is a stair climber, each day may seem like an uphill battle.

If you see a photograph of your best vacation, you may feel an extra reason to go to work and plan for the next holiday. Add these observations to your list and put it aside for a day.

After taking a day off, take your list and diagram and look at them through fresh eyes; note anything you might have forgotten. You are now ready to start implementing your Feng Shui cures.

Start with the energies of the Bagua. What is sitting in each of the corresponding corners? If your relationship corner is full of dirty laundry or broken items, it could hamper your current or future relationships.

Look at the two-column list you made. Does the placement of furniture and accessories and the use of colors and textures enhance areas and their energies or detract from them? How can you move items from one area to another, more beneficial spot? What can you remove, clean, rearrange, or reposition to enhance Chi? This exercise brings you face-to-face with what you have been living with on a daily basis.

To see how powerful Feng Shui cures can be, pick the most important thing on your list, and while using the Bagua combined with the five elements, correct that one thing. Note the day you made the correction on your calendar and then watch to see how fast a change is realized. From there, you can move down your list and begin to implement other changes.

Changes can be made on a small scale and still have life transforming effects:

> *One young man was having job difficulties, money problems, and lacked a romantic relationship. He was one of three people living in a house and had control only over his bedroom.*

> *I told him that working with just the bedroom was not a problem. In fact, since one third of our lives are spent there, and it is the most personal space we inhabit, the bedroom is where the most powerful cures can take place.*

*The first order of business was to clean. Then, by using colors and shapes of things he already had, we began to make Feng Shui adjustments. The client worked in the entertainment field, so using the Bagua, we moved his television into the self/career area. To energize his relationship corner, we placed a pair of candlesticks with deep rose colored candles. The symbolism of a pair was to encourage a partner to appear; the candlesticks with rose candles were to illuminate and generate a spark. A green plant was moved into his empowerment/wealth area, allowing growth to take place. A blue graduation cap tassel was placed on the shelf as a water symbol to feed the plant.*

*Within three weeks, his life had completely turned around. He got a new job in his chosen field, met a woman, and began a deep relationship with her.*

## Little Cures, Big Results

If you are living in a dormitory space and are having difficulty studying, look to see if the wisdom area is cluttered. Clear it out, perhaps by adding a bookcase to store books. Add illumination with a lamp or a bright, colorful picture for impact. Study habits and grades can quickly improve.

Are you left-handed or right-handed? Change your main lighting source to the side opposite your writing hand. When the lighting source is on the same side as the hand you write with, it casts a shadow across the writing surface.

Your eyes must make constant adjustments and they will tire more quickly. Simple cure, big result.

### Cures for any Age

The adjustment of personal space can greatly help children of any age. Often, children feel out of control in their lives and environments. Looking into children's rooms can give vital clues about what is going on in their life; it is their own small universe and personal sphere. Parents can help them make a change and see the results quickly.

### Does your child:

> Hate getting up in the morning? Change the bed so that it faces east, or put a mirror across from an east facing window. The morning sun will encourage him to rise and shine!

> Prefer napping in the afternoon instead of doing homework? Check to see if the desk is in front of a western facing window. The heat could be the culprit; put mini-blinds on the window or use a fan to circulate air.

> Have problems respecting you? Place a low maintenance plant such as a philodendron in the community corner of the child's room. This allows growth to occur in the relationship between parent and child.

> Have trouble with a friend? Put a ticket from the last rock concert they attended or a funny picture of the two of them in the relationship corner of their room and see what happens.

Whether they are for a child or an adult, small Feng Shui adjustments can start the flow of energy in your space and affect bigger changes than you ever imagined. When you begin, truly observe and evaluate your environment. Apply the principles of Tao, yin/yang, and Chi to the area. Compliment these by using the energies of the five elements and the Bagua. Then mark your calendar. You will be amazed at how fast things start to change. Experiment! Have fun! Simple changes in small places can allow new and wondrous events, people, and opportunities to enter your life.

*Graphics: Courtesy of Steve Reynolds, PO Box 636, Mariposa, CA 95338*

# Family and Space Relationships

## Pamela Tollefson

Many people want to improve their loving relationships and create better harmony among family members. They want their space to contribute to good communication, a happy daily routine, and peaceful coexistence. It is important to implement Feng Shui cures that appeal to a family's lifestyle, decor, and personal taste. Understanding the people who live and work in a space is important for creating a supportive environment.

Western astrology is a useful tool for gaining insight into interpersonal relationships. It uses the macrocosm of the planets' configurations and the relationship of their energy patterns to understand the microcosm of human interaction. The placement and the relation of the planets to each other at the time of birth becomes a road map for what a person is meant to do in this lifetime. When you use astrology in conjunction with Feng Shui, you can begin a path of self-knowledge, which can lead to greater understanding of family relationships in your home.

The astrological signs give you valuable personality information. For example, emotional water signs like Cancer, Pisces, or Scorpio have a *feel* for a space. The intellectual air signs, Gemini, Aquarius, and Libra *think* about how a space looks. Aries, the initiator of the zodiac, *reacts to* a space and starts implementing changes right away.

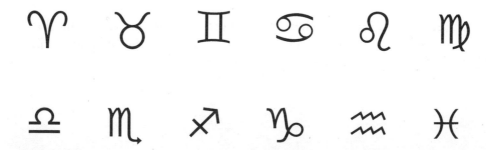

By looking at where your sun sign falls in your astrological chart, you get a glimpse into your style:

Aries underestimate their decorating skills. They are able to sustain the uncluttered, efficient home most people want.

Taurians are often messy, but they love luxury and have quality furnishings.

Geminis have many magazines, books, and bookcases. They crave light and need many work centers.

Cancers have very comfortable furniture. They love their kitchen and always offer food to their guests. The Cancer man will do anything to make his home a better place.

Leos make their home a stage. They are focused, striking, and flamboyant. They enjoy entertaining and want their house to enhance their personal appearance.

Virgos have perfectly clean, neat, and functional homes, but if you find a rare messy one, watch out because the mess will be unbelievable. Visual appeal is usually secondary to functional use.

Libras love beautiful homes. They admire charming floral patterns along with visual and spatial balance. They already have Feng Shui mirrors.

Scorpios have tall hedges surrounding their patios and lots. They need secluded private spaces. They are concerned about every detail in their daily routine.

Sagittarians have eclectic taste and home decor. They feature objects and statuary acquired while traveling.

Capricorns are well-organized; they have many file cabinets and traditional decor.

Aquarians usually have company, lots of seating, and the latest electronic equipment.

Pisceans have full laundry baskets and dishwashers. Their creativity can be seen in every room of the house. Even their clutter looks artistically arranged. They love to add fish tanks and water fountains to their spaces.

These descriptionsgive you a general sense of how each sign views their space. The key to your true aesthetic sense is determined by Venus, the planet of love and beauty. The sign in which Venus falls in your astrological birth chart,[1] tells you more about your aesthetic sense and favorite decorative concepts. You can use the combination of your sun sign and Venus sign to determine which approach would be best for implementing Feng Shui adjustments.

---

[1] *In astrology, the heavens are divided into twelve areas and given names: Aries, Taurus, Gemini, and so forth. Your birth or sun sign is based upon which of these twelve areas the sun was positioned in at your time of birth. Because all of the planets, including the sun, were in the sky on your birthday, they also can be identified and analyzed to provide life information. (For example: Sun in Libra and Venus in Cancer.)*

If your Venus is in Libra, for example, you are a natural for Feng Shui. Looking for balance and harmony is a lifetime goal. The visual takes priority over function; proportion and style are vitally important. If your Venus is in Taurus, you like to acquire great paintings, sculptures, and tactile arts. You love buying luxury items but can be very thrifty when replacing items like dishwashers and clothes dryers. The basics do not excite you. Combining your sun sign and Venus placement, you can gain insight into your sense of style.[2]

You can take this base of astrological information about you and your family and begin assessing your home. Spatial layout is another important factor in family relations. There are two common architectural features that plague family relationships:

**The location of bedrooms:**

Many modern houses have the master bedrooms protruding out in the front of the house. If the children's rooms are in the back of the house, in the command position, the children will run the household.[3]

---

[2]  *Astrology is a valuable intuitive science that requires quite a bit of knowledge. If you get stuck, please continue to read because Pamela provides excellent Feng Shui ideas.*

*For more information on how to incorporate astrology with your Feng Shui, as the ancients always incorporated the relationship of the heavens, earth, and man, please refer to "Astrology and Color," and how to overlay your "Local Space Chart" on your floor plan in, Earth Design: The Added Dimension.*

[3]  *Please refer to "Feng Shui and Children," p. 349.*

**The brick or blocking wall syndrome:**

This occurs when you encounter a wall directly after crossing a threshold. Walking into a wall when you enter a room creates blockage in your life, usually in the life area which that wall represents on the Bagua.[4]

**Case Study 1: Widow in the Wrong Room/Son in Command**

Blocked Wall
Knowledge
and Self-cultivation
Area

Parent in less
Powerful
Room than Child

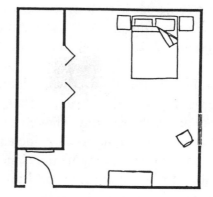

After the tragic death of her husband, Jane bought a new ranch-style house to live in with her three children. She was a Pisces who exhibited typical Piscean creativity, but she had little confidence in the direction her life had taken. She was in college but had been unable to concentrate, and her grades were dropping. She knew she had to improve her grades or leave the program.

When I examined the horoscope of Matthew, her fifteen year old son, I found that he had a totally opposite personality from his mother. Being a Virgo, the sign associated with being a perfectionist, he could handle the day-to-day routine of the house better than his watery Piscean mother. However, displaying the negative traits of his Virgo sign, he opposed his mother's every move.

---

4   *Please refer to "The Bagua," p. 35.*

In her effort to help Matthew accept the move, he got to choose the bedroom he wanted in the new house. He took the right rear bedroom, which put him in the command position of the home. Jane took a front bedroom. Though located in the powerful *helpful people* area of the Bagua, not being in the command position left her at a disadvantage.

Her room also had *a brick wall* created by a blocking closet wall. Jane walked into a blocked *knowledge* area every time she entered her bedroom. Is it any wonder her opportunities for academic success and self-improvement were stagnant?

To remove the blockage, we put in a full length mirror to open the space. Now, Jane could see herself as she turned, and it gave her a moment to reflect on her self-image. We also put a crystal in the closet to get her knowledge *out of the dark.*

Changing the balance of power with Matthew was not as easy. Rooted in his Virgo rigidity, he did not want to change rooms or make any changes for the sake of family harmony. Though changing rooms would have been the best solution, we did not want to increase Jane's friction with her son. Instead, we worked on strengthening Jane on every level. I supplied her with crystals to put in strategic positions, such as pull chains for her ceiling fan and bedside lamps. I suggested that she meditate to strengthen her focus and set aside a time and place for family discussions. Jane's self image greatly improved. She felt that she was able to take control of her family and the direction that her life was taking. She is now an "A" student, and Matthew will soon be in college.

### Case Study 11: An Angry Teenager

Blocked Wall in
Helpful People Area

Unsupportive Colors
Electromagnetic
Fields

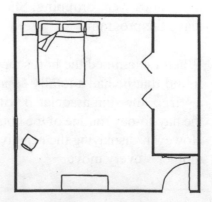

Adam was a very angry teenager with a lot of problems. His room was positioned at the end of a long hallway. Chi was funneled fast and hard down the hall and hit the blocked entry. Adam was also *banging* into this brick wall every time he entered his room; there were even dents where he had taken out his frustrations on the wall. This blocked wall was further complicated by Adam's astrological sign. Adam, a fiery and independent Aries, had a quick temper. His chart confirmed that he was his own worst enemy.

Adam's room reflected his unhappiness and contributed to his distress. Black and reddish-orange were his main decorating colors: Black seemed to contribute to his depression, and the reddish-orange stimulated his anger. The room needed repainting. I suggested changing it to a bluish green for a calm visual effect and to represent the colors of growth and knowledge.[5]

To open up the blocked wall, we put up a rock music poster, which we had framed with reflective glass. The poster was much more to his liking than a mirror. It gave the blocked wall some depth, and it made Adam happy.

I also sensed an irritating energy when I was in Adam's room. Suspecting an electromagnetic field,[6] I tested the room with a simple sound amplifier and found there was a magnetized water pipe above the head of his bed (The electricity had been grounded to the water pipe.)We moved Adam's bed out of the direct line of energy, catty corner to the door, and the magnetized water pipe was fixed. Adam is much calmer, his angry outbursts have dissipated, and he sleeps much better.

---

[5]    When you are working in a child's room, it is very important that get the child's permission. Ask if you may enter and talk directly to him or her about the room and the changes you think would be beneficial. Within reasonable limits, a teenager should be allowed to design his/her space in order to have it support and also reflect his/her personality.

[6]    Testing is especially important in the bedroom. You sleep there for eight hours and are very receptive to the energy around you in your subconscious state. The sound amplifier brings inaudible sounds into the audible range. *Please refer to "Energy Fields, Feng Shui, and Fragrance," p. 339.*

## Case Study III: The Clashing Sisters

Bed on Same Wall as
Bedroom Door

Astrological
Incompatibility

Arguing Doors

Entry Blocked with
Wall
and Scales

Clutter

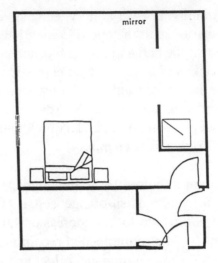

When doors do not line up and doorknobs clash against one another, expect disharmony and arguments among family members. Barbara, divorced with adult children, was a Taurus - a fixed sign that hangs on to everything, especially the past. She had turned her old Victorian home into a rooming house, and she had only her bedroom to truly call her own.

This room had a series of blocked walls and clashing doors at the entrance. In addition, Barbara had added another obstacle: a hospital style scale was right inside her door. Stagnant relationships, sibling rivalry, and weight, Barbara's three biggest concerns, were visible in her bedroom entrance. The bedroom door hit the closet door which was filled with clothes that did not fit. They had been given to her by her older, controlling sister for *when she had lost weight.* (Her sister was a Leo, who thought her personal appearance must be sensational.) Barbara had lost 100 pounds when her sister had been abroad for a year. But since her sister's return, Barbara had started over-eating again and had gone back to her feelings of inferiority and habit of hanging on to the past.

In Barbara's room, there was so much clutter that her sister had given her such as old clothes and travel mementos, that there was no room for Barbara. We began to discuss how to get rid of the clutter and leave space for new opportunities and people. Using the Bagua, we made adjustments to her marriage and partnership area to open the way for a new relationship. Little by little, Barbara has moved out a dozen boxes (especially hard for a Taurus who clings to things), lost twenty pounds, and has noticed a lessening influence from her sister. The process has been a gradual but important step to Barbara's self-empowerment.

### Case Study IV: Love and Space

Good romantic relationships are high on the list of what people want from Feng Shui adjustments. A Libra client had her bed in a placement that could lead to one of the partners leaving the relationship. The bed was on the same wall as the door and had a view of the office, which was an addition within the bedroom. Lori did not want to place a barrier to disguise the office because it would also obscure the fireplace her husband really liked. Libras thrive on good relationships and must play a significant role in their mate's life.

Her Capricorn husband was a workaholic. Capricorns generally get their fulfillment from working, but his total absorption in work coincided with the completion of the new office. He was obsessed with starting new businesses and had been ignoring his wife for some time.

She followed my other Feng Shui recommendations but could not get herself to move the bed. Her husband did end up leaving the relationship, and the old bed went with him. Lori replaced the bed with a style of her liking and put it in a good Feng Shui position. She has found that she no longer lacks male companionship.

### Love the One You Are With: Yourself

*A successful romantic relationship can be very elusive and hard to maintain in these complex times. Sometimes it is tempting to look for someone to bring financial security and unconditional love and to supply the elements you feel you are missing. But you need only look in your Feng Shui mirror to see the person you must love unconditionally and work to sustain financially, yourself. Be your best partner. Syncronistically, when you are whole, self-sustaining, and do not need a partner, the ideal partner will appear.*

By comparing your birth chart with the rest of the family and by checking the current movement of the planets, you can get valuable information on relationships. When planets are in close proximity or aspect, Chi or energy is created. If the energy is positive, great opportunities and relationships may result. If there is conflict between the planets, there may be tension. Some tension is necessary in life to help propel you forward. Who does not need a little push now and then? But too much tension and extreme incompatibility are not positive or healthy for living arrangements. Feng Shui cures can help you make changes to foster better family relationship and to regain balance in your home.

Astrology and Feng Shui masters over thousands of years have passed on their knowledge and astute observations of how the heavens and earth help determine who you are, but you are the only one who can take that knowledge and determine who you will become.

# Chinese Wisdom for the Modern Workplace

## Kirsten M. Lagatree

Based on the premise that people are affected by their environment, Feng Shui unites ancient beliefs with modern space planning, interior design, ecology, psychology, and common sense. The words Feng Shui mean *wind* and *water,* two natural elements of incredible energy. They are a symbolic shorthand for the power of nature and the importance of living in harmony with it.

> *Whenever Rose Murray travels on business, she rearranges her hotel room. "I drag the desk around so that I can see the door while I work. And if there's unattractive, depressing art on the wall, I take it down and hide it in the closet." As a telecommunications consultant, Rose is hardly an expert on interior design. But what this thoroughly modern, professional woman is practicing is the ancient Chinese art of placement, Feng Shui.*

In removing ugly art from hotel room walls, Rose makes her surroundings feel positive and inspiring. When she drags the writing table to face the door, she is following one of the most important rules of Feng Shui: do not sit with your back to the door. To be powerful, you must feel powerful. Sitting with your back to the door leaves you vulnerable to anyone who may come in unannounced.

## How it Works

The first principle of Feng Shui is Chi flow. In the office, the placement of your desk, files, furniture, and plants should allow unobstructed movement of this vital life force throughout your work area. If you have massive stacks of files or unwieldy piles of magazines stashed on and around your desk, you are blocking the free flow of energy that is vital to your power of concentration and creativity.

*Small business consultant Alice Bredin says she can tell the difference between the poor Feng Shui of her cluttered work space in Maine and the good Feng Shui of her tidy office in New York City. "In Maine, there are so many projects stacked up around me that I don't know what to do first." She adds that the energy flow in her carefully arranged New York office, where she is very organized, makes her feel in control. "I can focus and be highly productive."*

In addition to paying attention to good energy flow, heeding compass directions and their spheres of influence will affect the Feng Shui of your surroundings. The Bagua[1] delineates these basic components of Feng Shui. Each compass point governs a different aspect of life: wealth, health, careers, and relationships. Each point has a corresponding color, natural element, and number. They can be combined to create enhancements which encourage success in any area of life.

---

[1]   *Please refer to the Bagua graphic in "Riding the Wind and Harnessing the Water," p. 101.*

## Putting It to Work in Your Office

You can take advantage of the Feng Shui enhancements shown on the chart to enhance your workplace, your business balance sheet, and your own piece of mind. Here are some tips:

### To Increase Wealth

Wealth is one of the first aspects to consider when making changes in your office; it is a business' bottom line as well as your remuneration.

Put an aquarium with a water pump in your office. The moving water symbolizes cash flow, and the fish encourage abundance. *There are always more fish in the sea!* Place the aquarium, along with something black, on the north wall. North is the direction, water is the element, and black is the color that governs career and business success.

The southeast direction governs wealth. Add red or purple touches in groups of four to that area to take full advantage of your money corner. Depending on the nature of your business, you may want to put the computer or fax machine in the wealth corner.

> *California interior designer Annie Kelly says, "The easiest thing to do is put office equipment out of the way and in a corner, so you might as well put it in the wealth corner!"*

### To Augment Fame

Take advantage of your south wall to bring fame (recognition for your work/effort) into your career and life. Use the Bagua's corresponding symbolism for south in any creative combination that enhances the decor of your office. This personal anecdote underlines how powerful these cures can be.

*Before my book, <u>Feng Shui: Arranging Your Home to Change Your Life</u>, was published, I created a special Feng Shui enhancement on the south wall of my office by hanging a poster featuring nine red cardinals. The number nine corresponds to south, and birds are the animal for this auspicious direction. Red is the color of south and represents fame and fortune. As it turned out, the first date for my book tour was on ABC's "Good Morning America." Millions of people saw that show and countless opportunities came my way as a result.*

**To Enhance a Flagging Career**

Solutions do not always have to follow the traditional *rules* to be effective. Experiment and see what works best for you.[2]

*Corporate coach and counselor Edith Berke was suffering a sluggish time in her business. Her individual clients were dropping away, and her corporate clients, the bread and butter of her practice, were not calling. Edith consulted a Feng Shui practitioner who suggested moving a beautiful black ceramic fountain from the back patio into her home office. This unorthodox design change happened to be feasible, since the floors in her house were tile. Within two weeks after adding the color black and the element of water to the north wall of her office, Edith had a lucrative contract with a brand new corporate client.*

Changes do not always have to be meticulously planned and executed. The simple addition of plants and flowers contributes to the good Feng Shui of any office or study.[3] You will enjoy a more harmonious working environment and receive the benefits of healthy, smooth flowing Chi.

---

[2]   *Please refer to "Using the Components of Feng Shui Cures," p. 65.*

[3]   *Make sure they are healthy and well cared for. Fresh cut flowers should be removed before they wilt.*

## Location, Location, Location

Proper office location, auspicious placement of your desk, and correct positioning of lighting are of utmost importance for good office Feng Shui.

### Desk Placement

The location of your desk is the single most important consideration in the workplace.

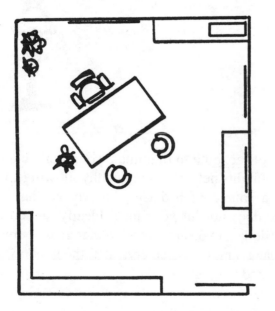

Your desk should be in a commanding position.[4]

That is, you should always sit facing the door and position your desk well inside the office to *command* a view of the whole room. You will think more clearly, your judgment will be sound, and as a result, your authority will be respected.

---

[4]    *Please refer to "Feng Shui and Children," p. 349, and "Family and Space Relationships," p. 249.*

*Kristin Frederickson, art director at a small New York publishing house, thinks it is impossible for anyone to work well with their back to the door. "There's such a detrimental feeling about not knowing what's going on behind your back. If you work that way, you are going to have paranoid energy around you, which will be felt by your coworkers."*

If it is not possible to arrange your desk to face the door, hang a small mirror over your desk so that you can see the entrance reflected. If you are facing the door but unable to see the rest of the room, use a mirror to improve your view.

## Lighting

Good light is essential for an office, both to illuminate your work and to create good Feng Shui. Bright lights help promote healthy, flowing Chi. Glare is a distraction and a source of bad Chi, known as Sha. Be especially careful that glare does not hit your face. Ideally, windows should be to the side of your desk.[5] If you are seated so that glare[6] comes across your line of vision, hang a multifaceted crystal at the window to disperse the Sha of the glare and to create good Chi.

## Office Location

The location of the manager or boss' office is the most important factor in determining the overall success of any business enterprise. Check the layout of your workplace to see if its placement is auspicious.

---

[5]  *If you are right handed, it is best if the natural light comes in over your left side so as not to block the light as you write; the opposite would be true for our left-handed friends.*

[6]  *You may want to determine the source of the glare and make such corrections as installing window treatment or moving to another good Feng Shui location.*

If you are in a position of authority at your workplace, keep the following in mind: The manager should have the office furthest from the front door and office traffic. From this vantage point, he or she will see the big picture and not be distracted by the minutia of daily transactions. The desk should not be close to the office door, or the boss may be viewed by others as not having sufficient control over operations and will not be treated with proper deference. Similarly, workers whose desks are further inside the office than the boss' are likely to be insubordinate; they will feel more in command than their superior.

For a more powerful presence at meetings, try to take the chair facing the door. This position will make you highly sensitive to the dynamics of the room. Do not sit with your back to a window. A solid wall behind you will provide more backing for your ideas and will lend authority to your presence.

## The Big Picture

The relationship between Feng Shui and finance can be seen on a much grander scale in any number of large, multinational corporations. The headquarters of the Hong Kong and Shanghai Banking Corporation in Hong Kong is a famous example. Reputed to be one of the most technologically advanced skyscrapers in the world, the forty-seven story building was sited and constructed according to the strictest Feng Shui principles.

Many visitors wonder at the odd angle of the escalators that lead from the plaza level to the main banking floor. The moving stairs appear to have been placed at random, but they were carefully situated to distribute maximum Chi and wealth evenly throughout the structure. Moreover, it is no accident that the building faces the sea and has Victoria's Peak at its back. These highly auspicious land forms endow this financial giant with their benefits: the mountain provides support and protection for the corporation's business ventures, while the ocean invites wealth to flow into the building.[7]

If you are feeling a bit skeptical about implementing this ancient art in your modern office, know that in many parts of the United States, especially areas like New York, Los Angeles, and Washington D.C., business deals rise or fall on good or bad Feng Shui. You might take a cue from Donald Trump, who routinely consults a Feng Shui master before embarking on new building projects. Trump says his international clientele prompted him to take the ancient practice very seriously. The billionaire real estate tycoon put it this way:

**"If they believe ... it's good enough for me."**

Graphics:     Courtesy of Frank Paine, 516 Paseo de las Estrellas, Redondo, CA 90277, (310) 243-3704

---

[7]    *This layout suggests the classic or armchair Feng Shui configuration when locating structures on a property, please refer to "Contemporary Architectural Design," p. 143.*

# The Way of Beauty through Feng Shui

## Katrine T. Karley

The earth is making a powerful energetic shift into the Age of Aquarius.[1] Feng Shui is an important tool in directing this increased energy and higher awareness. Its message: It is possible to create your own heaven on earth. The Chinese realized long ago that the beauty and perfection of heaven could be expressed in their everyday lives on earth.

Feng Shui is a process of discovering the beauty within yourself by creating a mirror of beauty in your surroundings. Understanding Feng Shui's relationship to beauty will unlock the potential for increased health, wealth, and prosperity. Start by taking a walk in nature to really experience it. Nature is beauty in its purest form. It is your healer, your teacher, and it should be incorporated into your home or office to make it a more beautiful, harmonious, and healthy place.

**When they are in concert, nature and beauty
create a sense of physical and spiritual well-being.**

Using nature's palette, with its infinite variety of colors, textures, and forms, and exploring how a space can benefit from these natural gifts is the beginning of the symbiosis of Feng Shui and beauty.

---

1  *Please refer to "Feng Shui in the Age of Aquarius," p. 387.*

## Incorporating Nature into Your Environment

Thoroughly explore the land outside your business, home, or development. Consider it a treasure hunt for beauty. Do this with a great sense of purpose; searching and working with the land will help create a *garden of peace* for yourself, your loved ones, and your business partners.

As you experience nature, collect whatever will benefit your inside space: flowers, rocks, shells, feathers, and drift wood.[2] Nature likes a great deal of variety within a given space.[3] Stay open to all the possibilities. Rocks and stones can provide the same benefits as fresh flowers! Their textures are great sources for grounding *earth* energy. They keep energy focused, which is an invaluable gift in the momentum of modern life.

Once you have found several items, it is time to discover how they make your internal environment more beautiful. Look at their texture, shape, and material for answers to the energy they will bring to your space. What energetic feeling do you get from a solid rock, a light and airy feather, a curved and rippled sea shell, or a branch of soft and silky pussy willows? All these objects adjust and encourage Chi to flow into places previously uninhabited by nature's life giving energy.

---

[2]  *In accordance with natural laws and the Native American tradition; before you take something from nature, ask permission and then leave a token or gift of appreciation such as some sage or even a strand or two of your own hair.*

[3]  *Sounds like good Feng Shui interior design!*

Color has the power, through its vibration, to influence and shift energy.[4] Each color vibrates at its own unique frequency and affects you on a level perhaps too subtle for your rational mind to perceive.

## Finding Hidden Beauty

Nature is a wonderful place to seek elements of beauty for your home or office, but many times you do not have to go looking for beauty because beauty finds you. Be receptive to serendipity.

*I was helping a client incorporate the natural elements. As I was looking at what she already had in her home, I realized there was a table with a special quality. It was covered with many books, photographs, and a tablecloth, and it needed only to be undressed to become a symbol of beauty and a magnet for Chi.*

The message is clear: take time to re-examine the objects and furnishings in your home. Is there something you are hiding or that is hiding from you?

**Feng Shui gently asks you to look at
your home in a different light.**

Be inquisitive. Ask questions. How do you view beauty in your home or business? Is there artwork? How is it arranged? Are there other art objects, plants, and eclectic details? What are your furniture and accessory choices? How much of nature have you brought into the space?

---

[4]     *Each body organ also has a specific color that relates to it, making color a powerful vibrational healing tool. Please refer to "Color and the Chakra System," p. 311 and "Five Elements for Better Health," p. 303.*

Take in your surroundings and listen to your inner response. Appreciate the beauty that you have already incorporated into your space, and acknowledge areas that you can improve. Regardless of your budget, beauty can play an integral role in your interior design scheme. Artwork and furnishings do not have to be expensive to be attractive.[5] Best of all, nature provides her art for free.

Hang your artwork and arrange your furniture and accessories with care. It is worth the extra time to position your objects according to the Bagua's eight areas of life: health, wealth, career, marriage, fame, knowledge, children, and benefactors.[6] Use the Bagua to place the objects where their color, material, and symbolism can best be used to effectively energize your space.

To get the most out of Feng Shui beauty, try a few cures in various areas of the Bagua.[7] In the relationship corner, place a clear bowl (crystal is a great Chi generator) filled with fresh water and a fresh flower petal every night to *clear the air*. It will absorb negative energy and purify it. Your bed, the sanctuary of your relationships, should inspire harmony and tranquility. Try soft sheets with rose or periwinkle petals.

---

5    *Though you do not have to buy expensive articles, please **do** buy quality items that will last. It is certainly not good Earth Design to add cheap furniture that has quickly worn out to our landfills.*

6    *Please refer to "The Bagua," p. 35.*

7    *Please refer to "Using the Components of Feng Shui Cures," p. 65.*

Hang a plant above the sink to keep wealth from disappearing down the drain; plants also heal and cleanse.

In the wealth area of your space, put a beautifully mounted and framed collection of coins to keep Chi circulating. Beautiful picture frames add the element of auspiciousness to anything. Use gold frames when possible, as they resonate wealth. The master Flemish painters always placed their art in gilded frames!

Project a new image of yourself to the world. Frame a nice portrait of yourself. Make sure it is a recent one taken with your new *outlook* sparkling in your eyes, and hang it in the fame area. Use a deep golden frame. Do not limit yourself. If you feel self conscious about hanging a self portrait, make a collage of pictures. Experiment and have fun!

Everyone has the ability to go far beyond their current set of circumstances and abilities. Step away from your cocoon of routine. Create what you will; your home is your canvas! Make life affirming changes in your environment, and watch the wonderful effects manifest themselves on the larger scale of your life.

Beauty can help ease the transition to the perceived uncertainty of the world. Change begins at home, with yourself. Starting the process can be as simple as wearing brightly colored clothing in vibrant reds, purples, and greens. Consciously acknowledge why you are making these changes. Invoke blessings and enlightened power with the six true words:

**Om Ma Ni Pad Me Hum.**

These words bring the body, speech, and mind into true spiritual alignment. Breathe deeply and store the intent and blessings in your soul, your source of power and beauty.

The path toward beauty begins by planting seeds. The coming years promise to be more powerful as the earth shifts into a new age. Plant your seeds along the path of beauty for a future full of radiance, splendor, and enlightenment.

## Making *Scents* of Feng Shui

Once upon a time, sleeping beauties laid their pretty heads on pillows perfumed with sweet smelling blooms and soporific dried hops. For a better night's sleep, use chamomile, lavender, neroli, marjoram, nutmeg, or valerian essential oils. They bring romance and peace into your busy life. Day pillows can have their fragrance[8] matched to the fragrance you like to use in individual rooms, such as lemon, geranium, or rose. Stuff a pillow creatively, utilizing a few drops of your favorite essential oil. This will accentuate beauty and promote better health. Master Lin Yun said, "The soul would pass away if there were no scents in the world."

---

[8]  *Please refer to "A Scentual Reminder of Feng Shui Remedies," p. 329 and "Energy Fields, Feng Shui and Fragrance," p. 339.*

# Feng Shui for the Healthy Body

# Energy Systems and Feng Shui

## Maggie Leyes

In 1953, Francis Crick and James Watson *discovered* the template of life, the 64 codons of DNA, the genetic code for all life. Three thousand years before, Chinese sages set down in the mystical text of the I Ching the template of life as they saw it reflected in nature. The oracle, composed of 64 hexagrams based on the binary elements yin/yang, could describe all conditions in the universe. In 1973, German philosopher, Martin Schönberger, put together the ground-breaking correspondence: the absolute one-to-one equation of the 64 hexagrams of the ancient Chinese I Ching and the 64 DNA codons.

This discovery is a powerful lesson for our times. Each civilization had come to the same conclusion about the nature of life and the universe. Western science found it under a microscope, and the East intuitively understood it mirrored in nature. What we can glean from this 3,000-year discrepancy between technology and intuitive knowing is two-fold: First, we must suspend our blind faith in scientific proof, opening ourselves to intuitive processes that can lead more directly to the answers we seek. Second, these answers do not always lie in what we create through technology but are inherent in nature and in ourselves.

**Harmony in our world is achieved by understanding what already exists and using that knowledge to bring balance into our lives.**

How did the ancient Chinese formulate such an *advanced* concept of the universe? They gained knowledge of the flow of Chi, or energy, by observing nature and working with it intuitively. That body of knowledge and experience grew into an art and a science, a method of understanding man's relationship to his surroundings, called geomancy or Feng Shui.

What was the nature of that relationship between man and his environment? Again, we can look to the I Ching for answers. It clearly shows the main tenet of Feng Shui revealed in the trigram, the basic component of the oracle.[1] The bottom line of the trigram represents Earth; the top represents Heaven, and the middle line represents Man. Heaven, Earth and Man[2] (Tien, Di, Ren) are the cosmic order; these energetic systems work in tandem to achieve harmony, balance, and the full range of human and cosmic experience. Remove one of the elements, and the entire matrix collapses.

**Heaven, Earth, and Man are three interdependent systems of energy that resonate together to form our universe.**

The art and science of geomancy that flourished in China reflected the quest to understand the intricacies of those three parallel systems. They understood that everything, all phenomena, when broken down into its simplest component was energy.[3] They perceived Heaven, Earth, and Man as resonant systems of energy in which the energetic patterns of one system were reflected and generated in the other systems.

---

[1]  From the concept of the trigram, three lines of yin/female and yang/male energy, flow the eight basic energies of the universe. In keeping with the poetic nature of the oracle, they were given archetypal, energetic names from nature: Heaven, Earth, Thunder, Water, Mountain, Wind, Fire, and Lake.

[2]  Heaven is the archetypal reference to the cosmos or space; Man refers to humanity.

[3]  Again, ancient intuitive knowledge and current scientific findings converge. Quantum physics has *proven* this,"...mass is nothing but a form of energy...mass is no longer associated with a material substance, and hence (atomic) particles are not seen as consisting of any basic "stuff" but as bundles of energy." Fritjof Capra, The Tao of Physics, Shambhala Publications, Inc., 1975 p. 202.

## Heaven

According to the ancient Chinese geomancers, patterns of harmony came from Heaven or the cosmos: first there was Wu Chi, the primal vibration or Cosmic Sound; this differentiated into Tai Chi or two tones, the yin/female and yang/male polarities, which then manifested as the 12 tones or Lu. These vibratory modulations affect Earth and Man in regular cycles of hours, days, months, years, and so on. Astronomy and Astrology are the sciences used to explain the cycles and how Man and Earth resonate with the energetic vibrations emanating from space. Tides, seasonal shifts in nature, human bio-rhythms, menstruation, and many other more subtle cycles are all influenced by these harmonics.

## Earth

**Whatever befalls the earth, befalls the sons of the earth.**
**Man did not create the web of life; he is merely a strand of it.**
**Whatever he does to the web, he does to himself.**
Chief Seattle, 1854.

Earth, like Man, in addition to a physical form or *body,* has an energy body. This energetic body is a complex network of lines and nodes that acts as a transducer of energy entering from other systems; it is the connection between the physical and the cosmic. It allows life energy to flow into the system which vitalizes the physical form.

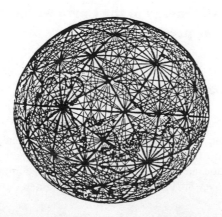

The Earth's energy body is composed of a web or energy matrix that surrounds the earth; it can be seen as a kind of energetic grid.

The lines that make up the grid are polarized channels. Chinese geomancers called the lines *lung mei* or *dragon paths*,[4] which flowed as either white tiger/yin lines or green dragon/yang lines. (In English these are called ley lines)

Where two paths met, a power point was formed. These Chi rich nodes were the auspicious sites chosen for temples or burial sites for emperors. The geomancers placed their buildings and monuments as terrestrial acupuncture needles to tap into the natural abundance of Chi, and to harmonize and distribute that Chi along the earth grid.[5]

These concepts of energy were known by ancient cultures across the globe. They understood it and used it to build their ancient sacred structures.[6] Stonehenge, the Pyramids of Giza, the Gate of the Sun in Tihuanaco among other megalithic monuments give us a clear picture of the three systems working in tandem. A site was chosen on a powerful, energetic spot that was connected to lines of earth energy. A monument was erected using sacred geometry and a highly resonate material, stone, to tap into the power of the earth. It was carefully aligned to act as a precise astronomical tool to utilize the energy of the cosmos, especially at auspicious times like solstices. Man was there to witness, experience, and merge with these energies emanating from above and below.

**These sacred structures united the energy of the Earth with the energy of Heaven in the presence of Man.**

---

[4]  *Please refer to "Feng Shui and Healing Architecture," p. 133.*

[5]  It is important to remember that these nodes are power points, and those who *control* these points, control the energy inherent there and the energy distribution to the rest of the grid (as well as the people who rely on it.) Through war, economic colonization, and alliances, the United States currently has access to or outright control over 80% of the Earth's major nodes.

[6]  *Please refer to "Earth Design: The Roots of Our Nature," p. 25.*

## Man

Feng Shui is sometimes seen as the right positioning of a building and its contents to insure proper Chi flow. The true essence of this art, however, is to harmonize the three systems of the universe: Heaven, Earth, and Man. Within this matrix, Man is a conduit drawing light, yang energy from Heaven and dark, yin energy from Earth in his vehicle of experience, his body.

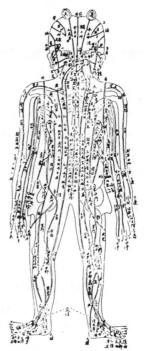

Man, like a true microcosm of the Earth, has an energy body to process this incoming energy. It is an intricate system, a web of energy lines, or meridians. There are 12 major meridians ten that regulate the major organs and two affiliate channels.

A peak of energy cycles through the meridians in two hour intervals, making a full cycle within a day, in keeping with the vibratory modulation of Heaven. A balanced flow of Chi along the meridians brings energy to the organs, *feeding* and harmonizing them. When the flow is cut off, or is somehow altered, the organs and body do not receive the energy they need and disease is the result.

**The most basic prescription for maintaining health is to keep a balance of energy flowing to all organs.**

Along these meridians or body *ley lines* are points of concentration that regulate the flow of Chi. These points or nodes can be manipulated to insure the proper flow of Chi through the body. As the geomancer manipulates Chi at the power points and ley lines in the Earth, the acupuncturist works with the body's meridians and points to bring balance and health to the patient. Acupuncture is a highly developed system of maintaining health through manipulation of the energy body.[7] It is based on true Feng Shui principles: achieving balance in Man's ultimate home, his body, brings balance to the surrounding resonant systems, Heaven and Earth.

## Acupressure to Access Your Energy Body

Everyone has the capacity to understand and use these power points. By learning to manipulate this energy, you can bring a balanced flow of energy to the body and the organs. Acupressure is based on the same system as acupuncture, but uses hand and finger pressure instead of needles. In using these points, intuition is the key. Though they can be found through mechanical means of measurements and diagrams, only by *feeling* the point can you know its exact position. You must also use your intuition to insure that it is appropriate to work with a particular point at that time.

### Remember, your body is the best teacher.
### If it does not feel right, do not do it.

Most points that need attention will feel sensitive and *different* than the surrounding skin: hotter, colder, more indented, and so on. The pressure used to stimulate these points varies; it should not be painful, though there may be slight discomfort or sensitivity. The length of time you should put pressure on a point also varies; apply pressure *only until the*

---

7    In a study done by Dr. Pierre de Vernejoul, Director of Nuclear Medicine at Necker Hospital in Paris, France, doctors injected a harmless radioactive substance called technetium into acupuncture points on patients' arms and legs. They used a special camera to trace its flow along the meridians. They saw the technetium move along the lines corresponding to the traditional acupuncture meridians. They also found that stimulating acupuncture points sped up the flow. And incredibly, when doctors stimulated a point on one side of the body, they got a similar result on the other side as well. (reference: Dr. Jongwan Kim)

*sensitivity decreases*, otherwise you will exhaust the point. You can *fish* for Chi by applying pressure to a point then pulling the finger away a number of times. This allows you to access Chi from the depths and then disperse it when you release your finger. If you want to tone and strengthen a point, you can give it a massage in a clockwise direction.

Much disease, especially in modern cities, begins with stress and tension that is held in the body. By releasing tension or blocks from the body, Chi flows more freely. It is important to remember that when you bring increased Chi flow to the physical system, you are also bringing it into the emotional and spiritual systems. A release of tension or an energy block on the physical level may also bring a release on an emotional or spiritual level.

The following is a series of acupressure points that can used in a meditation series or independently to remedy a specific imbalance. This information has been compiled with the help of two acupuncture physicians, Jongwan Kim, L.Ac., O.M.D., Ph.D., and Sachi, L.Ac., O.M.D.

Begin by sitting in a comfortable position. Keep your spine straight but relaxed and shoulders at ease. Breathe slowly and rhythmically through your nose. Let your belly be soft, it should expand outward (like a baby's does) with each breath. Your tongue should rest gently on the roof of your mouth with the tip touching the hard palette (major yang and yin energies meet here.) Let the outside world and your thoughts melt away.

### Sea of Tranquility

> Bring your hands into the classic prayer position with palms together and place them at chest level, the thumb joints should be gently pressing into the protrusion of the sternum. This is the *sea of tranquility* point (conception vessel 17), and is a central meeting point of all the yin meridians. As it also corresponds to a chakra,[8] it will bring a feeling of centeredness, release anxiety,

---

[8]   There are 7 main chakras or energy vortexes that are lined up the center of the body. This point corresponds to the heart chakra and can assist in opening it up. *Please refer to "Color and the Chakra System," p. 311.*

and help bring emotions into balance. Remain in this position during a cycle of twelve breaths, or as long as feels appropriate.

With this and each successive point, concentrate on rhythmic breathing, focus your breath and attention on the point while applying pressure, visualize any blockage or tension being released

## Meeting Valley Point

Bring your hands in front of you. With the thumb of one hand, press into the center of the mound in the space between the thumb and index finger on the top of the other hand. This point, the upper gate of Chi (large intestine 4), relieves headaches,[9] neck and eye pain, toothaches, and sore throats. It opens pores to help disperse toxins, and stimulates the intestines thus relieving constipation. This point tones *wei* energy, which is the first line of defense against colds.

This point mirrors the auspicious Feng Shui site configuration of the white tiger (thumb) and the green dragon (index finger.)

**Meeting Valley Point (Li 4)**

## The Third Eye and Sun Points

The third eye point, the yin tang, is located between the eyebrows. Apply pressure with the tip of your finger. This point will help release pressure in the eyes, relieve frontal headaches, runny noses, anxiety, and insomnia. This is also the site of a chakra and can clear your focus and perception, as well as stimulate intellectual and psychic abilities. The sun point, the tai yang, is located at the temples. Massage this point lightly on either side; do not use pressure. This point also works on frontal headaches and insomnia.

---

[9]  Different points relieve different types of headaches.

## Gate of Consciousness

Use your thumb tips to massage the Feng Chi or wind point in the depressions below the occipital bone on either side of the back of the head. This point, sometimes called the gate of consciousness (gall bladder 20), helps regulate nerve and sense functions in the brain. It is good for releasing neck pain and stiffness, a chronic problem for office/computer workers. It also works on colds, nasal obstructions, blurred vision, vertigo, and headaches.

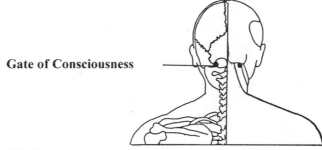

Gate of Consciousness

## The Bubbling Well

This point (kidney 1) is located on the sole, just below the ball of the foot. Grasp your foot in your hands and use you thumb pad to apply pressure. According to the Chinese, the kidney is the foundation of the body; it houses *jing*, or the material essence of life. This point is the base of meridian and when stimulated, energy *bubbles* forth. It brings calmness of spirit.[10] It also improves poor vision, and dizziness.

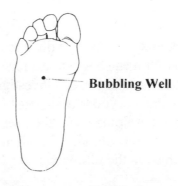

**Bubbling Well**

---

[10]   Using lavender oil on this point has a doubly calming effect.

## Building Energy

Two points, when used in tandem, help build energy: stomach 36 point, approximately three inches below the eye of the knee between the tibia and fibula, and spleen 6 point, four inches up, inside the medial ankle bone. Press them at the same time with either the thumb or finger pad. They can be used for general fatigue or even to combat jet lag.

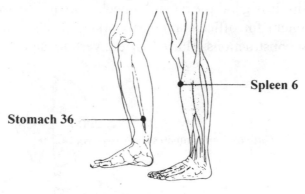

## Deep Relaxation

If you have been doing these points in a meditative state, you can now gently lie on your back in the traditional yogic *corpse pose*. For the next five minutes, continue your deep rhythmic breathing and visualize your entire body relaxed, free of tension, with energy moving freely to all your organs. This is the most important step, as it gives your body the chance to rid itself of any negative energy or blocks that you have released with acupressure.

Using acupressure points will bring you into contact with how your energy body functions. You can begin to exercise your intuition, to *know* which points need attention, and you can investigate other points that may be *calling* for acupressure. As you learn to trust your body, your ultimate home, you will begin to harmonize with the energy of Heaven and Earth. When Man is balanced and vibrant with abundant energy, so too are Heaven and Earth, which is the ultimate goal of Feng Shui.

# Using Feng Shui to Create Health

## Andrew and Sally Fretwell

Feng Shui and traditional Chinese medicine are two highly compatible disciplines. Both are based on the same fundamental principles of energy movement. The ancient scholars of China were keen observers of nature and her cycles. From these observations, they created a model of the universe based on two natural energy forces: one dark, passive, and contracting or *yin*, and one light, active, and expanding or *yang*. These two forces produced all known phenomena, which was subsequently divided into the five elements: *earth, water, wood, fire,* and *metal*. Both Oriental medicine and Feng Shui use the yin/yang and the five element principles as diagnostic tools.

Chinese medicine views the physical body as composed of many subtle energy fields. Illness is a result of these fields becoming distorted. These imbalances are due to a wide range of factors: prenatal shock, toxins in the environment, poor lifestyle habits, and inappropriate living spaces are just a few. They distort the "core frequency,"[1] the prime impulse for all life - the deepest energetic part of each individual and of all nature. In Chinese medicine, the doctor determines the underlying energetic imbalance and uses acupuncture, herbs, and lifestyle advice to create health and balance.

Feng Shui works in a similar way. Physical structures influence you on a subtle energetic level. If you have a strong constitution and good health but are living or working in an environment that has a distorted energetic vibration,[2] that imbalance will eventually weaken your physical state.

---

[1]    Core Frequency is a term that Audrey Ryan, a healer of extraordinary power, uses to describe the unique vibration of the individual and the universe.

[2]    *A distorted energetic vibration of a space, like that of a body, can be caused by many factors, such as an inappropriate layout or a poor site location. Please refer to "Contemporary Architectural Design," p. 143.*

Feng Shui principles allow you to identify the source of the imbalance in your environment and suggest cures to bring back balance and harmony. Feng Shui recommendations must be tailored to each individual, addressing their unique core frequency and their specific space or environment.

## The Link between Health and Your Living Space

These two powerful arts, Feng Shui and Oriental medicine, can be used in tandem to create optimum living and health conditions. The following are simple tools you can use to integrate them into your life to achieve balance and harmony.

## The Five Elements

The five elements: earth, metal, water, wood, and fire are archetypes or representations of all aspects of life's experiences. Humans and all of life - from the smallest sub-atomic particle to the largest spinning galaxy - go through continuous cycles: birth to death, dawn to dusk, the seasons of the year. These cycles can all be represented by the interaction of the five elements.

Because the elements also identify and highlight which organs or systems are out of balance, they become an incredible diagnostic tool for your health and are also useful for self empowerment. In addition to bodily functions, specific emotions, psychological qualities, and personality traits are associated with these five elements. By using them, you can simultaneously identify body, mind, and spirit issues that need to be resolved.

Below are definitions of each of the elements. The first column shows the effects when that particular element is stressed or when the body and organs are working harder than they are expected to work. The second column shows when they are balanced and function optimally.

Look through the lists and mark off which qualities or health issues apply to you. Use the lists for a general idea of which elements need support. For example, if you are always getting colds, look at the lungs and the metal element and also at earth with its relationship to the immune and lymphatic systems.

### Water - Stressed
Kidney/bladder problems
Fearful/phobias
Low back pain, sciatica
Impotence/frigidity
Holding on to things
Dissatisfaction with life's path
Frequent urination
Dark shadow/bags under the eyes
Aversion to cold
Workaholic
Water retention
Disorders of the central nervous system

### Water - Balanced
Happy with life's journey
The ability to flow with life
Vitality
Adaptable
Strong will power
Gentleness

### Wood - Stressed
Liver/gallbladder problems
Anger/complete absence of it
Impatience/easily frustrated
Always on edge
Eye problems
Problems with equilibrium/coordination
Tendon problems
Lack of flexibility/stiffness
Addicted to doing
Tension cramps, especially in the shoulders
Muscle spasms
Bitter taste in mouth
Irregular menses

### Wood - Balanced
Patience
Flexibility mentally
    and physically
Good organizer/planner
    and decision maker
Perform well under pressure
Clear thinking
Bold and decisive

### Fire - Stressed
Heart/small intestine problems
Cardiovascular diseases
Insomnia
Restlessness, forgetfulness
Hypersensitive
Over excited/craves stimulants
Speech disorders
Exuberant in public/depressed when alone
Hard hearted
Pain in chest region

### Fire - Balanced
Feeling fulfilled
Lively
Charismatic
Enthusiastic
Ability to sense rhythm of
    any experience
Knows one's limits
Loving and caring

**Earth - Stressed**
Stomach/pancreas/spleen problems
Worry, always thinking
Immune system problems
Digestive problems: gas/belching
Lack of absorption
Lymphatic problems
Loose bowels
Anemia
Hemorrhoids
Overweight or under
Always thinking of food
Over nurturing
Inability to receive
Feeling stuck/can not move forward

**Earth - Balanced**
Grounded/peaceful
Good imagination
Deep understanding
    and compassion
Able to go a long time
    between meals without
    craving food.
Able to nurture others
    without depleting self
Sympathy
Good digestion
Ability to delegate

**Metal - Stressed**
Lung/large intestine problems
Sorrow
Isolation
Cynicism
Asthma
Skin allergies/problems
Hay fever
Judgmental/narrow viewpoint

**Metal - Balanced**
Clarity
Optimism
Organized
The ability to let go
Courage
The ability to create order
    out of chaos
Good aerobic ability

## Feng Shui Recommendations

Based on the information from the lists, you have now identified which elements are out of balance in your body and life. To bring them back into harmony, you can make inner adjustments based on lifestyle advice and outer adjustments based on Feng Shui recommendations.[3] To begin implementing changes, overlay the Bagua diagram on your home or on any individual room. Place the central circle in the center of your room or home. The fire area of the Bagua will always be at 12 o'clock in relation to the entry door.

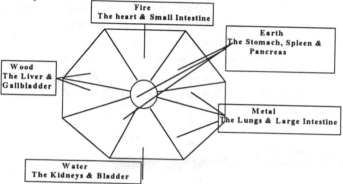

Look around your home or office for a correlation to the unbalanced element you have found. Sometimes it will not be obvious, but there will always be something. The following example will illustrate how this process works.

*Jean was suffering with lower back pain, pain in the ovaries, and a very stressed and hectic life-style. The elemental influence at the time of birth was metal.[4] Metal people are generally overachievers and find it difficult to relax. Their metal nature creates a more serious outlook, and they tend to neglect the lighter side of life. Using the lists of stressed/balanced elements, we found that the first two symptoms were related to the*

---

[3]  If you require a more in-depth evaluation, contact a qualified Chinese physician.

[4]  In our work, we also use the birth date of the client to determine their elemental influence at the time of birth. Yakashi Yoshikawa's The Ki, St. Martin's Press, New York, 1995 is a good reference book for more information.

*water element and the last to fire. We confirmed through Oriental diagnosis that the kidneys/adrenal glands and reproductive organs were all under stress.*

*In her apartment, the front door was in the water position of the Bagua. From there, our attention was drawn down a long narrow corridor and out a back window that was in the fire position. Her home was channeling excessive Chi along this corridor; her home was being overly charged along the central water/fire area of the Bagua.*

*Our recommendation was to add a soft fabric over the entry-way or a screen to the corridor to allow Chi to move in a more balanced way. On a physical level, we suggested she change from her very rigid metal-type exercise regime to a fluid, water-type one such as in-line skating. We also suggested that she add more routine to her life and make some dietary changes. Long relaxing baths in the evening were prescribed as well. Two weeks later, she phoned to say that all her physical symptoms had disappeared.*

## Recommendations for Stressed Water

In the water area of the Bagua, look for stagnation: clutter, broken objects, unfinished business, dirt, stuck doors, and/or leaky or bad plumbing in any area of the home. Look for over-stimulation or over-use of water elements in this area: large fish tanks, fountains, pictures of water, or over-emphasis on the color blue. To help free up water energy, try painting, free-form dancing, or any activity that develops flow and dispels fears.

On the psychological level, evaluate your life path. Are you satisfied with the direction toward which you are moving? Ask for support and practice letting go.

In addition, keep your kidneys and lower back warm. Stay away from coffee; it has a strong effect on the adrenal glands. Avoid excessive salt intake, and drink only when thirsty.

## Recommendations for Stressed Wood

In the wood area of the Bagua, look for stagnation. Remove artifacts that give the impression of stiffness and immobility, such as heavy pieces of furniture. Replace them with lighter, more flexible pieces. Bamboo is a good material to use for this area.

Develop a more flexible approach to life and learn to relax. This could mean getting regular massages and gently exercising. Long walks in nature help to balance the wood element. Resolve old feelings of anger.

In addition, limit your intake of animal foods. Increase fruits, vegetables, and whole grains. Avoid an excess of greasy foods, fat, cholesterol, and alcohol because they put stress on the liver. Adding the element of silliness and game playing can be very therapeutic.

## Recommendations for Stressed Fire

In the fire area of the Bagua, look for over-stimulation: a high concentration of electrical objects in one place: televisions, air conditioners, stereo; many doors; reflected images that are distorted; pictures that are busy and have a lot of activity. Try introducing calm, peaceful images and things that uplift and inspire. Beautiful artwork and paintings work very well here.

Create a rhythm in your life. Make order; focus on one thing until it is completed. Understand that fulfillment comes from a balanced approach to life. Introduce Tai Chi into your schedule for physical as well as spiritual balance. Take time to read and do things that you truly enjoy. In addition, eat at regular times, and always sit to eat. Avoid all stimulants, especially coffee and alcohol.

## Recommendations for Stressed Earth

In the earth areas of the Bagua, look for accumulation. Clear out everything that no longer serves you. House cleaning is very good for stressed earth. Create space and allow energy to move. In the bedroom and living room, make sure that the open space in the room balances the amount of furniture and objects. If things look full, create more space for movement. Get organized; complete any unfinished paperwork or projects.

Learn how to receive; if someone does you a good turn, accept it graciously without feeling indebted. Commit to completing things. Set easily attainable goals, and once they are achieved, congratulate yourself. Set boundaries and stick to them; learn how to delegate. Nurture yourself the way you nurture others and practice self love.

In addition, practice any sport or exercise that physically challenges you.

## Recommendations for Stressed Metal

In the metal area of the Bagua, and in the entire space as well, look for an overly pristine, cold, or an excessively ordered approach to design. Add elements of fun, color, and comfort. Avoid pictures that suggest isolation and aloneness; replace them with warmer, more joyful pieces. Because the metal element relates to contraction and solidity, add the water element to help things become more fluid. Do not over use white; add more terra cotta or earth and water colors.

Understand that life also needs spontaneity and joy. Learn how *not* to do; discover the joy of floating down life's stream. Celebrate life; watch comedies with friends. Spend more time with others, especially children. Allow yourself to be vulnerable and to express deep feelings.

In addition, scrub the skin all over your body everyday with a hot damp cotton wash cloth. Do exercises that allow the lungs and heart to open. (The bridge pose in yoga is very effective.) Eat foods rich in chlorophyll: leafy green vegetables, blue green algae, alfalfa.

While Oriental medicine and Feng Shui give you effective tools to bring your body and environment into balance, the most important evaluation that you can make is *that you are OK right now*. Your true self is perfect. It is admirable to want to improve your physical and emotional life so your perfection shines through, but to love, respect, and accept yourself as you are is the best Feng Shui you can ever practice.

# The Energetic Basis of Good Health

## Jeanne D'Brant

Feng Shui can have profound effects upon your health and well-being. Blocked Chi in your environment can create blocked Chi in your emotional well-being and your physical body. In traditional Chinese Medicine, the proper movement of Chi or vital energy through the body's meridians or channels is considered critical to good health. If the energy is obstructed or imbalanced, ill health will result. In Feng Shui, the harmonious flow of Chi in the home or work space is also vital to a healthy and supportive environment. Blocked or excessive Chi movement within a space can also have adverse consequences on your health.

How can you tell if your Chi is flowing properly? Examine how you feel. Vibrant health shows in a firm step, a clear eye, a positive outlook, and an abundance of energy. Symptoms such as pain, muscle spasm, fatigue, headaches, indigestion, depression, and worry can all indicate that Chi is not balanced or flowing harmoniously.

Traditional Chinese Medicine, with 4,000 years of history, is one of the oldest systematized healing traditions on earth. One of its primary goals is prevention of disease; it treats the whole person, not just the symptoms. Acupuncture, Chinese herbs, Qi Gong (Chi Kung),[1] and Tuina[2] all have the common the goal of balancing Chi in the meridians and body regions.

---

[1]     One fundamental way of moving Chi is to practice Qi Gong (see Glossary p. 427.) Daily practice ensures the harmonious flow of Chi by freeing blockages of stagnant or unbalanced Chi. Excesses are balanced as the channels open and harmonious flow is established.

[2]     Tuina is a Chinese healing therapy incorporating massage and acupoints.

## Understanding Chi Flow

The Chi of the human body should flow harmoniously in a connected circuit. The pathways or electrical lines it flows through are called the meridians. Along these lines are the many vortex points which function like resistors in an electrical circuit; they modify the rate and intensity of Chi flow.[3] It is at these points that the acupuncturist makes her intervention.

In recent years, Germans and other Europeans have moved to the forefront of Chi technology. They have developed specialized machines that can quantitatively measure Chi flow.[4] The VegaTest Method, for example, is an advanced technology for monitoring a person's bio-energetic state[5] using electronic instrumentation. It measures Chi flow in the body's organs, meridians, and subtle energy fields.

The VegaTest measures electrical conductivity of the acupuncture points along the meridians. There is normally a very large drop in electrical resistance at the site of an acupuncture point versus the skin surrounding it. The electrical state of the points varies according to the physiological state of the person. Shifts in resistance along the acupuncture points fall into demonstrable patterns, which can indicate disease and dysfunction. Electronically monitoring the conductivity of the points along the acupuncture meridians can give you a wealth of diagnostic information.

The VegaTest also shows if these Chi imbalances are related to Feng Shui in several ways: It differentiates between geopathic stress from the earth and electromagnetic disturbance generated by appliances, power lines, and transformers. These external influences can be mitigated through Feng Shui.

---

[3]    *Please refer to "Energy Systems and Feng Shui," p. 275.*

[4]    Mora work and Bio-Electronic Vincent are bioenergetic therapies that are widely available in Europe and on a limited basis in the United States. Please contact the author for more information.

[5]    Bioenergetic state is derived from Einstein's equation of energy and matter. We know that there is an interface between energy and molecular vibration with physical structures and organ functions.

## Electromagnetic Fields

While the debate continues about the safety of exposure to electromagnetic fields, particularly related to children, minimizing your exposure to these fields in your home and office is considered prudent.[6] Understanding what these fields are and how they affect you will help you identify them in your surroundings so you can protect yourself.

Everything electrical has a charge; that matter exists in two polarities, *positive* and *negative,* is a fundamental construct. Charges move in currents; a direct current (DC) flows evenly; an alternating current (AC) flows unevenly, changing direction between 60 and 120 times *per second.* Every electrical charge has an electrical field around it. When another object enters that field and has a like charge (both objects positively charged) it will be repelled; if it has an opposite charge, it will be attracted.

When electrons flow in currents, a magnetic field is created around the current (as well as an electrical one). If the current is direct (DC), such as the one in the human body, the field is relatively stable. If the current is alternating (AC), such as the one in electrical appliances, it is not. The magnetic fields that whirl around appliances induce currents in anything nearby that conducts electricity, especially the human body. Fragile DNA may be adversely impacted by these fields. Children are especially vulnerable because they are growing rapidly and have many cells in the fragile state of cell division and DNA replication.

Fields not generated by electrical equipment can often be attributed to geopathic stress of such natural land formations as underground streams, mineral deposits, and geographic faults. These natural phenomena pose a greater challenge; you can move a computer or TV but cannot lift your house off a fault quite so easily!

---

[6]  *Please refer to "Energy Fields, Feng Shui, and Fragrance," p. 339, and "Feng Shui and Children," p. 349.*

A person showing electromagnetic stress will have imbalances in his/her flow of Chi through the meridians and the acupuncture points, which will manifest as a wide range of disease and sickness. Imbalances in Chi flow, whether caused by EMF's or a myriad of other factors, can be identified and treated according to the five element theory of Feng Shui.

## The Five Elements

According to the Chinese five element theory, Chi manifests in five properties of matter: earth, wood, fire, metal, and water (in addition to yin and yang.) Each element is associated with two of the twelve major body meridians. Fire is the exception; it is associated with four. The following table shows each of the five elements and its corresponding meridians, organs, and qualities. It demonstrates how a deficiency or excess of a particular element can cause dysfunction of organs and negative emotional states.[7]

---

[7]    This is not by any means complete enough to make a thorough diagnosis; other factors such as the creative and the destructive cycles of the five elements must be factored in. *Please refer to "The Five Phases of Energy," p. 81.*

## Feng Shui Cures to Regain Balance and Heath

The inherent nature of Chi is to flow in a smooth and unobstructed manner. When it does not flow harmoniously in the body, there is also a corresponding imbalance in the outer environment.

**Renewed balance is achieved by treating the outer environment to stimulate change in the inner environment.**

A doctor of Chinese medicine will treat the acupuncture points, suggest dietary change, herbal supplements, and/or Chi-moving exercises.

Feng Shui offers cures to balance the energy in your personal living space, thus balancing the outer environment to create harmony and health inside.

**Metal Imbalance**

If your entrance door[8] opens onto a wall, your Chi will be blocked and you may feel easily defeated in life. According to the five element theory, defeat is associated with an imbalance of metal. This disequilibrium could lead to lung and large intestine disorders, organs that are related to the metal element. As a cure, try placing a picture of a nature scene or a mirror on this *brick wall* to give the entryway a feeling of depth.

---

8  *For additional cures, please see "The Room of First Impression," p. 207, and "The Entry: New Beginnings," p. 201.*

Asthma (lungs) is a metal imbalance and is often related to grief, the emotion of the lungs. Those individuals with breathing difficulties should avoid living in dark or stark spaces that give the feeling of loneliness and coldness. Painting your bedroom a soft color may be an appropriate solution.

**Earth Imbalance**

Joint pain and arthritis are related to an imbalance of the spleen, the organ related to the earth element. This condition can be improved by employing Feng Shui cures to conditions in your life that create worry (the related emotion). If you live next door to a taller building, you may feel *oppressed* by your *greater* neighbor. Using a Feng Shui cure of mirrors to reflect back the energy of the taller building should ease the worry of having your Chi suppressed.

Singing is also associated with earth. Those with an earth imbalance should be encouraged to break forth into song as often as possible! Other uplifting cures for worry are playing music - particularly vocals, or opening the windows to enjoy hearing the birds sing. Arthritics must guard against Sha[9] (negative Chi) emanating from damp basements and moldy corners in their homes.

**Wood Imbalance**

Liver imbalances, the organ related to wood, are common in the United States. This is due in large part to the fast-paced, aggressive lifestyle and to over-consumption of fats, dairy products, drugs, and alcohol. To offset this condition, balance the wood element by using indoor plants or the color green.

---

[9]    *Please refer to "The Power of Chi," p. 49.*

Secret arrows[10] and other forms of Sha can arouse defensiveness and anger, emotions related to wood and the liver. It is unfortunate that Western architecture relies so heavily on right angles and linear structures. This society is defining itself as angry and competitive with unbalanced Chi by the structures it lives in! Mirrors, crystals, and vines can be used to obscure corners that are projecting secret arrows. Creating harmony in the home with curves and flowing lines is an essential antidote to living in modern Western civilization.

## Water Imbalance

Adrenal exhaustion due to stress and burn out is another consequence of fast-paced modern life. This water element imbalance is very prevalent. Allergies, insomnia, fatigue, and poor concentration are symptomatic of overstimulated adrenal glands.

It is easy to remedy this problem by representing the water element in the home or work space; a fountain or a bowl of fish will do quite well.

In one of my treatment rooms, patients can lie down and listen to the soothing sounds of a bubbling fish tank. It is the room most often requested!

---

10    *A secret arrow is a line of unseen, negative energy that appears to be pointed into a space or at its occupants. It might be a sharp, angular corner jutting into a room or a long shadow from another structure that crosses into your space. Please refer to "Contemporary Architectural Design," p. 143, and "The Power of Chi," p. 49.*

## Fire Imbalance

Fire element imbalance can manifest as problems of absorption and assimilation in the digestive system. There may also be vitamin and mineral deficiencies. The heart is also a fire element organ. Heart disease is rampant in industrialized societies, which is due directly to the cultural need to push to succeed. In addition, the fire element is associated with metabolism and the circulation/sex (hormones) meridians.

An imbalance of fire can be countered by use of the color red, a very auspicious color to the Chinese, in appropriate areas. Other Feng Shui cures include wood stoves and heaters as well as decorative objects with points.[11]

---

[11]  Those individuals with heart disease, life threatening illnesses, or any health difficulty are advised to seek the advice of a holistic and/or traditional health practitioner.

## The Bagua and Health

### Chi of the five elements fills the universe
### which in turn spreads to all things.[12]

As everything is inter-related, the Bagua[13] is an important tool for balancing health as well as a space. If an area of the Bagua is missing in your home due to the structure's shape,[14] its corresponding element will also be deficient. If the home is missing an element, it will affect the health and well-being of person living there.

Activating the health area of the Bagua is another important step. Below are some examples of adjusting your space to heal your body.

> For liver troubles and gallstones, place cures in the east or family/health area of the Bagua; this will strengthen the wood element.

> For hormone problems/digestive difficulties, place cures in the fame or south area.

> For skin and hair conditions/weak lung function, adjust the metal area in the children or west region.

> For fearful persons who suffer in cold weather, activate the north or career area for the water element.

> For diabetes and immune disorders, activate the central or Tai Chi area and the earth element of the home.

---

[12] From the ancient Chinese classic <u>Tiau Yuan Ji Da Lun or Great Treatise on the Universe.</u>

[13] *Please refer to "The Bagua," p. 35.*

[14] *Please see "Outdoor Feng Shui," p. 155, for additional cures to remedy missing areas of the Bagua.*

A qualified practitioner of Chinese Medicine would also suggest other areas for adjustment according to the Shen (creative) and Ko (control) cycles of the five elements.[15] A Feng Shui practitioner might use color cycles corresponding to the five elements to produce the same effects.

You are a complex being living in complex times. Yet maintaining your health can be greatly simplified if you keep a balanced flow of Chi in your life - both internally and externally. There are endless ways of accomplishing this goal, from acupuncture to implementing Feng Shui cures in your home. Many people seek relief for their physical complaints by going to a doctor for a pill or a cure-all treatment, yet emotional change is imperative for the healing process. Affecting your psyche with Feng Shui techniques is an important adjunct to creating good health.

---

[15]  *Please refer to "The Five Phases of Energy," p.81.*

# five Elements for Better Health

## Lillian Lesefko Garnier

Feng Shui has never been more popular. News stories, magazine articles, and television shows are all talking about this ancient art. Though it has reached a wide audience, one important factor has been overlooked. The principles of Feng Shui are often understood as absolute rules instead of guidelines to be adapted to a particular space and set of circumstances.

The Los Angeles Times' "Hot Property" section carried an article about a house built in Malibu according to *perfect* Feng Shui specifications. *Perfect* meant that it faced south, towards the water and had appropriate rooms in the symbolic corners.[1] It was wonderful that someone cared enough to build a house this way, but the idea that this house was perfect missed the mark.

Traditionally, the Chinese proudly faced their building toward their vast imperial conquests which laid to the south. Fame and south became intrinsically linked. Based on the Bagua, south is also associated with the element fire. So, is this traditional southern orientation *perfect* for a home in Malibu?

Southern California is already full of fire. It has a hot climate; energetically, it is a very active place, not to mention the real fires that sweep through the area with regularity. What if the person who bought this *hot property* with *perfect Feng Shui* had heart disease? The owner would need to calm this energy down, not move into a house that augments it!

---

[1]  *Please refer to "The Bagua," p. 35.*

## The Five Elements

The five element theory is a solid base of information. You can then take traditional Feng Shui principles and adapt them to your own needs. The ancient Chinese discovered that the world could be broken down into five energy types, and they were given archetypal names from nature: water, wood, fire, earth, and metal. The system not only described the principle energies, but it was used to understand smaller sub-systems such as: colors, shapes, textures, time, the human body, organs, and environments.

In Feng Shui, the five element theory is used to determine which element is dominant or deficient in a space. Cures, based on elemental correspondences, bring the elements back into alignment. Used as guides, the five elements can help you make positive energetic adjustments to your space according to your needs. The result is a balanced environment that heals and nurtures.

In the human body, all five elements are represented in a person's make-up, although one or more may be dominant. The manifestation of the elements is visible in the body's constitution, coloration, facial features, character traits, and habitual behavior. As with a space, the elements can be used as a tool to balance any disharmony.

## Understanding the Five Elements

The first step to using the five element theory is to understand how each element manifests itself.

**Water**

The water element is present in a view of the ocean,  lake, river, stream or swimming pool. It is amorphous, like a building that has been added on to so many times that it no longer has a defined shape. These buildings at times inspire creativity or even confusion.

People who are water types usually need to live near it. They have either large bones or wide hips, shadowing under their eyes and around their chins, depth of expression in their look, and either high, rounded foreheads or strong chins.

The colors associated with water are black and blue, the corresponding direction is north, and the organ is the kidneys.

**Wood**

The wood element can be seen with trees, in wood paneling and furniture, wood carvings, or plants. It is symbolized by tall columns which mimic the shape of trees. These buildings, such as high rises, multi-storied houses, and cabins, inspire growth and a connection between heaven and earth.

People who are wood types usually have olive-colored skin and are either tall and angular like trees, or short and energetic like bushes. They have sinewy arms and legs and strong eyebrows or jaws. They are aggressive or assertive, direct, and have a strong temper and a lot of drive. Wood people usually love nature and have a lot of trees or plants in their environment.

The color of wood is green, the corresponding direction is east, and the organ is the liver.

**Fire**

The fire element appears in angular designs with sharp edges and points as well as in structural features like fireplaces and barbecues. Buildings in the fire shape excite the mind and emotions and are good places to generate ideas. Many libraries and churches have these shapes.

Fire people are usually willowy with bright eyes, big smiles, and reddish coloring on the neck and chest. They are charming, fun, mischievous, easily excitable, and change emotional states rapidly. They love change, bright colors, and environments that stimulate.

The colors of fire are red and orange as well as pastel pink, purple, and peach, the direction is south, and the organ is the heart.

**Earth**

The earth element is represented by anything made from stone, brick, ceramics, tile, and adobe. Buildings made of these materials have heavy walls and by necessity are low to the ground. Earth buildings are excellent for holding onto things and keeping things safe. They are long lasting, hard to damage, and promote stability, ideal for warehouses and museums.

People who have the earth element dominant in their constitution will have rounded limbs and soft flesh. They are warm, kind and look huggable. Earth women look like earth mothers, even when slim, and the men look like big bears. They have plump cheeks and generous mouths. They like to collect things and invariably have knickknacks around the house.

The colors of earth are brown, yellow, and clay colors, the direction is the center, and the organ is the stomach.

 **Metal**

Metal is a dual element. It is well represented by the Chinese coin, round with a square hole in the center. Metal shaped buildings are either rounded: a dome, curved walls, or squared: very boxy and modern. These buildings bring money, an ideal shape for a bank. Houses with high ceilings and a lot of glass are also metal homes; metal is reflective and needs a lot of space.

Metal people love minimalism. They like blank walls and monochromatic color schemes because it calms their futuristic minds. They are organized, clean, and contained, living very simply or very regally. Physically, they are fair skinned with small bones, broad shoulders and prominent cheekbones. Aquiline features, long noses, and carved chins and jaws dominate their faces. They give things away easily because they do not like to accumulate things.

Metal colors are white and all metallic shades: gold, silver, chrome, brass and bronze. The direction is west, and the organ is the lung.

## Balancing the Elements

Each person has a dominant element to their constitution that, if overemphasized, will eventually cause disharmony. If this primary element is overused, it overshadows the other elements and may lead to a deficiency or lack of the other elements. For example:

> *A man with a dominant metal element had always lived with glass, chrome, and a lot of windows. He went through changes that made him realize that he was lacking warmth in his personal life, and he realized that he was lonely. Metal environments can be stark and impersonal, so he started by adding fire colors. He began a collection of earthy objects to fill all the empty space around him. He learned to bring balance into his life by incorporating other elements into his environment.*

Deficiencies are also evident when someone has an intense craving for a certain element. People tend to be unhappy without their dominant element around them.

> *One client was a definite water type; he had big bones and a lot of stamina. He was not getting enough of the water element from his environment, as his illnesses and injuries showed. His complaints: low back pain, knee injuries, and hearing problems, all signs of water deficiency in Chinese medicine.*

> *I suggested he move closer to the water or add water to his environment with a fountain. His girlfriend began to laugh and told me that sometimes he was so obsessed with water that he would go home and turn on the faucets just to hear the sound of it! He quickly found a fountain for his home and office, (It is much more economical to recirculate a small amount of water than to run the faucets.), and he has had significantly better health ever since.*

People crave the element that dominates their constitution as well as the element they need. Like the old game, Paper, Rock and Scissors, the five elements can *help* each other or *harm* each other, as is evident in their growth and destruction cycles. Water feeds wood, wood feeds fire, fire makes ash for earth, earth grows metal, and metal (minerals) becomes water. Conversely, metal cuts wood, earth blocks water, water puts out fire, wood uses earth, and fire melts metal.

It is crucial that people get fed by the mother element and avoid being harmed by the suppressive element.

> *A client wanted me to help him in the area of relationships. He explained that they always started hot and heavy but then washed out. This was definitely a fire and water problem! His house was missing his marriage and partnership corner.[2] Outside, where it should have been, was a waterfall and a barbeque: fire and water canceling each other out. In the kitchen, the marriage corner was a laundry area with a washer and dryer, fire and water again. In the marriage corner of the master bedroom, there was a fireplace and an aquarium, and in the master bath, a Jacuzzi and fire pit. Every place with fire, also had water.[3]*
>
> *To fix the imbalance, we moved the barbecue to a different spot in the yard. In the kitchen, we made the laundry area into a pantry, moved the fish tank from the master bedroom and created a tropical rain forest garden in the fire pit location. Within a month, he began a relationship that is still rewarding to him three years later.*

---

[2]  *Please refer to "The Bagua," p. 35.*

[3]  *I find this so coincidental in my practice. The greatest personal issues keep manifesting again and again in the space. It feels as if certain houses are selected to help play out some karmic responsibility.*

Working with the elements guarantees personalization of the Feng Shui principles. These cures can be used to balance a surplus or lack of any element. Be creative in the application of the elemental principles. Use your imagination and watch how healthy you become when the elements are balanced.

## Five Element Feng Shui

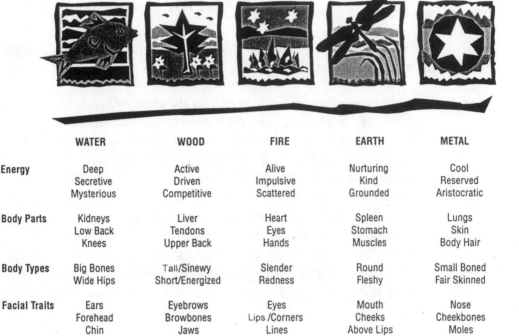

| | WATER | WOOD | FIRE | EARTH | METAL |
|---|---|---|---|---|---|
| Energy | Deep<br>Secretive<br>Mysterious | Active<br>Driven<br>Competitive | Alive<br>Impulsive<br>Scattered | Nurturing<br>Kind<br>Grounded | Cool<br>Reserved<br>Aristocratic |
| Body Parts | Kidneys<br>Low Back<br>Knees | Liver<br>Tendons<br>Upper Back | Heart<br>Eyes<br>Hands | Spleen<br>Stomach<br>Muscles | Lungs<br>Skin<br>Body Hair |
| Body Types | Big Bones<br>Wide Hips | Tall/Sinewy<br>Short/Energized | Slender<br>Redness | Round<br>Fleshy | Small Boned<br>Fair Skinned |
| Facial Traits | Ears<br>Forehead<br>Chin | Eyebrows<br>Browbones<br>Jaws | Eyes<br>Lips /Corners<br>Lines | Mouth<br>Cheeks<br>Above Lips | Nose<br>Cheekbones<br>Moles |
| Emotions<br>Physical to Transformed | Fear to<br>Wisdom | Anger to<br>Human Kindness | Excitement<br>to Love | Worry to<br>Instinct | Grief to<br>Gratitude |
| Shape | Amorphous<br>Curved<br>Add ons | Tall Columns<br>Tree/Bushes<br>Skyscrapers | Angles<br>Sharpness<br>Corners | Low<br>Heavy<br>Permanent | Round<br>Square<br>Open |
| Colors | Black<br>Blue | Green | Red/Pink<br>Orange | Brown<br>Clay | White<br>Any Metal |
| Needs | Water<br>Time Alone<br>Creativity | Trees<br>Plants<br>Focus | Color<br>Light/Heat<br>Talking | Comfort<br>Things<br>Family | Order<br>Purity<br>Boundaries |
| Values | Truth<br>Spirituality | Work<br>Intensity | Fun<br>Variety | Helping<br>Stability | Past/Future<br>Aesthetics |

# Color and the Chakra System

## Nancy SantoPietro

The transformational power of Feng Shui is derived from its keen ability to understand and decode the healing aspects of nature and recreate them indoors. By understanding what makes a forest of trees soothing or a beautiful sunset inspiring, we can recapture the magic of the outdoors and bring that force inside. One of the most profound healing aspects in nature, which affects our lives on a daily basis, is the presence of color.

Color is the most plentiful and visible of all gifts we receive from nature. It is the first thing we see when we open our eyes, and it is the last thing we see each night before we go to sleep. It affects everything from our choice of clothing to our moods. The more we understand how color impacts our lives, taking our cues from mother nature *the world's greatest artist*, the more we will know how to use these properties to heal ourselves and our world.

Almost everything in nature is defined by color: the hot yellow sun, clear blue waters, midnight-blue skies, red roses, green pastures, purple eggplants, and pink grapefruits. Our emotions are conveyed more thoroughly by adding a visual description of color to them: green with envy, red with rage, or feeling sad and blue. Color impacts our lives and creates rich, saturated images that encourage us to react and emote. The universe has provided us with a color spectrum to beautify our world, stimulate our senses, and nourish our spirits.

According to various spiritual teachings, before we incarnate into a physical body, our souls first exist on an ethereal level. On this level, the soul is made up of units of sparkling white light. This light is often described by individuals who have had near-death experiences. These units of white light, or soul, are our individual *vibration* and are as unique and specific to each of us as are our fingerprints and DNA. Our vibration acts as a personal computer that stores all the information needed for this lifetime. This information ranges from the relationships we will draw on to the type of lessons we are here to experience.

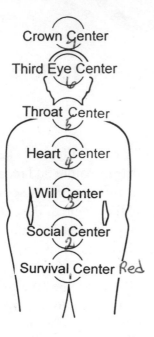

In the body, white light is broken down into the seven colors of the rainbow and are concentrated in seven areas called *energy centers* or chakras.[1] Each chakra oversees different characteristics and aspects of our lives. Although these little computer centers have the awesome responsibility of keeping us alive, they require very little from us to keep them active.

Their fuel is absorbed from the colors we encounter within our homes, in nature, food, and clothing. Learning to harness and access this color energy from our environment will empower us to change our lives for the better. By exploring the many facets of the chakras, we can better understand how the use of color in Feng Shui will adjust our patterns of energy and create harmony and balance in our environment.

**The Survival Center**  Red (1)

The first chakra is located at the base of the spine; its energy pattern resonates to the color red. It oversees all issues of money, the ability to complete projects, and survival: taking care of ourselves, providing such basic needs as food, proper housing, and work. It is our root center and

---

[1]    Chakra is a Sanskrit word that means spinning wheel of light.

provides the grounding energy needed to stay clear and focused in life. This center governs all physical and health aspects of the genitals, legs, knees, feet, and procreation.

**The Social Center** ( 2) *Orange*

The second chakra is located approximately two inches below the navel; its energy pattern resonates to the color orange. This is the *feeling center* and oversees our emotions. The energy in this center collects information regarding culture, family dynamics, issues related to the father, as well as our sense of who we are in the world. It oversees self esteem and how we come to define ourselves in relation to others. We store our childhood issues and traumas here; these can range from abandonment to incest, as well as addictive behaviors such as drinking, binging, and drugs. Sexual energy, intimacy, and raw creative energy are activated from this chakra. It governs all physical and health issues related to the lower intestines, ovaries, and lower back.

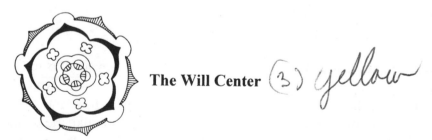

**The Will Center** (3) *yellow*

The third chakra is located in the solar plexus area in the opening where the rib cage parts; its energy pattern resonates to the color yellow. This center oversees the energy behind our will and our ability to focus on a specific direction or purpose. This is the center where our intellectual mind and our ability to reason is stored; it is from this center that we analyze, process, and distribute our thoughts, form new ideas, and tap into our willpower. It activates our drive and moves us through our goals. We store our fear and anger here. This center governs health issues related to the stomach, intestines, liver, gall bladder, adrenal glands, and middle back.

**The Heart Center** *(4) green*

The fourth chakra is located in the center of the chest; its energy pattern resonates to the color green. Through this center, we are able to feel love for ourselves and unconditional love for others. It connects us with the oneness uniting all living things: people, nature, animals, the mineral kingdom, the Universe, and God. This is the center where we derive our true personal power, security, confidence, and trust. All healing is generated from this center, as it connects directly to the two minor chakras located in the palms of the hand. In health, it oversees our upper back, chest, shoulders, arms, hands, lungs, and all physical and emotional issues of the heart.

**The Throat Center** *(5) Sky Blue*

The fifth chakra is located in the center of the throat; it resonates to the color sky blue. This is the center of our identity and the sense of who we are as individuals. This chakra's issues of identity differ from the "who am I?" of the second chakra. It does not collect information like the social center; instead it actively shows the world who we are. It oversees communication and all forms of creativity, from art work to writing. Issues related to authority, teaching, leadership, organizational and managerial skills are generated from this center, as well as anything having to do with the voice, singing or speaking. This center oversees adolescence, that period when we form our identities and show them to the world. This energy center oversees all physical and health-related issues regarding the throat and neck.

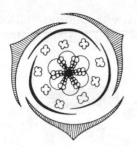

The Third Eye Center (6) *indigo*

The sixth chakra is located on the forehead between the eyebrows; its energy pattern resonates to the color indigo. This center is the *eye in our mind* that oversees all aspects of our intuition or *inner knowing*, when we *know* without fully understanding how or why. It is the center of truth, where we intuitively see an outcome or a particular situation for what it truly is without attaching our emotional needs or wants to it. This is where we store and access the energy for our psychic sight and clairaudient capabilities. This center governs all physical or health issues relating to the eyes, ears, and nose.

The Crown Center (7) *purple*

The seventh chakra is located at the top of the head; its energy pattern resonates to the color purple/violet. This center oversees our connection to our destiny, our specific path here on earth. The crown center acts as our personal compass, directing and pointing us towards the next part of our journey. The energy emitted from this chakra acts as a transmitter, drawing and repelling people and situations that will guide us on our path. In the esoteric realm, this center connects us to our *higher self* and provides the energy used for creative visualization. This chakra also connects us with the gifts that our soul is here to contribute to the world. It governs all physical and health-related aspects of our skull, brain, and pituitary function.

### Fueling Our Chakras from Our Surroundings

One of the ways these spiritual energy centers get fueled and nourished is by absorbing their corresponding colors from the environment; colors act as nature's *food for the soul*.

The mechanism that the physical body uses to absorb the energy from color is called the *aura*. The aura is the subtle light that glows, surrounds, and penetrates the physical body. It acts like a sponge, absorbing color from the environment and feeding it to the chakras.

The presence of color in our homes and lives is so important because without it we starve our souls and deplete our energy system. Feng Shui and the adjustment of color in our surroundings insure that we receive a correct balance of energy for each of our chakras.

Black Hat Sect Feng Shui uses the creative color cycle of the Bagua and the five element color system to create a balance of colors in homes and offices. It creates an environment that has a positive impact on our internal energy systems, the chakras. The main sources for absorbing color from our environment into our auras and physical bodies are: interiors, environment, nature, clothing, and food.

## Interiors

Home and work interiors have a profound effect on our chakras. The colors of our walls, floors, and furniture all activate, balance, or depress our Chi. The best colors for our homes and offices are those that make us feel energized and happy.

### Avoid color schemes that are too intense.

If you like deep purple, instead of painting four walls of a room with it, which would be very overwhelming, try using it in the fabric of your couch or as part of the design on your bedspread. You can introduce it into your surroundings through such objects as lamps, pictures, and accessories.

### Avoid an all neutral color scheme.

Having an all neutral color scheme in your home lends itself to apathy and indifference. People who use exclusively neutral tones may be trying to *neutralize* their feelings. Color invokes feelings, and no color invokes neutrality. If you are partial to these colors or if you already have these colors on your walls, *please do not panic.* [2] Try to introduce some color into the space by painting a room or one wall or by hanging colorful artwork.

### Assess your total color quotient

*One client had every wall in his apartment painted off-white. He was a vibrant, enthusiastic person who did not seem to be affected by the lack of color in his space. Before I commented and explored the color scheme with him, I asked him what type of work he did. He responded, "I am an artist and I work with paints all day long." I quickly realized that he was saturated with color at work and needed his home to be in neutral colors to balance out and calm his Chi. The home environment that he created helped him achieve the perfect balance of the color spectrum, for him.*

Look at all the places that you come in contact with throughout each day. If you do not have much color in your collective environment, you probably will not have a very colorful life. It is your choice!

---

[2]  Give my suggestions thought and see if they ring true for you. If not, let them go. Make sure you have the final say about any changes that you make.

## Environments

Environments that we come in contact with every day, such as bus stops, grocery stores, a friend's apartment, or a doctor's office, can also affect the balance of our chakras. How we feel in these places: safe, pressured, nurtured, or uplifted, will determine the state of our Chi and the balance of our chakras.

**Think about how a certain place *feels*.**

> Take notice of where in your body you sense the feelings a particular place gives you. This will put you in touch with which chakras are reacting to specific colors and situations. For instance, while you are waiting in a doctor's office, look around at the color scheme in the waiting room. How does it make you feel? Do you like the colors? Hate them? Do they calm you? Give you anxiety? Start interpreting and describing colors by using specific adjectives describing how they make you feel or react. This will help you develop a sensitivity to how your environment affects you.

**Notice the Feng Shui of the space.**

> Use your knowledge of Feng Shui and your newly acquired sensitivity to color to help you make decisions about which grocery store you choose to shop in, which restaurant to dine in, even which chair to sit in. If the circumstances allow, honor your energy system and base your decision on the chakra colors that you need to *fuel* on that particular day.

## Nature

Another common way we absorb energy is through the vast amount of color available in nature. We are surrounded by green trees, blue skies,

**Notice the colors in nature you respond to most favorably.**

Do you gravitate towards cool blue waters or the lush green of a forest to find peace and relaxation? Which colors do not attract your attention? Be aware of colors that soothe you, stimulate you, and make you feel alive. Make a list of your favorite places or things in nature. Ask yourself what it is about those places that are peaceful, comforting, or soothing. List the colors associated with those images and how they affect you.

**Integrate nature into your home.**

Hang a photo or picture of your favorite place in nature that reflects the colors and attributes you found on your list. Place copies of that image in strategic spots. Make eye contact with it as often as you can, and feel yourself drawing in the energy and the balancing effect of its color. Make eye contact with similar colors in your environment to further enhance your healing experience. Absorb the colors into your body through your eyes, using clear, conscious intention to help you to visualize your body being filled with its healing ability.

## Clothing

A very powerful way to consciously work with color is through clothing because it is color energy that touches our *mobile home*, our body, and our aura. Our wardrobe provides us with a daily opportunity to adjust our color energy. It is not a permanent state of color; it can change and fluctuate with our moods and imbalances.

**See clothing as a flexible system for energy adjustment**

Choose clothing that lifts your spirits, stimulates your creativity, or helps you express love. Connecting to your chakras will allow you to make the right color choices, which will make you look and feel good. Color and clothing can make the person or make the person *invisible*. The more you tune into yourself and connect to your color needs, the more you can give your soul the best nourishment it deserves.

## Food

Traditionally, the nutritional value of food refers to its vitamin, mineral, or caloric content. When we are balancing our chakras and Chi, we must evaluate the nutritional value of our food through its color scheme and corresponding element parts. Certain foods, based on their color and/or the energy they impart, activate different chakras and contribute healing energy to our bodies.

### Eat foods associated with the seven colors of the chakras

You can ingest and absorb the colors from nature to heal and balance your energy. If you are dealing with emotional, second chakra issues regarding your childhood or family, eat more oranges or carrots to help you cope; orange-colored foods will help balance those emotional issues. Be aware that sometimes a center is *overactive* and needs *less* of the color it resonates to. Also take notice of your food cravings to see if you are gravitating towards any one particular food color group. Your body might be telling you that a particular energy or chakra is out of balance.

Think about the foods you eat and need, then consciously make choices that will not only appeal to your appetite but to the hunger of your soul.

The methods available to harness color and improve our Chi are vast, yet all have a common denominator that make them effective, *mindful application of thought*. It is the ability to apply the thinking mind and focus it in a specific way for a specific result. When we work with the energy of color and Feng Shui, our belief in a higher force along with our conscious intentions are the only tools that we need to create change. Our thoughts are powerful. We must learn to use them responsibly and with consciousness to change our lives and create happiness.

# Feng Shui: A Life Healing Tool

## Hope Karan Gerecht

People often feel the need for change but are unsure of what it is that needs changing. They turn to Feng Shui to begin making adjustments on the physical level because they want a nicer looking environment. What they do not realize is that Feng Shui takes them toward a much deeper energetic change by exploring and enhancing the many facets of their lives.

Feng Shui is a healing tool that works on both the physical and energetic levels. Physically, you bring more balance and beauty to your home. Thomas Moore, in his book <u>Care of the Soul</u>, states that beauty is the only thing the soul recognizes and grows by. Energetically, Feng Shui adjustments bring about a deep sense of comfort and a high level of inspiration.

Life is a wonderous mystery that is constantly unfolding through personal vision and goals. Feng Shui helps remove any blockages, allowing more movement in your life. As energy begins to move and shift, you can direct that additional energy toward the areas of your life you wish to enhance.

**The highest aim in Feng Shui is to apply increased personal Chi and insight to a place where you feel a heart-centered attraction.**

Feng Shui can help your life grow in unexpected and welcomed ways. After you make adjustments and see their results, you can re-evaluate and look toward new goals that have grown out of these personal changes.[1]

An interesting way of viewing Feng Shui is through its description as acupuncture for the home.[2]

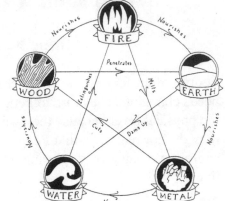

The five element theory,[3] which underlies both acupuncture and Feng Shui, provides a new perspective as you look at the various colors, shapes, and the movement of energy in your home.

Combining the symbolism of an object with a ritual[4] as it is placed in your home speaks to your soul on a deep level.

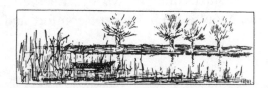

An environment with a balance of the five elements and symbolic belongings that act as reminders of important goals invites the focus of your life to move toward a deeply spiritual, and mindful place.

Often you have no idea what form the changes will take once they manifest. The following story shows how the addition of the nourishing element of fire initially manifested as increased joy, then later as love.

---

[1]  *Please refer to "Utilize All Your Resources," p. 189.*

[2]  *Please refer to "Energy Systems and Feng Shui," p. 275.*

[3]  *Please refer to "The Five Phases of Energy," p. 81.*

[4]  *Please refer to "The Magic of Ritual and Feng Shui," p. 369.*

## Jeannie's Story

I had not spoken to my longtime friend Jeannie in a number of years. Our lives had taken us in different directions. One day, she called to tell me her Mom had passed away after a four-year battle with breast cancer. Within that past four-month span, she had also lost her grandmother and a close aunt. Each loss further deepened her grieving process. She had been working to heal herself with acupuncture and grief therapy but felt that she still needed more balance and stability in her life.

Jeannie decided to turn some of her attention toward her surroundings, and she invited me to give her some Feng Shui recommendations. First, I assessed Jeannie's core energy: her Feng Shui natal element was *earth,* which is nourished by the *fire* element.[5] Jeannie confirmed that her acupuncturist was currently using a treatment that focused on supporting her fire and earth element energetics.[6] I found it interesting that two ancient Chinese artful sciences, acupuncture and Feng Shui, had reached the very same conclusion. Nothing is coincidental; the physical body is directly related to its surroundings.

While performing an assessment of Jeannie's home, I found that it had virtually no fire represented: no red, nothing angular or triangular, no candles, not even much sunlight. The predominant elements in her home were water and metal, both of which dampen and reduce the fire and earth elements.[7]

---

[5]  In my Feng Shui practice, I incorporate the teachings of four prominent schools. This system is taught by Derek Walters, author of The Feng Shui Handbook. *Please refer to Derek's article, "The Seven Portents," p. 93, and The Feng Shui Horoscope section of* Earth Design: The Added Dimension.

[6]  *Please refer to "The Energetic Basis of Good Health," p. 293, "Using Feng Shui to Create Health," p. 285, and "Five Elements for Better Health," p. 303.*

[7]  *Please refer to the destructive and creative cycles of the elements in "The Five Phases of Energy," p. 81.*

Jeannie lived on the top floor of a one hundred year old home that had a back circular staircase. Its corkscrew effect and the open risers on the staircase made it difficult for Chi to rise and enter Jeannie's second floor living space. We added a plant under the staircase, and greenery spiraled around the handrails to invite Chi up to her home. For extra measure, we entwined a bit of shiny gold accent into the upward growing trail of greenery.

Jeannie entered her home through the back door, which lead directly into her kitchen. I wanted to shift the focal point away from the stove and refrigerator, neither of which presented great first impressions.[8] A circular, stained glass art piece and two large hanging plants created a new focus to greet Jeannie as she entered. A mirror placed behind her stove doubled two fire elements: her burners[9] and the sunlight from an adjacent window. A three-paneled mirror with a broken pane was hanging in the family-health area[10] of the kitchen. I shared with Jeannie the importance of not having anything broken in her home because broken things lower the Chi of everything around them.

In the center of Jeannie's home was a very small yet busy hallway with six doors leading off it. We hung a beautiful, glass prism wind chime in the center to encourage the smooth movement of Chi at this very busy intersection.

Jeannie's living room required a number of changes. It offered a great opportunity for incorporating the fire element, one of our main concerns because of her elemental energetics. We replaced black upholstery and draperies with a dynamic geometric print that included fire and earth tones. To ground some earth energy for this earth lady, we laid a multi-hued striped rug in subtle tones of cinnamon, gold, brown, and cream. She loved it!

---

8    *Please refer to "The Room of First Impression," p. 207.*

9    Traditionally, burners are a symbol for wealth, so doubling them with mirrors also invited increased wealth.

10   *Please refer to "The Bagua," p. 35.*

We hung a mobile with a sun in red and gold between the entrance to the living room and a window in a direct line with the door. The mobile encouraged Chi to slow down and circulate throughout the room instead of making a rapid exit out the window because of the front/back door alignment problem. We also angled the furniture to invite the eye and Chi to move around the room.

Her helpful people area had a television/stereo cabinet with a pile of twisted wires which did not allow the cabinet doors to close. I recommended that she drill a hole in the back of the cabinet so the wiring could be concealed and the cabinet doors could close. It is important that utilitarian items such as electronics or wiring are concealed in cabinets, placed behind folding screens, or draped with fabric, so the eye sees only beauty.

We moved tall bookcases so they no longer towered over the seating area. We moved one of them to her office to open up the living room and to allow for more graceful movement in this small room. Above the bookcases, we hung artwork to pleasantly lead a visitor's attention around the room.

In Jeannie's bedroom, there was a large door in the ceiling leading to the attic. Regardless of where Jeannie placed her bed, the attic door was above it, and it made her uneasy.

The feeling of the room was instantly lightened when we hung a beautiful red and white floral, oriental paper fan over the opening.

I made sure that the bottom angle of the fan did not point toward Jeannie's bed and create a secret arrow.[11] We then arranged Jeannie's bed in a command position[12] with a full view of the door, and we moved a heavy dresser away from the foot of her bed. She was now able to get deeper, more revitalizing rest in her balanced bedroom.

---

[11]    *Please refer to "The Power of Chi," p. 49.*

[12]    *Please refer to "Feng Shui and Children," p. 349.*

I asked Jeannie if she knew anything about her apartment's previous tenant. This was an important concern since energy tends to repeat patterns. The previous occupant had done well in her work but had not had a relationship during the four years she lived there. Jeannie and I did some clearing and blessings rituals[13] to change the energy of the space. I also shared Master Lin Yun's transcendental cures with Jeannie:

### For the Mind
Creative visualizations for that which Jeannie wished to have enter her life.

### For the Body
A hand mudra, or a position symbolizing the brushing away and clearing of old patterns.

### For Speech
Prayers to focus the mind on the highest awareness.

All three activities worked to support the spiritual essence of her home.

Two months after our changes, Jeannie called me and said, "I don't understand why Feng Shui works; I only know that I am happier now than ever before. I feel more stability and have more balance in my life."

Jeanne knows Feng Shui helped her complete her grieving process. She was able to take the vacation of her dreams to Australia, New Zealand, and Fuji. She also began a long-term relationship and was thoroughly enjoying her work. Feng Shui had helped her discover the magical unfolding of the subtle and profound beauty, benefits, and blessings of her life.

---

13   *Please refer to "The Magic of Ritual and Feng Shui," p. 369, and "The Bones of Your Home," p. 399.*

# Feng Shui for the Healthy Home

# A Scentual Reminder of Feng Shui Remedies

## Dennis Fairchild

Fragrances have long woven their scents through the fabric of history. Ancient Egyptians were famed for their use of aromatic oils as beauty and health remedies as well as for religious and medicinal purposes. During times of plague, it was believed that perfumers were immune and did not fall ill because they were exposed daily to essential aromatic oils. In the eighth century, Wang Wei proclaimed,

**"Look in the perfumes of flowers and of nature for peace of mind and joy of life."**

Even today, fragrant essential oils[1] - liquefied Ma Nature - keep us under their spell. Rationally, we know that the limbic system, or *smell part* of the brain, plays a significant role in how we perceive places and situations. Intuitively, we understand that the power of smells and aromatic oils goes far beyond our simple enjoyment of them.

These *flowers in a drop* possess the life force or Chi of a plant's flowers, leaves, ersatz stems, fruit rind, berries, resin, or roots that are distilled into an aromatic botanical. Much of the lore about aromas as Feng Shui cures has been lost over the centuries. Reintroducing their *secrets* is the first step to revitalizing this ancient and powerful body of knowledge.

**Essential oils are 21st century tools for all Feng Shui enthusiasts.**

---

[1]   Essential oils refer to 100% natural extracts, not manufactured, chemical copies or oils that have been processed or treated. *The fragrances available in the order pages are of the purest quality. These essential oils are produced from several hundreds or thousands of plants to extract just one pound of oil through a state-of-the-art low pressure/temperature distillation process.*

Bring fragrance into your space. Begin with just a few scents. Buy small bottles and store them in a cool, dark space. If essential oils are hard to locate or garden space is limited, try using scented candles or incense, always aiming for quality and purity. Keep a journal of your fascinating results. Whatever your choice, never overlook or disregard the magic of aroma!

## Essential Oils in Action

**Basil:**

It usually hides out in the kitchen spice rack! Ancient Chinese herbalists and Feng Shui practitioners have sung praises about its magical potency as a supplement to self-esteem and as an expectorant and laxative. In its native India, it is the herb of Vishnu, Krishna, and Shiva and revered as a plant of great holiness. In addition to its delicious culinary qualities, many African tribes grow basil around the main entrance of the home to ward off poverty and the evil eye.

In your Feng Shui garden, plant basil in the northern/career area[2] to develop fortitude and awareness of who your enemies are. It does not grow close to other plants or its own kind, and so it is said to promote individuality, luck with solo work, and personal ventures. To insure clarity, crush fresh basil leaves and rub their fragrance on your fingers next time you have a writing deadline. Dab a few drops of its oil onto the bulb of your desk light when working on projects. Avoid using basil if you are pregnant.[3]

---

[2]  *This refers to how the Bagua is overlaid in your garden, see "The Bagua," p. 35 for more information.*

[3]  Like food, some people are sensitive to certain aromas and essential oils. Because certain essential oils are known to stimulate the uterus during a woman's first trimester, like basil, juniper, and rosemary in particular, they should be used gingerly and with caution. At other times, go with the flow and let your nose be the guide.

**Bergamot:**

Weight Watchers unite! Bergamot's citrusy floral scent curbs the appetite, lifts depression, and relieves anxiety. Best used with lavender and rose geranium, try adding a few drops to your moisturizer or evening bath and get rid of the diet pills. Plant bergamot in your garden's southern/acknowledgment from peers area, to ward off superficial friends or gossip. Used around the patio, it will repel insects.

**Chamomile:**

From the Greek *chamos*-on the ground and *melos*-apple, chamomile remains one of Europe's favorite "upbeat" herbs and lawn coverings. Globally recognized for its soothing sweet fragrance, royals and writers alike pay it homage. Buckingham Palace reserves a large space for this golden beauty to grow. Beatrix Potter's Peter Rabbit was given chamomile tea to calm him after his adventure in Mr. MacGregor's garden. And Shakespeare's Falstaff says of this indestructible yellow-budded plant: "Though the chamomile the more it is trodden on the faster it grows, yet youth the more it is wasted the sooner it wears."

Governed astrologically by the Sun, it is said to bring peace as well as harmony to lovers and household members when planted in the garden's southwest/relationships area or in the western/family area. When it is freshly picked, place a bouquet in the eastern/health area of a room of someone prone to anxiety, panic attacks, or mental confusion. And while you are at it, brew them a fresh cup of its tea.

**Cinnamon and Cloves:**

These spicy scents, a favorite potpourri ingredient, stimulate the taste buds. A great trick of realtors is to simmer apple cider and cinnamon on a stove top when showing buyers a prospective new home. Its tantalizing, flavorful aroma excites taste buds, prompting folks to drool and get excited. Try this ploy next time you need family support in home projects, decorating, or Feng Shui-ing.

Difficult to cultivate in North American gardens, store ground or whole cinnamon sticks and cloves in separate dark glass containers in the eastern/health section of the kitchen to promote good eating habits. Place them in a small bowl next to your word processor and take a whiff when writer's block occurs. One caution, keep it away from the skin, as its stimulating factors are irritants.

## Eucalyptus:

The pungent, antiseptic-green smell of eucalyptus is commonly used in medications to aid sinus problems and alleviate head colds. In the northeastern/knowledge areas of a home, the clean smell from fresh stalks stimulates clear thinking, which is great for students, budding authors, and aspiring actors!

Plant eucalyptus in the northwest corner of your garden to promote clarity when traveling and an awareness of which friends are truly on your side. After work, soak in a bath with several drops of eucalyptus oil when you have trouble on the job. Its cleansing properties will *wash* away frustration, making you more apt to see matters realistically and uncover solutions.

## Frankincense:

Frankincense oil or scented candles are a must for a proper Feng Shui household. One of the Wise Men's gifts to the baby Jesus, its esoteric aromatic qualities are universally known to cleanse the air of hatred and prejudice. Its unique, sweet balsam-like scent has purified homes and temples for centuries. Blend a few drops with lavender in an oil base for body lotion, great for arms and legs that have been overexposed to the sun.

**Jasmine:**

The climbing jasmine vine, originally found along the ancient trade routes from Iran to China, remains a favorite Asian Feng Shui remedy. Its pleasingly sweet, floral fragrance helps troubled homes where infidelity, divorce, or arguments occur. Considered an antidepressant as well as an aphrodisiac, it is effective in cases of impotence and lack of confidence. Interestingly, in Christian floral folklore, it is a flower of the Epiphany and attributed to the Virgin Mary.

Place a few drops on the light bulb of a lamp near the bed stand of anyone who is depressed to lift their spirits and to cleanse their thoughts of animosity or low self-worth. For luck with money, plant fresh sprigs in the southeast/money section of the garden. In the eastern/health sector, it will aid in rapid recovery from surgery and prevent fear of the unknown. Many Japanese keep fresh bouquets in the rooms of newborns to insure pleasant dreams and promote individuality. Governed by Venus, the planet of love, it is said to bestow divine hope, grace, and heavenly felicity.

**Juniper:**

In Christian legend, the Virgin Mary took refuge with the child Jesus behind a juniper bush when fleeing from Herod to Egypt. Ancient Asians thought that the pungent smoke produced by the green branches would keep evil spirits at bay. Even today in Wales, chopping down a juniper tree is regarded as a misfortune, resulting in the likely death of a family member.

Oil of juniper is used in making gin and in treating urinary ailments and dropsy, possibly due to the effects of too many gin martinis. While fasting, sipping the juice from their purple berries benefits people with lung disorders and an infusion from the tree restores lost youth. A favorite of Princess Diana, juniper helps relieve cellulitis by detoxifying and enabling the body to throw off toxic wastes that accumulate. It is a flower of Libra and symbolic of longevity, asylum, and protection. Plant juniper beneath bedroom windows to enhance martial bliss. Avoid using juniper if you are pregnant.

## Lavender:

An ancient symbol of love and cleanliness, lavender was once believed to grow only in old maids' gardens. It is the flower of Mercury, the planet of communication and winged liaison between gods and mortals. In aromatherapy and Feng Shui lore, its attributes include easing personal pain and emotional suffering, and its relaxing scent relieves apathy and fear. It is widely used in perfumes, massage oil, and facial steam and is a favorite remedy against insomnia, headaches, and jet lag.

It is most effective when planted far from entrances or bedrooms. On home sites, it is better to be seen than smelled or mistrust could occur amongst family members. Add a few drops of its essential oil to your evening bath to increase intuition.

## Lemon:

Lemons originated in the East along the old caravan trade routes through Persia. They also helped put Christopher Columbus on the map during his second voyage to the New World. In Christian art, a lemon is sometimes depicted as the fruit of the Tree of Knowledge and symbolizes love's fidelity. Governed by the sign Capricorn, its zodiacal attributes are everlasting commitment and perseverance.

Lemon juice mixed with distilled water was given as an antidote against the plague and was discovered to prevent scurvy on lengthy ocean voyages long before its magical properties were categorized as vitamin C. It remains a popular aroma for perfumes and antiseptics as well as a garnish for many drinks and vegetables.

Lemon trees on a property should be planted in the eastern/children area and western/health area of front and back yards to promote unity and vitality among household members. Dwarf varieties of the lemon tree or growing the lemon grass herb are favorable additions to every Feng Shui kitchen and are said to foster better eating habits. Ancient herbal philosophy says that adding the juice of a lemon to your evening bath water relieves mental pressure and negative thinking.

The smell of lime is juicier and more refreshing than its sister. It carries the same attributes and is a favorite scent used in men's shaving products and cologne. Place a bowl of fresh limes on the upper right-hand side of your desk to clear up marriage and relationship hassles.

**Orange:**

The orange's sunny fragrance, blossoms, and color encourage cheerfulness. Orange is also associated with generosity because of its unusual ability to produce fruit, flowers, and foliage at the same time. One of the labors of Hercules was to obtain some of these *golden apples* to prove victory and strength over adversaries.

Feng Shui masters[4] in Japan present new home owners with baskets of fresh oranges to attract happiness. The ancients suggested spraying or rubbing orange oil or burning orange scented candles and incense in the bedroom to promote good sex. Realtors favor spraying basements with the smell of oranges to increase salability while conducting an open house. Orange trees planted in bunches of three in a yard, rather than an entire grove, are also said to increase profits when selling property.

**Peppermint and Spearmint:**

Their cooling, refreshing aroma is an historical antidote for comforting people with emotional stress and fatigue. In the Feng Shui language of smell, its scent says, "Let us be friends and relax as individuals." Herbalists say that a tea from their leaves stimulates appetite and conversation and is good for the memory. Plant these sweeties in the northwest/friends or northeast/knowledge areas of your garden to improve friendships and help from others. Peppermint oil is not advised for use during pregnancy.

---

[4] *Master Lin Yun suggests bathing with nine circular pieces of orange peel to help restore depleted Chi and regenerate energy.*

**Pine:**

The clean, fresh scent of Scotch or Norwegian Pine relieves emotional stress and fatigue. Its needles and essential oils have been used to disinfect castles and cottages for ages. It is dedicated to Neptune, the god of the sea, because pine wood was used in the construction of the first ships. Tradition says it is one of the trees from which the cross of Christ was made.

Add a few drops in a pot and simmer on the stove, or dab some on cotton balls and tuck them around the house. Beware of using it on plastic surfaces as it tends to mar. A dozen drops added to soapy water makes cleaning easier and benefits the housekeeper's temperament as well as everyone who inhales its deep, woody smell.

**Thyme:**

Thyme is the plant that bees, fairies, and nature devas seek out. It is associated with activity and courage. Feng Shui herbalists recommend its potent aroma as an aid for melancholia. Add it to a simmering pot with frankincense to clear the air, encourage deep breathing, and curb bronchitis. A little goes a lon-n-g way with this oil, so use it gingerly! Grow thyme in the northern/career or southeastern garden corners to attract extra money, but as tradition dictates, never grow it indoors.

**Rose:**

The rose, whose origins are from ancient China and Japan has perhaps been the subject of more prose and verse than any other flower. In classical legend, it is known as the plant of beautiful silence. Ruled by the planet Venus, it is also the Christian symbol of charity, forgiveness, and mercy. Devotional beads were originally made from rose leaves. A rosebud of any kind symbolizes hope and youthful beauty; a rose in full bloom signifies secrecy.

White roses bestow the ability to cut through the thick of matters. An abundance of red roses, however, is said to generate pettiness amongst homeowners and should be reserved for the south part of the lot only. Too many of these scarlet beauties attract thorny disagreement. Yellow roses act as magnets to attract intellectual discussion and objectivity.

## Fragrance in Action

Place a few drops of essential oil in a pan of boiling water, in a bath, on a light bulb, or sprinkle a few drops on a handkerchief and breathe the scent at work. Experiment with these essential oils for a healthy Feng Shui home:

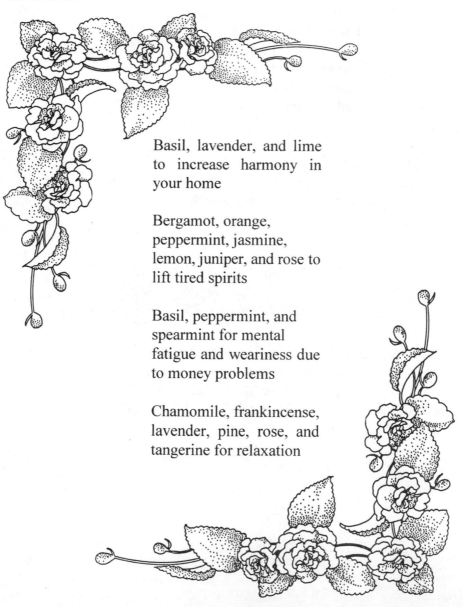

Basil, lavender, and lime to increase harmony in your home

Bergamot, orange, peppermint, jasmine, lemon, juniper, and rose to lift tired spirits

Basil, peppermint, and spearmint for mental fatigue and weariness due to money problems

Chamomile, frankincense, lavender, pine, rose, and tangerine for relaxation

## Also try:

Allspice to increase compassion
Angelica for inspiration
Caraway for faithfulness
Cedarwood as a sedative
Cloves for dignity
Coriander to uncover hidden worth
Dill to promote sleep
Geranium for comfort in the home
Honeysuckle for enduring bonds of love
Laurel for glory, self-worth
Lilac for childhood innocence
Lily of the valley for return of happiness
Magnolia for dignity
Pink carnation, for females only, to secure relationships
Rosemary for remembrance; avoid when pregnant
Sage for domestic virtue, good health
Violet for clear thinking, modesty

Human beings have always turned to nature for serenity. In flowers, trees, and herbs we find the loving hand of God. The essence of aromas in Feng Shui is to heal, comfort, and uplift the hearts, minds, and bodies in a home with the scents of herbs and flowers. What could be more simple or beautiful?

# Energy Fields, Feng Shui, and Fragrances

## Elaine Paris

In the ancient Chinese art of Feng Shui, the life energy force is called Chi. Chi gives life to the mountains and movement to the streams. It is the force that links all life together. Each person has individual Chi, which intermingles with the Chi of all the rest of creation. Feng Shui is about finding and nurturing balance and harmony between our personal Chi and the Chi that flows through our living and work environment.

Life force energy is constantly vibrating, pulsating, and evolving. In nature, your personal Chi moves in harmony with the Chi of the earth and universe. The electrical field of living things is a direct current (DC) of electrical pulsations. Electrical current flows in one direction, and its frequency is harmonious and coherent.

In the modern world, man-made energy patterns, such as electricity, electromagnetic fields, toxic air, and synthetic building environments, all create disharmony in the natural flow of Chi.In particular, objects connected to the electrical power system operate on an alternating current (AC), which changes its direction of flow.[1] Its pattern is disharmonious and incoherent to our own. Thus, in the electrical world of our cities, our personal Chi is affected by incoherent AC frequencies that resonate differently and discordantly from our bodies electrical DC field.

---

[1] In the United States, the electrical power is a 60 hertz system, which means that the flow of the current changes its direction 60 times per second. Europe is on a 50 Hz system.

## Our Electrical Body

The human body has both an electric and a magnetic field. The electric field is 62-68 hertz of direct current. Each cell in your body generates a charge of approximately 1.17 volts at a specific frequency unique to the organ or system where it is found. This special frequency is called a *signature* frequency.[2] A magnetic field also surrounds each cell. It is generated by the movement of the cell's electricity and its response to the natural magnetic field of the earth. The electric and the magnetic fields of the body work together to adjust and maintain a state of homeostasis or equilibrium.

The hypothalamus is the most important part of the human brain for assisting the body in maintaining its equilibrium. This part of the brain mysteriously responds to the natural electric and magnetic fields of the earth as well as to the electric and magnetic fields within the body.

## Electromagnetic Fields

Electromagnetic field is a global term for two different fields: electric and magnetic. Electric fields are the charges surrounding electric appliances like TV's, computers, or coffee makers. They are ever present, whether the appliance is turned on or off. Magnetic fields are created when the electrical charge is moving. They are present only when the object is turned on.

---

2      Gregg Branden, <u>Awakening to Zero Point: The Collective Initiation</u>, 1994, p.57.

Electromagnetic fields are broken down into a spectrum arranged according to frequency and wavelength.[3] High frequency radiation includes gamma rays, x-rays, and ultraviolet rays. These rays give off *ionizing* radiation, which means they have enough energy to permeate cells and break down chemical bonds.

Middle and low frequencies of radiation do not emit enough energy to enter the cells of the body and are therefore *non-ionizing*.

Middle frequencies are visible light, infrared radiation, radio frequency, radar waves, television, and microwaves.

Microwave radiation is emitted by: video display terminals, electric security systems, telephone relays, citizen band radios, satellites, and broadcast transmissions, to name a few.

Microwaves are dangerous because of their thermal effect, their ability to heat and cook tissue, and their non-thermal effect, their ability to cause biological changes without the body heating up.

Extremely low frequency or ELF radiation is emitted from 60 Hz power lines and appliances. Until recently, ELF radiation was believed to be safe; however, recent research indicates that this may not be the case. For example, I can easily demonstrate how the individual frequency/energy field of eight of my clients was significantly altered by the presence of

---

3     Frequency is the number of waves emitted per second, and wavelength is the distance between two successive peaks of the wave. The higher the frequency, the shorter the wavelength and the greater the number of waves.

electromagnetic fields within their own home environments and the negative effects that resulted.[4]

**The body's energy field pulsates at a different frequency
than that of the synthetic world.**

## Synthetic Environments

Most spaces in which we live and work are synthetic. Many present-day buildings have metal/iron support structures with metal frame walls and sides. The walls, both exterior and interior, are covered with synthetic materials and filled with synthetic insulation. Often, the air is recycled because the windows cannot be opened to bring in a fresh supply.

**We have created toxic and stagnant energy fields
where we live and work.**

Modern heating and ventilation systems create electro-static charges in synthetic paints, carpets, and furniture in spaces with high electromagnetic fields, such as in an office filled with computers and electrical appliances. As non-polarized charges seek polarized particles, these synthetic materials are always searching for the home of the opposite electrical charge. Mucous membranes in the eyes, nose, and mouth are excellent magnets; this leads to eye irritation and allergies.

If you work at a computer all day, particularly if the room is lit by fluorescent lights, how do you feel at the end of the day?

4    References: "The Effects of Electromagnetic Fields on Signature Sound Frequencies," *Sound Advice*, Athens, Ohio, October, 1994, by Sue Ruzicka, and Two excellent references by Robert Becker, The Body Electric - Electromagnetism and the Foundation of Life, William Morrow Publishing, 1985; and Cross Currents, G. Putman's Sons, 1990.

Are you tired? Do your eyes burn? Is it difficult to concentrate? How many colds do you get a year? Do you have allergies? All of these conditions are things for you to recognize about your own personal energy status.

These synthetic environments create stress on the body at the cellular level. High levels of stress, high blood pressure, chronic illness, chronic fatigue syndrome, and allergies may all be related to the disharmony between personal energy fields and artificial living and working environments.

### Detecting Electromagnetic Fields

Negative electromagnetic fields affect personal Chi as well as Chi in the home. There are several devices for identifying these energy fields: A gauss meter identifies and measures the intensity of electromagnetic fields. The Tri-field meter measures electromagnetic fields, electrical fields, and microwaves. The EMF Natural Tri-field meter identifies more subtle energies: noxious energy zones of the earth, energy patterns in the atmosphere, and subtle spirit energies. For the logical mind, these last two meters provide quantifiable readings of what you cannot see, but is felt by your body.

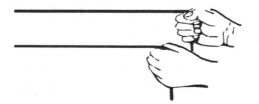

The ancient art of dowsing is another method to identify subtle energies of all types.

It provides a means by which the person serves as an energy probe to tap into the energy in the surrounding environment. It is an intuitive method of using inner knowing. The key is to quiet your conscious mind and allow the energy to flow through your dowsing device. Dowsers use different devices: L rods and pendulums are the most popular.

Your body can also serve as a dowsing tool. Anyone can dowse; however, the more experience you have, the greater the validity of the results.[5]

## Balancing Electromagnetic Fields

The electromagnetic fields and electrostatic charges from electronic appliances can be redirected by using a dielectric device[6] which collects harmful radiation and rebroadcasts it as a life energy field. The main component of a dielectric device is a special quartz material that is a nonconductor of electricity.

For homes and offices that have a high electromagnetic field (2+ millegauss), use a Tri-Pak Resonator on the electrical fuse box. You can dowse to check for correct placement and use the EMF Natural Tri-Field meter to measure its effects.

Dielectrics such as the Smog Buster are used for computers, televisions, video players, and cellular phones. The Crystal Catalyst Bead is designed to protect the body from harmful radiation. Pendants containing various gemstones that work with specific frequencies of the body are also good choices.

## Frequency, Fragrances, and Energy

Essential oil is the resin extract from a plant that contains its aroma. It has bio-electric properties that make it a powerful tool for working with the energy fields of both your body and your environment.[7] The air you breathe indoors is often out of balance. It is over loaded with positive ions, partly from the electronic devices you have. When sprayed or diffused into the air, essential oils add negative ions and shift the frequency of the atmosphere.

---

[5]    The American Society of Dowsers, St. Johnsonbury, Vermont, can provide information on classes and the nearest local chapter in your area.

[6]    *Please refer to order pages for more information.*

[7]    *Please refer to "A Scentual Reminder of Feng Shui Remedies," p. 329, and "Feng Shui and Children," p. 349 and to order pages for fragrance products.*

## Each aroma adds a different frequency to the air
## and a new energy to a room.

Using essential oils is not a modern remedy; it dates back to ancient times. Translations of Egyptian hieroglyphics and Chinese manuscripts indicate their use before the time of Christ. Ancient civilizations used aromas and resins from plants in religious ceremonies, purification rituals, and for healing. Fragrance had spiritual meaning, linking humanity to the gods.

To this day, Native Americans use sage and cedar to purify the air and cleanse the energy field. In India, incense has been used for thousands of years to purify energy fields. Today in Europe, particularly France, aromatherapy is a major modality in medicine. Many of the oils are antifungal, antibacterial, and antiviral. Modern research continues to measure and document the positive effects of essential oils.

Quality is a very important factor when you are choosing essential oils. There is a difference in the frequency of an essential oil, depending on how and where the plant is grown, when and how it is harvested, how it is distilled, and how it is packaged. Essential oils made from organically grown plants with a slow steam distilling process are best. Plants, like all living things, have Chi, and organically grown plants have more vibrant Chi than those that are grown with the use of chemicals and fertilizers.

Research has shown the frequency of the organically grown plants to be superior.[8] Each essential oil has a unique frequency measured in hertz. Essential oils have frequencies between 52 and 320 hertz, versus that of processed/canned food at 0 hertz, fresh produce at 15 hertz, dry herbs from 12-22 hertz, and fresh herbs from 20-27 hertz. Oils that have a frequency of over 100 hertz are spiritual oils (rose is 320) and are good oils to use in Feng Shui. Oils under 100 hertz work better on the physical body.

---

[8]    Research done by Tainio Technology.

In Feng Shui, essential oil can be used for working to change the overall frequency of the environment, and in rituals[9] as well. Mix nine drops of essential oil with four ounces of distilled water in a spray bottle. The oil can be chosen intuitively or by dowsing. Below are blends that can be used in Feng Shui cures.

### Healing Fragrances[10]

If there are children around and there is a sense of chaos, use a blend called *peace and calming* comprised of the following oils: citrus, ylang ylang, tanactum, and patchouli. After spraying it, the energy settles, the children calm down, and there is a sense of tranquility.

Use *purification*: a blend of citronella, lemon grass, lavender, and melaluca when there is a sense of a negative or heavy frequency in the work place, heavy frequencies may even be caused by the staff holding negative thoughts toward each other.

At home, if an argument has transpired, use the single oil pepper to clear the negative energy from the atmosphere; then, follow that with *purification* or *peace and calming.* Here again, you can either dowse or use your intuition to determine which oils to use.

You can use a variety of essential oils in a ritual to elevate the energetic vibration of your home or office. This can be done when moving into a new home or office; for releasing spirits or entities that are present; or for a general cleansing of the space's energy. *Release,* a blend of ylang ylang, lavender, geranium, and sandalwood, works well for any negative or dense energies that might be present. If there is negative spirit energy present, first use essential oil of pepper, then follow with *purification* to cleanse and create new life energy.

---

9    *Please refer to "The Magic of Ritual and Feng Shui," p. 369.*

10    *Please refer to order pages for more fragrance information.*

The following is a general guideline for performing your own ritual.

Use a prayer or chant to call *the forces* (angels, guardians, spirit helpers, whatever your belief system may be) to assist you.

Clearly state the intention for doing the ritual utilizing your senses (visual, auditory, and kinesthetic predominantly), take several minutes to set this intention.

Move through each of the areas of the Bagua, begin at the front door and continue in a clockwise manner.[11]

At each area (Gua) of the Bagua, spray release nine times and focus your intention on releasing any energies that are stagnant or holding back your progress in the specific area of life represented by the Bagua. Then spray *purification* nine times. Focus your intention during this phase on new energies that you want to manifest in this life area. Here again, use the senses (visual, auditory, and kinesthetic) to create a powerful visualization.

A prayer of thanks or a chant is then said before moving on to the next energy area (Gua). Move through each area of the Bagua until you reach the starting point.

To complete the ritual, focus your attention on the energy of the entire home or office and spray *release* nine times to release any negative energy left. Then spray *purification* nine times and visualize positive and supportive energies manifesting.

Finish the ritual with a closing prayer or chant. This ritual is most effective when done between 11 and 1 (a.m. or p.m.)

If you want to sell your home and release any energy you have attached to it, use the following blends of essential oils: *forgiveness:* rose, melissa, helichrysum, and angelica, as well as *release,* and *purification.*

---

[11]   *You may want to follow the traditional order of Tracing the Nine Stars, please refer to "Spirituality and Feng Shui," p. 357*

Before beginning the ritual, remove any pictures or other items that personalize your home. By packing these items you set the intention to sell your home and move.

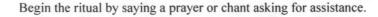

Begin the ritual by saying a prayer or chant asking for assistance.

Start at the front door, and proceed as in the above ritual, moving in a clockwise direction through each area of the Bagua.

Focus on the energy of that Gua and the experiences related to that particular area. Spray forgiveness nine times and focus your intention on forgiving yourself and others. Then spray *release* nine times and see those experiences being healed and released. Spray purification nine times to shift the energy of the space and prepare it to be received by a new owner. Say a short prayer in this area of the home and proceed to the next energy area of the Bagua.

When you have completed all areas of the Bagua, focus your attention on the energy of the entire house. Spray *forgiveness* nine times, *release* nine times, and purification nine times. Visualize the entire home as one energy field. See your energy as the owner being totally released from the house, and a new energy coming in.

Say a closing prayer thanking yourself and all others (persons in physical form as well as those is spirit form) for assisting you.

Essential oils provide a tool for you to balance the frequency of your home or office on a daily basis. Their use brings a smile to your face and balance to the space.[12]

Understanding how EMF's are generated and what their effects are is the first step toward solving the problem. If the problems of EMF's and electrostatic fields are left unaddressed, there will always be disharmonious energy in the space. There are many different tools available to use for electromagnetic fields in homes or offices. One of the most pleasant is using essential oils. They are not only an excellent cure for Feng Shui, but they also keep you feeling vibrant and alive.

---

[12]  *True! The use of fragrance is a wonderful "scentual" Feng Shui cure for many different energy problems.*

# Feng Shui and Children

## Susan H. Ruzicka

Everything in the universe is energy. Children are especially receptive to the movement of energy in their environment. Feng Shui adjustments can be used very effectivly to create a supportive environment which nurtures the child and promotes growth of mind, body, and spirit.[1]

The age of the child is an important consideration in using Feng Shui cures. Children two to twelve years of age show an immediate outward response to adjustments, so a gradual implementation of Feng Shui changes is recommended. Too many changes made at one time can create a chaotic environment. Be aware of how the energy of the adjustments is affecting your child.

> *During one consultation, four children, ages three to six, were present (only one lived in the home). They were playing and running around. There was a front/back door alignment problem,[2] so the Chi was moving too fast. As I did the heart calming mantra,[3] all four children stopped in their tracks and were quiet. As I made adjustments with the client, the children's behavior remained calm. Two days after the consultation, the client called and reported fewer fights and arguments than before, and the children played more quietly when indoors.*

---

[1]  *Children are more receptive to energy flow because they have not yet internalized the Western rationalistic mind set, which teaches us to negate what cannot be explained about the energetic realm.*

[2]  *The problem arises when there is a direct path between the front and back doors. When you walk in the front, your eyes focus directly through to the back sliding glass doors and the outside. If your line of vision follows this path, Chi will too. Please also refer to "The Room of First Impression," p. 207.*

[3]  *Please refer to "The Magic of Ritual and Feng Shui," p. 369 and "Spirituality and Feng Shui," p. 357.*

Children can participate with their parents in making Feng Shui adjustments. Children ages four to six seem especially receptive to doing the three secrets reinforcement.[4] Several clients related that their children were repeating the six true words: "Om Ma Ni Pad Me Hum" *daily* in the area where adjustments had been made. The children had sensed deeply the power of the adjustments and the ritual in combination.

## Implementing Feng Shui Adjustments for Children

### Bedroom Placement

The placement of the child's bedroom can have a significant effects on his/her psychological growth. The parent's bedroom should always be located in the command position. The command position is the room furthest from the front door but within the Bagua.[5] It is the position of control for the home. A child whose bedroom is located there *runs the home*. What is this doing to the child? Feeling the energy of being in charge carries a lot of responsibility. The child then tries to live up to a task which is beyond his/her age and capabilities. The child may be acting too grown up and missing his/her childhood. This situation may also manifest as low self-esteem or behavior problems like: temper tantrums, controlling and manipulative tendencies, and/or pouting.

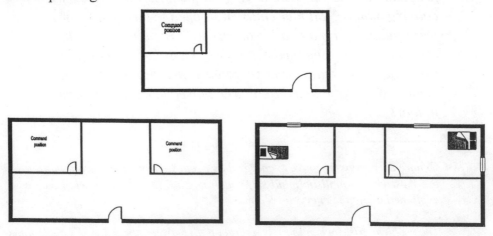

---

4    *Please refer to "The Magic of Ritual and Feng Shui," p. 369 and "Spirituality and Feng Shui," p. 357.*

5    *Please refer to "The Bagua," p. 35*

In the top illustration, the command position is located in the left back corner of the house, the wealth section of the Bagua. Notice that the front door is on the right side. In the lower left illustration, the front door is in the middle; therefore, both rooms are in the command position. In this last case, as in the lower right graphic, the parents should use the larger of the two rooms and place their bed in the command position of the room.

Think about your own childhood. Was your bedroom in the command position of your home? Recall experiences that you had in this house/room. How did you feel about your capabilities? What was your relationship with your parents like? Many times parents who had their childhood bedrooms in the command position will put their child in this same position.

It is in the best interest of the child to change the location of his/her bedroom. Approach the issue of changing bedrooms with your child by citing the benefits of the new location. Involve the child in the moving process. Do not move the child's belongings without his/her permission. A good bedroom placement for young children up to the age of twelve is in the *children* section of the Bagua. The energy of this area is more supportive and stimulates creativity.

*I have many wonderful stories of parents that have regained control over their home and their lives after moving the child out of the command position. Parents are happier and so are the children. One mother stated that her child was beginning to act like a child again instead of like a worried small-adult. By moving the bedroom, the child is able to evolve at a rate that is more in line with his/her age. He/She is faced with the energy of children's issues instead of feeling the pressure of adult issues.*

If moving the bedroom is impossible, another cure is to place a picture of the parents or guardians in the child's bedroom.

> *One client had a teenage daughter whose bedroom was in the command position. He placed a picture of his wife and himself in his daughter's bedroom where she could not see it. Within twenty-four hours, she came to her father and asked if she could change her bedroom to another room in the house.*

Another bedroom placement that is inappropriate for children is one that falls outside of the main Bagua. The child may not feel safe in his/her room. There will be a sense of separation and loneliness, and he/she will not want to sleep in his/her bedroom. (Does your child end up in your bed more often than his/her own?)

Again, the best cure is to move the child's bedroom to one that is inside the energy of the Bagua but not in the command position.

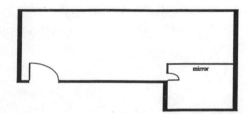

If there is not another room available, place a mirror on the wall nearest the inside of the Bagua to reflect and symbolically pull the room back inside.

**Furniture**

Children's furniture should not be an afterthought; it has a significant impact on the child. The furniture should be scaled to size for children so they can reach the top of the dresser, chest, book shelf, and toy hutch. This allows children to have control of their own room. This sense of control leads to sound psychological patterns of self confidence, positive self-esteem, and expansive creativity.

Spaciousness from the child's viewpoint is also important. What may feel spacious to you may not be for the child. Get down to a child's eye level and view the room from there.

Bunk beds, though seemingly practical, are not a good option for children. The child sleeping on the top does not feel safe, while the child on the bottom feels overpowered. In addition, many bunk beds are constructed of metal. These metal bunk beds hold a high electromagnetic field that may prevent the child from sleeping restfully. Separate the bunks into twin beds, or if that cannot be done, find another style bed.

## Clutter

Clutter is typical in American homes. What is in our space often reflects what is going on inside us. When there is clutter on the *outside,* there is usually clutter on the *inside*. For the child, a cluttered environment can lead to confusion, inability to focus, frustration, and disempowerment, especially for those children with attention problems.

A child needs a space that is orderly and has definite boundaries. You and your child can work together in the space (whether it be their bedroom or a common living area) with the intent of clearing and organizing that spot. Work on a specific and manageable area so you both can see immediate results and not become overwhelmed with the task.

This cleaning and organizing can spur a similar process on an inner, emotional level. Use this opportunity to teach your child that everything has a birth, a growth, and a death cycle. By releasing things you no longer need, you are making space for new experiences to enter.

## Front Door Entry

**Whoever enters the front door is
the master of the house.**

In many homes, the owners enter through the garage or the back door. In most cases, the children enter through the front door more often than the adults. So, guess who is in charge of things? If the child is also in the command position bedroom, he/she has double power for running things in the household.

It is important that the adults enter the house through the front door at least several times a week. This will bring a major shift of energy in the family's group dynamics. The parents will be putting themselves back in charge.

## Electromagnetic Fields

Many children's bedrooms are filled with electronic devices: a computer, television, video machine, and telephone. This creates a space with a high electromagnetic field (EMF) that prevents sound and restful sleep. High EMF's are linked to hyperactivity, tiredness, allergies, headaches, eye problems, depression, the inability to stay focused, and chronic disease.[6]

The best solution is to remove electronic devices from the bedroom. If not, the next best solution is to shut off the electrical power to the room at the fuse box or unplug the devices before going to sleep. This will create a sleeping space that has no electrical energy, thereby making it a space where the body can fully relax.

## Fragrances

Essential oils contain bio-electric properties that change the energy field of a room. They are wonderful Feng Shui cures for children, who are especially receptive to their energies. When sprayed in the air, they will quickly shift the energy in the room.[7] Used in a diffuser, they help maintain a constant energy in the space. They can also be applied on the body but must first be mixed with a carrier/base oil like almond.

There are many Feng Shui adjustments that can help support your child's healthy growth in life and love. But in the excitement of making these changes, remember to be sensitive to your child's responses to the adjustments you make. It is easy to forget how sensitive and vulnerable children are. Before you begin, write in a journal the specific behaviors that you notice about your children and yourself. As you make the Feng Shui adjustments, note the changes of behavior. Review your journal entries periodically, and you will see some surprisingly good changes in your home's Feng Shui.

---

[6] *For an indepth look at EMF's and solutions for them, please refer to "Energy Fields, Feng Shui, and Fragrances," p. 339.*

[7] In a spray bottle, add nine total drops of the essential oil mixture to 4 oz. of distilled water. The frequency of the oil is not altered when mixed with distilled water.

# Feng Shui
# for the Spirit

# Spirituality and Feng Shui

## Crystal Chu

Black Sect Tantric Buddhist (BTB) Feng Shui, as taught by Master Lin Yun, includes three features that are unique and different from all other traditional Feng Shui approaches: the incorporation of contemporary science and Western knowledge, the concept of visible and invisible elements, and the use of transcendental cures and blessings, which is the spiritual aspect of Feng Shui.

Since ancient times, humans have found ways to harmonize themselves with nature, the universe, and their living and working environments. Over time, their experiences, wisdom, and knowledge were systematically incorporated into a body of knowledge called Feng Shui.

### Feng Shui is choosing and creating the most suitable living and working environment

Due to the vast distances in ancient China and the lack of communication between territories, many different schools of Feng Shui developed. They were based on similar universal knowledge but developed different approaches and techniques. Traditional schools of Feng Shui are based on such factors as a person's numerology and fate along with the cardinal points of the compass combined with the topography of the land and building layout. They place more emphasis on the visible elements, concepts you can see. Professor Lin developed and created his own school of Feng Shui, which uses similar conventional, *visible* approaches and also incorporates the *invisible* or transcendental/spiritual aspect.[1]

---

[1]    Though these teachings are labeled Black Sect Tantric Buddhist Feng Shui, you can practice it no matter what your religious belief or religion is. You can visualize your own deity, omnipresent source, God, Nature and/or Universal Energy.

| INVISIBLE ELEMENTS | VISIBLE ELEMENTS | |
|---|---|---|
| 1. Three Secrets Reinforcement<br>2. The Ever-Changing Eight Trigrams(Bagua)<br>3. Interior House Ch'i Adjustment<br>4. Exterior House Ch'i Adjustment<br>5. Blessing -- The Turning Dharma Wheel<br>6. Blessing -- Tracing the Nine Star Path<br>7. Blessing -- The Eight Door Wheel Arrangement<br>8. Blessing -- Site Purification<br>  - demolition<br>  - ground breaking<br>  - grand opening<br>  - wedding<br>  - others<br>9. Predecessor's Situation<br>  - injury/death v.s. longevity<br>  - moving to a smaller house v.s. moving to a larger house<br>  - lay off v.s. promotion<br>  - divorce v.s. get married<br>  - bankruptcy v.s. well-off<br>  - burglary v.s. safety<br>  - others<br>10. Others | 1. Ch'i of the Land<br><br>2. Shape of the Lot<br><br>3. Shape of the House<br><br>4. Floor Plan<br><br>5. Others | |
| | **Interior Factors:**<br>- position of the bed<br>- position of the stove<br>- exposed beams<br>- stair case<br>- pillar/column /post<br>- door<br>- position of the desk (studying, dinning, office)<br>- color<br>- brightness<br>- others | **Exterior Factors:**<br>- road/street<br>- bridge<br>- tree<br>- roof<br>- pointed roof ridge<br>- temple/church<br>- water<br>- telephone line post<br>- transformer post<br>- color<br>- others |

Professor Lin's BTB Feng Shui is a multi-discipline approach. His Feng Shui theories and practices incorporate contemporary sciences and such Western knowledge as medicine, physiology, psychology, ecology, architecture, interior design, and color theory with traditional knowledge, yin/yang theory,[2] and five elements knowledge. Spirituality is what makes BTB Feng Shui truly unique as well as accurate and powerful. This spirituality is the *invisible element*. The adjustments used are spiritual or transcendental solutions to *cure* problems.

---

[2]    *Please refer to "The Bagua," p. 35.*

[3]    *Please refer to "The Five Phases of Energy," p. 81.*

## Spiritual Elements of Feng Shui

### The Spiritual Energy of the Land

When you check the Chi of the land, you look at various factors, such as the health and condition of the animals, plants, and people as well as the events and spiritual circumstances surrounding them. Dowsing can be used to determine whether a site has spiritual energy or not.

> *The Rosslyn Chapel in Edinburgh, Scotland, a renowned spiritual center, was built in the mid-fifteenth century. The legend surrounding it says that the Holy Grail may be hidden there. Niven Sinclair, the founder of the Friends of Rosslyn, invited Professor Lin and Michael Bentine, the most famous dowser[4] in England, to analyze the spiritual energy of the chapel. The British Broadcasting Company interviewed both men about the energy flow under the chapel and in the surrounding grounds. When questioned about what makes Rosslyn Chapel so full of spiritual energy, the Chi of the land or its illustrious religious history, Professor Lin replied that it was due to the very strong spiritual energy or Chi of the land.[5]*

### Spiritual Omen of a Place

The spiritual aspect of Feng Shui is what you feel about a place. Everyone has had the experience of walking into a home or building and feeling very uncomfortable, although there may be no real reason for feeling that way.

---

[4] Dowsing detects the energy in a plot of land, and was used extensively to check land suitability before building a spiritual center. Its use was banned in 1540 by the King of England as it was considered an occult practice.

[5] *Please refer to "Energy Systems and Feng Shui," p. 275.*

> *You go to look at a house that is for rent or sale, and after parking the car, you find a hearse obstructing the entrance. The agent tries to open the house and the key gets jammed in the keyhole. As you exit the back door, you see a bird that has fallen from its nest...*

These are omens or signals, and your intuition begins to process the feeling that something is not right with this house. This is the invisible or spiritual aspect of Feng Shui.

## Transcendental Cures

To rectify Feng Shui problems, the Black Sect Tantric Buddhist approach is to use transcendental cures,[6] Xei-Tze method,[7] and blessings. The three secrets reinforcement needs to accompany any cure that is performed. The three *secrets* are: body (mudra or hand gesture), speech (mantra or prayer) and mind (visualizing the goal you want to achieve). These three tools reinforce the effects of a Feng Shui remedy.

### The Constantly Turning Dharma Wheel Blessing

When you are checking out the Feng Shui of a home or building and want to bring forth the best effort, a blessing should be performed. The Constantly Turning Dharma Wheel uses the six-syllable mantra, *Om Ma Ni Pad Me Hum*, which is recited in a cycle. Begin by chanting Om Ma Ni Pad Me Hum; the next line begins with the second syllable Ma Ni Pad Me Hum Om, and you continue in a rotating sequence as follows:

---

[6]   Mundane solutions are logical, easily comprehended, and accepted by the majority of people, whereas transcendental cures seem to defy logical and rational explanation. For example, if a couple has marital problems, a mundane solution would be to consult a marriage counselor, a transcendental solution would be to hang a mirror on opposite walls of the couple's bedroom.

[7]   Xie-Tze (literally minor additions) method solves and rectifies Feng Shui problems by hanging crystal balls, wind chimes, bamboo flutes, mirrors, and so on. These cures are easily used by anyone, and there is much literature about them.

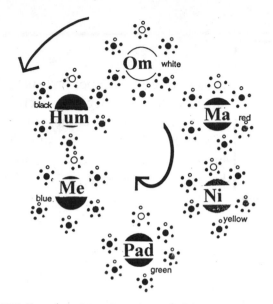

**Turning Dharma Wheel**

Om Ma Ni Pad Me Hum
Hum Om Ma Ni Pad Me
Me Hum Om Ma Ni Pad
Pad Me Hum Om Ma Ni
Ni Pad Me Hum Om Ma
Ma Ni Pad Me Hum Om

While chanting the six-syllable mantra in a reversed rotating sequence, visualize a wheel made up of a set of the six-syllable mantra. The set is each syllable in its own circle with its corresponding color.

| | |
|---|---|
| **Om** | white |
| **Ma** | red |
| **Ni** | yellow |
| **Pad** | green |
| **Me** | blue |
| **Hum** | black |

In turn, visualize each individual syllable of the larger wheel surrounded by a smaller wheel made of a set of the six-syllable mantra. If you can, move this visualization one step further and add a third level, another set of the six -syllable mantra around each syllable of the second wheel. This process can continue on to infinity. Visualize these sets of circular six-syllable mantra like a wheel in motion, constantly turning.

To use this Dharma Wheel, visualize it in front of you as you enter the main door of your house.

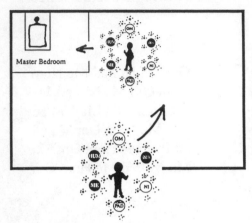

It can be used to expel bad luck, sickness, and any negative occurrences from every corner of a room, house, office, or site. It brings auspiciousness, good health, and prosperity.

**Tracing the Nine Star Path[8]**

This blessing uses the eight sides and center of the Bagua.[9]

It can be performed from one position and can be extended through your entire house or area, including the front and back yards by means of visualization. This takes practice and cultivation of your spiritual development.

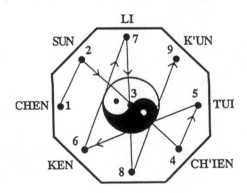

---

[8]  *I wanted guidance on what I was supposed to do next along my life path. I walked the nine stars on the new moon in Aries, which I felt was the most auspicious time for new beginnings. As I physically walked through each specific Gua in my home, I thanked the individual energies for their past support, and asked how they were to serve me during the next cycle, I asked to be guided on how I should focus my energy and expressed appreciation for future support. By the following full moon, the message was clear: The vision of the Feng Shui Anthology had been created. Jami Lin*

[9]  *Please refer to "The Bagua," p. 35.*

Before beginning, visualize the constantly turning dharma wheel with the powerful mantra in front of you.

You can begin on a smaller scale by working with the living room. You can physically move into the first area of the Bagua, *chen* (family) or just bring your visual focus to there. Visualize your whole family living in harmony and enjoying a happy family life and good health.

Now focus on the *sun* (wealth) corner and visualize financial stability and growth for your business or professional path.

Continue with the center of the house or space which represents health and the wholeness of everything in your life. Visualize and bless your family's good health.

Next, focus your mind on the *chien* (benefactors/helpful people) corner and visualize helpful people showing up at the right time and place to help you. Since this position also indicates travel and male occupants, visualize safe journeys for you and your family and that any males living in your home will enjoy good health, along with successful careers.

The next area is *tui* (children) corner. Visualize your children growing in love and health and that they will do well in school.

Continue and focus on the *ken* position, which represents knowledge and the cultivation of the family. If someone is pursuing a higher degree, or if your children are still in school, visualize them doing very well.

*Li* is the next position; it represents your fame, so visualize accordingly.

For the eighth step, focus on the *kan* position, the foundation or basis of the family (and career).

The last is *kun* or marriage corner, where you can visualize and bless your relationships.

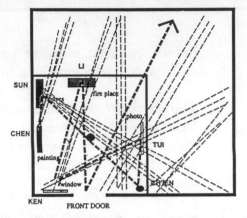

Professor Lin performs this blessing masterfully, incorporating the energy of the people present to further enhance the effect.

When Professor Lin enters a place, he usually stops at the chen position. He will direct the people's attention to this corner by pointing out a painting hung there while asking if anyone knows the artist. With everyone's attention riveted to this point, Professor Lin Yun will perform his blessings for a happy, healthy, and prosperous family for the occupants. Moving to the next Gua, there might be a table in the sun or wealth corner, and Professor Lin Yun might comment on the beautiful flower arrangement. Again, with everyone's attention drawn to the flowers, all their Chi is concentrated at the place that Professor Lin is blessing. He is then able to use this collective energy along with his powerful visualization to add more Chi to his blessings. With this method, he blesses people's homes, offices, and land which, includes the many aspects of their lives: their wishes, marriages, families, careers, children, and health.

## The Eight Door Wheel Arrangement Blessing

Another important blessing to adjust your home's Chi is the Eight Door Wheel Arrangement.

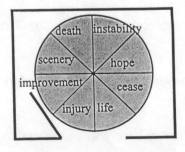

There are eight situations used to describe your luck: *life, injury, improvement, scenery, death, instability, hope,* and *cease.*

Of these, life, scenery, hope, and improvement are positive, and instability, injury, cease, and death are negative.

*To perform this blessing, visualize a wheel containing the eight situations spinning clockwise on the floor at the entrance. The eight situations should be arranged as in the diagram. As you step inside, use your intuitive first impression to determine which of the eight situations is the one you stepped on; this is the energy or Chi that is dominant in the house. If you step on life, internalize this energy and take it with as you move into the chen (family) area of the living room or home (either physically or through visualization). Then follow the Tracing the Nine Star Path route and bring this life into all the areas of the Bagua. Life is the most positive of these eight situations, and the energy you want to bring into your home. Therefore, if you step on any of the other seven situations as you enter, stop and turn the wheel until life is under your foot. Now that you have changed the situation and are bringing life into the house; proceed as above.*

## The Site Purification Blessing

If there is going to be a major event happening involving your home or another building: such as a demolition, ground breaking, a wedding reception, a grand opening, or to expel negative energy, you can use the Site Purification Blessing.

*Begin the blessing by mixing a measure of cinnabar (a reddish Chinese herb powder), nine drops of distilled spirits (the liquor and cinnabar are used to fend off negative forces and bring forth good luck), and a bowl of uncooked rice. Stir it with your middle finger until it forms an even texture; a mantra is chanted while stirring to empower the mixture. Visualize your Chi diving into the body of Buddha and then returning to you with the Chi of Buddha. In union with Buddha, you now possess the wisdom, compassion, and power of Buddha. Visualize Buddha leading you as you perform this blessing.*

Grab a handful of rice and sprinkle it outward. Visualize the rice feeding the roaming spirits so they will not disturb the site. Then, sow the rice to symbolize planting the seed of blessedness into the ground. While doing this, visualize an auspicious radiance coming from all directions from a myriad of Buddhas. This will assure that the event will be carried out smoothly, that your family or business will prosper, and that all family members or company employees will enjoy harmonious relationships. In conclusion, hurl three handfuls of rice up into the air, so as to elevate the positive energy of the family or business, bless them for peace, success, good health, and prosperity.

## Enhance Spiritual Growth through Meditation

The blessings and transcendental cures you perform become more effective the more you cultivate yourself spiritually. One way to do this is to practice meditation. Meditation will train you, broaden your wisdom, and expand your vision. It balances your physical and mental health, your temperament, and elevates you spiritually. In Black Sect Tantric Buddhism, there are many meditation methods, including the following Heart Sutra meditation.

## Heart Sutra Meditation

1.  Calm yourself by reciting the mind or heart calming mantra: *Gate, Gate, Para Gate, Para Sum Gate, Bodhi Swaha*, nine times. Visualize calmness.

2.  Visualize a *Hum* sound coming from afar. As it approaches, it becomes louder. The sound turns into a small white ball and enters your body through your *third eye* (that space between and just above your brows). See it travel down to your *dantien* (your energetic center located near your navel) and circle clockwise 9, 21, or 27 times.

3.  Visualize this white ball rising to your throat, nose, third eye, crown chakra (top of your head), and down the back of your neck, your spine, up through your genital area and back to the dantien. Repeat this process twice more for a total of 3 times.

4.  Make the small white ball turn red and see it rising again to your third eye. As it rises, the color changes from red to orange, yellow, green, blue, indigo and purple. When the ball turns purple at the third eye position, see it vibrate and change colors in the reverse order. Do this once.

5.  When the ball turns back from purple to red at the third eye position, visualize your Chi being carried by the red ball out of your body and toward an image of your deity or Buddha. Let the Chi of your astral body pay respect to Buddha, and enter Buddha's body through Buddha's third eye, and move down to Buddha's dantien. Allow your Chi to expand and fill Buddha's body. Visualize your Chi moving and causing the Buddha to also move.

6.  Visualize your Chi intermingled with Buddha's Chi, leaving the image and entering back into your energetic body, then into your physical body. Now, Buddha is you and you are Buddha. You are in union with Buddha as one entity. You have Buddha's perfect wisdom, great compassion, infinite power, color, and image.

7.  Visualize a fire burning in your head, your body, right down to your toes. This fire burns away your whole body, leaving the Buddha's Chi.

8.  Visualize a large eight-petaled lotus flower growing from your feet up, creating a new you, fresh and purified. Visualize another eight-petaled lotus flower blooming in your heart. On top of this lotus flower are two disks. One is a white disk or sun and the other is a red disk or moon. The sun disk turns constantly while the moon disc is stationary. Both disks radiate Buddha's light.

9.  Visualize your Buddha's light radiating to the myriad of Buddhas in the universe and the Buddhas' lights shining back on you.

10. Visualize your light shining on all sentient beings in the six realms of cyclic existence, releasing them from all sufferings, so they can be happy and at peace. Visualize their light shining back on you.

11.    Visualize your light shining on your spiritual teachers, relatives, friends, home, and offices. See your light filling up their bodies and/or the places and expelling all obstacles, sickness, and negativity. See them being replaced with good health, happiness, and auspiciousness.

12.    Make a wish and recite the *Gate* mantra nine times.

This appears to be a long meditation, but with practice it will no longer be difficult. This meditation not only builds your spirituality but also broadens your wisdom. It will transform your life, becoming easier, more smooth flowing, and happier.

Each home and building is unique, due to different energy flows, architectural design, floor plans, and many other factors. To practice Feng Shui from the Black Hat perspective, in addition to adequate Feng Shui training, exposure, and experience, you need spiritual cultivation. It allows you to make a thorough reading of your home, to help you properly identify all Feng Shui problems, diagnose spiritual omens, prescribe correct adjustments and cures, and maximize the benefits of Feng Shui with blessings. It does not matter if you believe that Feng Shui works or not. It has a great impact on your life and can bring you untold benefits.

# The Magic of Ritual and Feng Shui

## Helen and James Jay

One Autumn morning, we were getting ready to perform a ceremony and blessing ritual on our new property. Inspired by the beautiful day, our young son Anthony asked if we might go up to the high mountains to look for antlers that the deer had shed. His questions made us stop and reflect on how much more children are in tune with Nature's energies than we grown ups are. It is this intuitive understanding of the changing energetic realm that is at the heart of Feng Shui.

Feng Shui rituals are important tools for strengthening the link between our earthly, physical existence, the energy of the Earth, and the cosmos. When this link is connected, balance, peace, and harmony follow. Since ancient times, rituals have been used for celebration, spiritual connection, renewal, and blessing. The Chinese, for example, viewed their world as filled with spirits. Their rituals were designed to insure protection and favor from the spiritual realm.

The ancients had the keen ability to directly experience the energies of the Earth. Intuitively they understood their dependence on Mother Earth; they saw her as their supreme deity. Rocks, streams, plants, mountains, air, and oceans were considered her flesh; any alteration or destruction was an act of sacrilege. They lived respectfully on the land and left the Earth as they found it.

The ancients used ceremony and ritual to honor the Earth's gifts and to help them become part of the universal consciousness of nature and the cosmos. They consulted the spirits and asked for protection and bounty. Before hunting, they asked the spirit of the animal kingdom for forgiveness and later gave thanks for the take. Ritual was an integral part of their daily lives.

As settlements and cities began to surface, a dramatic new age with a radically changed lifestyle emerged. The plowing of fields and construction of living environments redirected the free flow of the Earth's Chi. New rituals were born to honor the spirit of the Earth and the changes being made to her.

Certain natural sites[1] were chosen for the special energy they possessed. Wells, springs, rivers, and lakes became common places of celebration and ritual. Mountain tops, valleys, and woods were also honored. This era heralded the beginning of *sacred space*. In this Nature-centered outlook, many rituals were developed and specialized for the sacred space selected. Each space had its own unique purpose and intention: fertility, healing, divination, birth, or death.

In modern times, people live within well-defined boundaries that are out of sync with the natural surroundings. Our large cities offer little connection to the natural world.

**The need for ritual and reconnecting with Nature and Spirit is greater now than ever before.**

How often do you walk in the park or spend time in the country? Do you ever take the time to lie beneath a tree to feel that overwhelming sense of peace and belonging that Earth gives? It is this sense of feeling connected that is at the heart of ritual.

**It is your birthright; you must reclaim it!**

How do you make your environment into sacred spaces? How can you reconnect with the Earth? Albert Einstein had wise advise. He said, "The significant problems we face cannot be solved at the same level which created them." The solution must *transcend* the problem, and ritual provides this link.

---

[1]     *Please refer to "Energy Systems and Feng Shui" p. 275, and* <u>*Earth Design: The Added Dimension,*</u> *Chapter 3.*

So how do you bring ritual into your life? The following are powerful rituals that can be performed to transform your space and your life.

**Let go of old attachments and bring in new energies!**

## The Elements of Ritual

### Offerings

All rituals should contain some form of offering. Candles and incense are commonly lit to offer light and fragrance[2] to the spiritual realm. Other items such as food, drink, flowers, evergreens, or personal items can also be used.

### Sound

Sound is universally used in ritual to call forth Spirit. Chanting a mantra or prayer is an offering and ritual of the highest form. A mantra can consist of pure, sacred sounds or *bijas* like the sound *Om*, or they may consist of words with a particular meaning. A mantra sends the message of the Divine into the environment and calls on celestial help.

In Sanskrit, the word mantra means a tool for thinking (from *man - to* think and *tra* - tool). Mantras have been employed since antiquity as a means of clarifying and focusing the mind, offering praise, thanks and gratitude, and calling on the spiritual realm for help.

Two commonly used mantras in Feng Shui are the heart-calming mantra: Gatay, Gatay, Para Gatay, Para Sum Gatay, Bodhi Swaha, and the six true words: Om Ma Ni Pad Me Hum.[3]

---

[2]    *Please refer to "A Scentual Reminder of Feng Shui Remedies," p. 329.*

[3]    *Loosely translated: I am one with Nature, I am one with God.*

The **Heart-Calming Mantra** or Heart Sutra[4] is considered by many to be one of the most important teachings of the Buddha.

> *Shariputra, listen carefully to these syllabic sounds which contain the entire Perfection of Wisdom, as a vast tree is miraculously contained within a small seed. This is the mantra which awakens every conscious stream into pure presence. This is the mantra of all mantras, the mantra which transmits the principles of incomparability and inconceivability, the mantra which instantly dissipates the apparent darkness of egocentric misery, the mantra which invokes only truth and does not acknowledge the separate self-existence of any falsehood: gate gate paragate parasamgate bodhi svaha (gone, gone, gone beyond, gone beyond even the beyond into full enlightenment, so be it!)[5]*

On the **Six True Words**, L. Austine Waddle in his classic study of Tibetan Buddhism said:

> *And no wonder this formula is so popular and constantly repeated by both Lamas and laity, for its mere utterance is believed to stop the cycle of rebirths and to convey the reciter directly to paradise. There is no mantra that can be considered superior to the mani, which includes not only all the functions, but also all the power and blessings of all other mantras. The learned sages of the past, like the great Karma Chagme, for example, were unable to find anywhere in the scriptures a mantra more beneficial, quintessential, or easier to practice than the mani; so it was this mantra that they took as their main practice. Even just hearing the mani can be enough to free beings from samsara.[6]*

## Movement

Bring movement into your ceremony. Dancing and ritual actions put the body in motion and involve you directly with the energies of the ritual. Hands held in a mudra or prayerful fashion crystallize your intention in

---

4    *Please refer to the Heart Sutra Meditation in "Spirituality and Feng Shui," p. 357.*

5    Lex Hixon, Mother of the Buddhas, Quest Books, 1993.

6    Patrul Rinpoche, The Heart Treasure of the Enlightened Ones, Shambhala Publications, 1993.

the ritual. These specific hand gestures are often portrayed in images of the Buddha.

**A mudra helps to evoke a calm and centered state of mind.**

Two commonly used mudras in Feng Shui rituals are the **Heart Mudra** (left hand resting on right, with thumbs lightly touching while placed in the lap 2-3 inches below the navel) and the Angali Mudra (palms held together at chest level similar to Judeo-Christian hands in prayer).

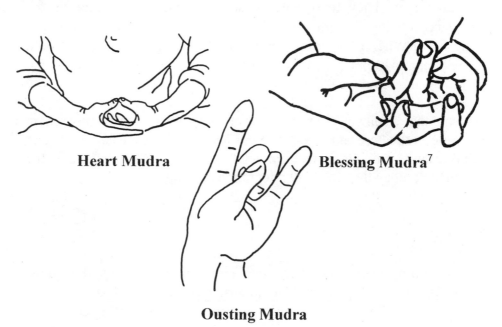

**Heart Mudra**          **Blessing Mudra**[7]

**Ousting Mudra**

Other common mudras are the **Blessing Mudra** (a portable mandala formed by the hands) and the **Ousting Mudra** (first and little fingers pointing out while the thumb holds the middle two fingers) which is used for breaking up negative energies.

---

[7]   This Mudra creates an offering mandala. The two ring fingers together represent Mt. Meru or World Mountain in ancient Indian cosmology. The fingers around Meru represent the continents of the world: the hungry ghosts dwell below and the high devas and gods above. Also above are the realms of pure form and formlessness, and the Buddha fields above the pure land.

## Intention and Visualization

Intention and visualization are the unseen ingredients that give the ritual its power of transformation. Visualization also helps to focus the mind and unleash its power to manifest reality. This brings to life the creative potency of one's thoughts and dreams.

## Three Secrets Reinforcement

Sound, movement, and visualization form the pillars of the three secrets reinforcement. They represent the speech, body, and mind of the enlightened being. The three secrets reinforcement is an integral part of Feng Shui. When performing any ritual or placing a cure, you should recite a mantra or prayer, hold your hands in a gesture of mudra blessing, and focus the mind on a visualization or prayer.

It is said that when you are mindful, every action is a focused movement of being in the here and now.[8] The unification of the speech, body, and mind enables you to focus completely on the ritual and give it the mystical potency that only full attention can bring.[9]

## Timing

Lastly, timing should be taken into consideration. A ritual is most powerful when it is performed at an auspicious time. Full moons, new moons, solar eclipses, lunar eclipses, astronomical, or astrological events were traditional times for ritual ceremonies. Also New Years Day, birthdays, specific hours during the day (between 11am-1 pm or 11 pm-1 am are especially auspicious), or any time of trouble or bad luck.

---

[8]    *Please refer to "Zen Feng Shui," p. 409.*

[9]    *In quantum healing, Dr. Deepak Chopra suggests that your thoughts are molecular energy that combines with such physical matter as furniture, accessories, or other cure items. The thought and item become molecularly connected through your intention. Master Lin Yun confirms that idea or visualization in this way, Feng Shui is 110% effective, while placement alone is only 10% productive.*

## Rituals

### Bamboo Flute Ritual

*The melodic notes of the bamboo flute fill the air. The listeners are transported to an ancient time, and the breath of the musician is transformed into a vehicle of spirit. Thus, the music of the simple flute made of bamboo has the power to lift our spirits and enhance our Chi.  --Anonymous*

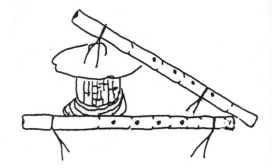

The simple elegance of the bamboo flute represents peace and safety. Traditionally used to herald news of peace, the music of the bamboo flute brought happiness to those who heard its beautiful sounds. In Feng Shui, the flute has many functions:

1.	It brings peace and safety. When still a shoot underground, bamboo already has its joints. This symbolizes the innate integrity of the bamboo. Although it grows high and lofty, it always remains humble. Hang flutes to bring a sense of peace.

2.	It provides support. When properly hung, bamboo flutes can lift any oppressive element. Flutes hung on overhead beams will counteract their oppressive effect. Always hang them in the direction of growth; this assures an uprising force.

3.	It fights evil. Flutes hung over the door can counteract negative influences of the first room entered, a staircase, and so on. They can be used to drive away evil spiritual influences.

4.	It can be used to accent any area of the Bagua.

5.	It can be used for rituals.

The following is a powerful bamboo flute ritual from the Black Sect Tantric Buddhism tradition, as taught by Feng Shui Master, Professor

Thomas Lin Yun. This ritual can be used when moving into a new home or opening a new business location.

1.    Place a bamboo flute, mouthpiece up, in an empty flower vase. Tie a 9-inch red string around the vase. The red string is important, as it symbolizes the removal of any negative energies. Performing the Three Secrets Reinforcement, chant the Six True Words: Om Ma Ni Pad Me Hum 108 times. Visualize the sound of the mantra infusing the flute with great spiritual power.

2.    Carry the flute and vase into all the rooms of the house or building. Visualize the flute bringing safety and peace and removing all evil from the premises. You may use the order of the Nine Star Path[10] blessing.

3.    Place the vase with the flute in a prominent place that can be seen upon entering the building. Or take the flute out of the vase and hang it on the wall. It can be used to reinforce an area of the Bagua by hanging it in the corresponding location. In order to enhance your wealth, for example, it may be hung in a wealth corner of a room or of the building.

4.    Again, perform the Three Secrets Reinforcement as a final blessing, and close the ceremony. Visualize that all is well in this location and that you will experience good health, long life, and abundance.

## Burning Ritual

Burning is an ancient method of transforming energy. As a substance burns, it releases energy in the form of heat and smoke, which then travels skyward. A burning ceremony is a symbolic method of letting go of mistakes and failures and ushering in a new start.

Joss[11] papers are brightly colored, ornate papers in varying sizes with special spiritual symbols printed on them.

---

10    *Please refer to "Spirituality and Feng Shui," p.357.*

11    *Joss translates into luck or fortune, when wishing someone "Good Joss," it is to bless them with good fortune, good luck, and auspiciousness.*

*Please see the author's biography for information on obtaining joss papers and in the order pages.*

For thousands of years, joss papers have been burned as an integral part of Taoist and Feng Shui rituals.[12] Different papers have distinct intentions: longevity, money, prosperity, good health, and fertility.

The act of burning these papers in a ritual sends messages to the spirit world, and you receive blessings and help in return. They are burned in accordance with your most sincere earthly wishes. This ritual is performed whenever you move to a new location, on such designated ceremonial days as New Year's Day, or in times of bad luck or trouble. One package is known as The Wish Fulfilling package. It is a bundle of brightly colored papers wrapped with a depiction of the 3 immortals of Taoism.

Here is a simple burning ritual that can be performed for financial or relationship problems, and which can also be modified for other problems.[13]

---

[12]   *James and Helen graciously sent us a Money/Relationship Joss Package. On the full moon, at midday, during the final week of putting the anthology together, Maggie, Rita, Elizabeth and I performed an "unlimited success and all levels of abundance ceremony" for the book, for all the wonderful authors, and for you.*

*On each new moon, I burn all the red envelopes I have collected during the past cycle, as I set the intent of my clients' blessings to help them manifest their desires through the Feng Shui we did. You can also burn sage, incense, or candles. Consider burning an old lover's letters to release unwanted feelings.*

[13]   The Taoist/Buddhist tradition of Raymond Lee, Feng Shui master and Buddhist priest in San Francisco, suggests not eating beef on the day of the ceremony.

1.      Go to your backyard, porch or balcony. If they are not available, use a fireplace or wood stove. Be aware of fire safety. Use a fire-proof bowl or receptacle, and have a lid or cover handy in case the flames get out of hand.

2.      Light candles and then incense. If you do not have an incense burner, use an apple or orange to hold the incense. Ask that spirits come to the light of your candles and accept the offering of incense.

3.      For money problems, mention the name of your business or job and ask for help from the spiritual realm to increase your wealth. For relationship problems, ask for spiritual help and understanding to create healthy partnerships. Repeat a prayer of your choice nine times while holding your hands together in a mudra or prayer-like fashion. Visualize money flowing into your life and that your relationships are healthy, loving, and strong.

4.      Burn the papers from the package all at once or in small groups.

5.      Perform this ritual during the day. The hours between 11:00 a.m. and 1:00 p.m. are especially auspicious.

## Creating Your Own Ritual

You may choose to create a personal ritual.[14] Sincere intention is the most important ingredient. Feel free to experiment. It is not uncommon to feel a bit apprehensive or nervous at first. Relax and open yourself up to new possibilities.

 As nature proves, everything comes full circle. What became of Anthony's excursion to the high mountains to find deer antlers? On that same Autumn day, we finished our blessing ceremony by walking around the perimeter of our sacred space, our land.

We traveled up hillsides, through thickets of manzanita, oak, and pine trees, enjoying nature. At a small bend in the trail, Anthony suddenly stopped in his tracks. On the path was a full set of deer antlers. It felt as though our ritual had been acknowledged by the spiritual realm, and the deer, no longer needing his old antlers, had left them as a gift to bless our new beginning.

---

[14]     *Please refer to "Using the Components of Feng Shui Cures," p. 65.*

# Self, Society, and Good Feng Shui
## An Experience of Guided Self Awareness

### Melanie J. Lewandowski

Think of a healthy and well-balanced society, one with abundance and satisfaction for each individual. This society would be safe and secure, with a strong sense of wholeness of self and of family, and with the world at peace. Know that this society begins with each one of us. We have the power within us to create the life we desire while contributing to the greater purpose of mankind. The method is simple, and the result is of great magnitude.

In looking at the self as the source for a healthy society, we begin with Chi, the vital life force. We are all born with a basic quality of Chi, and depending on life factors, the state of our Chi changes. Education, a healthy living environment, purposeful work, and empowering relationships strengthen our Chi. Involvements with negative-thinking people and living in spaces cluttered with the energy of poor self regard and past disappointments are ways our Chi is weakened. Strong Chi creates good fortune; weak Chi magnetizes misfortune.

Chi can be thought of as a vibrational frequency. Like high frequency bands that move information around the world through radio, telephone, and television, we too share subtle energies with those with whom we come in contact. We communicate with words formed of vibrations, through body language, and with the energy of our thought forms. Think of the times we are *on the same wavelength* with a friend, or when we meet someone for the first time and feel a sense of familiarity. These occurrences happen when our Chi is in harmony with another's energy.

Chi also relates to the energy of land and space. When the earth's Chi is clear and strong, good fortune manifests for those who live there. People report that after they consciously design their homes according to Feng Shui principles and raise their home's Chi level, good fortune spreads to neighboring areas.

*One woman reported that while achieving her dream of marriage in a short time through Feng Shui adjustments, she observed several single neighbors in the company of compatible partners soon afterward.*

*A person living in a row house spoke of the new sense of peace and harmony in her neighborhood after her Feng Shui changes. The corner drug trafficking virtually disappeared, and family arguments heard through neighboring walls were no longer evident.*

Chi of the self expands to the home, influencing and mixing with the Chi of the family members. The Chi in the home spreads to the neighborhood, which expands to the Chi of the town, the state, and outward. A change in the self ripples gently outward to influence all of society.

## Achieving a State of Self Awareness - a Meditation

As you delve into the area of self-cultivation and Feng Shui, take a moment to bring yourself into a state of awareness of your daily life. You may choose to tape this brief meditation and conduct this exercise while listening to your tape. When making the tape, be sure to leave a long enough pause between each visualization. You may want to have a pen and paper available to jot down your impressions when you have completed the meditation. Your impressions will provide a wealth of information about yourself.

Sit in a comfortable position with your hands to your side, feet resting on the ground. Visualize a small red ball pulsating in the area 1 ½ inches below your belly button in the point called the dantien. Feel the heat of this ball filling your body, clearing your Chi as if your mind and body are a clean slate. Now visualize yourself in your day-to-day life. (*pause*)

Notice the way you move through your day-to-day activities. Where are you and who are you with? Do you have a weighty feeling about the actions you take and the experiences you encounter, or do you have a sense of ease and grace? (*pause*)

Notice how you interact with others. Are you experiencing fear and anxiety, unable to be fully present with the situation or people at hand, or are you strong and compassionate in your approach? (*pause*)

Think of your family relations. How do you and your family members relate to each other? Is there conflict and lack of harmony, or is there a sense of mutual satisfaction? (*pause*)

Do you have a nagging sense about a change that needs to be made, or do you feel a sense of satisfaction, encouragement, and growth in your life? (*pause*)

Now move on to experience your personal space. Bring the presence of the red ball back to your dantien and feel the heat radiating in your body, clearing your Chi as if your mind and body are again a clean slate. (*pause*)

Stand at the front door of your home; open the door and walk inside. Notice the feeling as you move into your home. What visually catches your eye? Now close the door behind you.

Move slowly through your home, bringing your visual and energetic awareness to each of the following areas: the entrance (*pause*), living room (*pause*), den (*pause*), dining room (*pause*), master bedroom (*pause*), and children's rooms (*pause*).

Return to the front of the house, taking one last moment to embrace the essence of your home. (*pause*)

Exit, closing the door behind you. Feel yourself centered and complete. Feel the red ball pulsating in the dantien. Feel the red ball dissolving, your feet firmly rooted into the ground. Feel yourself stronger from this awareness and open for your inner self to guide you to the steps that are next for you in your Feng Shui experience. Stay with this awareness for three to five minutes.

**Notes from Meditation**

## Recreating the Self

When your Chi is strong, you are clear, bright, and self assured. You know who you are and are able to be in the essence of your wholeness with yourself and others. You become a mirror for others to positively enhance their experience of themselves as well as a positive example for social change. While there are many ways to guide you on this path, a Feng Shui perspective follows:

You display your internal identity through the clothing you choose, the cars you drive, and the way you design your home. The home is a visual, physical, and energetic manifestation. You are connected with the energies in your home while you are in it as well as when you are out in the world. In the way a mother and child always have a connection and a knowing of each other regardless of physical distance, a similar energetic connection exists between self and space.

While you update your image according to changing fashion, lifestyle, and body shape, you can also benefit from updating your environment to support your evolving inner self. A periodic look through personal belongings and asking if the items represent your current or emerging self is a valuable exercise. Personal growth is most successful when there is room for new experiences and their supporting energies to enter. Memorabilia from former partners, or *heirlooms* kept for obligatory reasons rather than personal desire, may be keeping you anchored in the past with no room for the new.

Feeling supported and centered empowers you in the ever-changing situations of life. A well-positioned bed with a wide-angle view of the door[1] and a solid headboard or wall behind allows you to sleep calmly and in an energy of openness and trust. This state will facilitate the clearing of Chi to be ready for the next day's experiences.

Bedroom colors also powerfully influence your Chi. A rose-colored bedroom brings the essence of romance and matters of the heart while light green or blue provide vibrations of hope and cultivation. Most auspicious for seniors is yellow, as it provides gentle earth energies of nourishment.

As you position objects around you to support and nurture your Chi, you can also align yourself through the direction of the breath.

---

[1]    The bed should not be in direct line of the door, however. *Please refer to "Feng Shui and Children" for information on the command position, p. 349.*

When rising in the morning, clearing Chi can easily be accomplished with the *Inhale-Exhale Breath,* a very special healing exercise from the teachings of Master Lin Yun and Tibetan Tantric Black Sect Feng Shui.[2] Inhale-Exhale Breath provides improved health, self esteem, and the ability to clearly speak for yourself. Also, it simply feels good!

> Positioned with feet firmly on the ground, sitting on the edge of the bed, bring yourself into a state of calmness. Feel yourself clear and open.

> Take a long inhalation through the nostrils, feeling bright, clear, strengthening Chi filling your body from head to toe.

> Hold the breath for a moment; then, exhale through the mouth with eight short breaths, then one long one. While exhaling, feel your Chi clearer and stronger, and feel that any tightness, anxiety, lack of clarity, or illness have been removed from your body. Continue the inhale and exhale sequence for a total of nine times.

> When this exercise is complete, it is advantageous to stay present with the feeling of your crystal-clear Chi for a few minutes.

> You will then want to feel your Chi firmly rooted in the dantien, one and a half inches below your belly button. You will feel your feet firmly rooted in the earth. As you stand, you will feel yourself connected to the heavens and to the earth, standing fully in your magnificence, able to encounter all people and experiences with confidence and joyful anticipation.

When you have been introduced to some of the ways to experience the Chi of self and space, it is possible to energetically define a way of enhanced well-being to live by.

---

2    Transcendental cures are only to be shared when honoring the tradition of the red envelope. *Please refer to "the Red Envelope" in the Glossary, p. 427.*

## Redefining the Self in Space and the Self to Others
### *A Meditation*

Sit comfortably and gently close your eyes. Take a few deep breaths and visualize yourself in your bedroom just after awakening. Feel the Chi of the earth radiating in the space and in your heart through the sun's warm rays.

Feel yourself calm and centered. You may even choose to do the Inhale-Exhale Breath exercise at this time. See yourself as strong and clear as you stand up and move about the room, feeling the connection with heaven and earth.

Notice how your Chi feels and what it is telling you about preparing for the day, the colors that are important to wear, the items to take with you, the foods to eat.

Experience yourself interacting with your family in a positive and peaceful manner, sharing the upcoming day's activities. Feel yourself interacting with your family in a way that makes you feel that your bright Chi is being transmitted to them and theirs to you. *(pause)*

Watch yourself moving through your daily activities with a sense of ease and strength. Feel the lightness and sense of purpose in the interactions you have with the people with whom you come in contact. Feel the awareness that with each interchange an empowering link of energy or Chi is passing between you, as if you were weaving a web of harmony with each person and situation. See the people you interact with moving forward in their lives in a more positive and productive manner. *(pause)*

Bring yourself to the end of the day and take a moment to reflect on the past experiences. Feel yourself accomplished and at peace. Know that your being is an important part of the universal plan, and that the world is a meaningful place for one and all. *(pause)*

Take a moment and see if your inner self guides you to any important changes you need to make at this time: rearranging your furniture, opening up your entrance way, choosing a color that would be useful to wear often.

Take that awareness with you as you feel yourself centered and whole, a bright shining essence, radiating warmth and filling your space with your Chi, and feeling the Chi of the earth and your space radiating back to you.

**Notes from Meditation**

With this shared information and a sincere desire, you can alter the course of your life and contribute to those around you. Lin Yun once shared, "Please take time before time takes you," words that are of great importance in this ever-changing world you live in. The cultivation of the self is the single most precious gift you give to yourself. A few minutes of reflection invested in daily conscious activity, adjusting the Feng Shui and Chi of your environment and the Chi of the self, can create a society of new, powerful consciousness.

# Feng Shui in the Age of Aquarius

## Cynthia Murray

We are on the cusp of the Age of Aquarius; it has been prophesied about and referred to in songs and books. The Age of Aquarius is now upon us. The approach of this age is creating an energy shift of such power that all aspects of our lives will change dramatically. We are entering the uncertainty that precedes the new order.

A pivotal dynamic of this new age is the relationship between energy and matter; it is said that energy will become more important than matter. Success or satisfaction will be measured more by personal accomplishment than material gain. Material success will be more a by-product of living in accordance with our higher purpose than a barometer of our worth.[1] We will rely less on empirical science and more on intuition.

As an intuitive art that links energy and matter, Feng Shui is an important bridge for our transition to the Aquarian Age. Feng Shui uses form to create energy shifts and uses energy to create form.[2] It helps us better

---

[1] *"Walk the Talk Now!" The work that you love is in accordance with your higher purpose.*

[2] *Energetic symmetrical form has always been an integral part of the relationship between the earth and the rest of the planets. Notice the energetic and planetary symmetries, courtesy of The Munich Planetarium, of the paths of the planets as viewed from planet earth.*

*Mercury*    *Venus*    *Mars*    *Jupiter*    *Saturn*

understand the connection between energy and matter. Feng Shui is a safe, comfortable, and understandable way to use the familiar material world to access the energetic or invisible world.

## From an Astronomical Perspective

Astronomically, the Aquarian Age relates to the procession of the equinoxes, a phenomenon caused by the wobble of the earth's axis. The entire cycle lasts approximately 25,920 years.

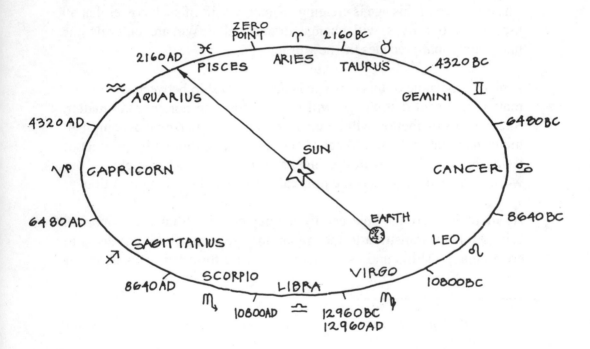

During that time, the sun, relative to the earth's equator at the vernal equinox, appears to move through each of the twelve zodiacal constellations. The period of time the sun remains in each sign is approximately 2,160 years, and it is called a "cosmic moon." The transition time, or cusp, between cosmic moons is approximately two centuries, and energies from both zodiacal ages are in play on our planet. We are currently shifting from the Piscean Age to the Aquarian Age, and we are experiencing the dynamics of both ages.

**The Aquarian Age is a time when:**

We will truly understand that our thoughts are energy that create matter.

We will rely less on material technology and more on spiritual understanding and intuition.

We will not confine our understanding of reality to information received from the five senses. Instead, we will become *multi-sensory* beings, increasingly aware of and in communication with invisible energies.

We will shift from a parent/child mentality, in which we rely on external elements for our well-being to an adult mentality in which we will take responsibility for creating our own reality.

We will depend less on external and traditional religions for our understanding of and connection to God.

We will become more aware that we can access divinity directly and that the Divine resides within everyone and everything.

## The Shift in Progress

In order for the new dynamic to enter the planet, current systems must be re-evaluated. We are currently experiencing the crumbling of socio-economic structures like communism and capitalism. In the United States, there is the impending end to such institutions as Medicare, Welfare, and Social Security. Job security is a thing of the past. Our medical systems do not promote true health.[3] Many marriages end in divorce and the traditional nuclear family has virtually disappeared. We are not even sure we can be parents anymore as we turn our kids over to day care and/or lobby for a twelve-month school year. Through this dysfunction, we are witnessing the breakdown of the current parent/child mentality by which we rely on societal or impersonal structures to take care of us.

Our scientific knowledge and technological progress have surpassed our spiritual maturity and personal development. Designed to improve the quality of life, technology has polluted our planet and contributed to the illness of living beings on the Earth.[4] Machines and appliances, designed to make our lives easier, have contributed to our feeling scattered, pressed for time, and out of touch with nature. Many of us come home at the end of the day only to interact with our choice appliance: television, stereo, computer, video game, telephone, or exercise equipment.[5]

**The popularity of Feng Shui is due to our feeling disconnected from the ability to create balanced, harmonious living and working environments that truly support well-being.**

## Thoughts Create

Thoughts are energy that influence the material world. The idea of being consistent in thought, word, and deed is an age-old concept reflected in many different philosophies; it will help us thrive in the new dynamic.

The connection between energy and matter can be used to create through our intention, whatever we desire: personal growth, improved relationships, a new home, or success in a lawsuit. Energy is impersonal and does not support achievement of spiritual goals over material gain.

---

[3]  *Please refer to "Using Feng Shui to Create Health," p 285, "Five Elements for Better Health," p. 303, and "The Energetic Basis of Good Health," p. 293.*

[4]  *Please let us be better Earth Designers.*

[5]  *Please refer to "Energy Fields, Feng Shui, and Fragrances," p. 339.*

### All is available.

Energy can also be used as a mystical tool, as a way to increase consciousness of a transcendent reality and to acknowledge the invisible. All is knowable through our connection with The Source. When we make this connection and live accordingly, material needs are met automatically, sometimes before we even know they exist.

In the past, those who wanted to pursue mystical learning would retire to a monastery or other spiritual environment. Today, the strong energy of the shift into the Aquarian Age has made this path widely available to all. A mystical path can be pursued by anyone, from a stay-at-home suburbanite to an urban business person during the course of ordinary daily life.

### There is great potential in using Feng Shui as a guide to the new reality.

Feng Shui has enormous potential to help people connect to their higher purpose. Becoming conscious about the link between the internal and external environments helps us become more conscious of our overall lives, our choices, our purpose, and our use of power.

The use of the energetic principles of Feng Shui to create material, worldly, or ego-based success can result in *spiritual materialism*.[6] This aim is not wrong; it is merely a low level goal. It is fun to use energy and form to create on the material plane. Caution must be taken when we create what we think we want, as there is the potential to pay less attention to our deeper needs. When we create from our deeper soul level needs, the universe automatically provides what we need on the material level.

---

6  *In Feng Shui methodology, all is possible through the creation of being in service for the highest global as well as personal good. The universe is abundant and unlimited.*

## The Aquarian Dynamic and Higher Energies

One aspect of the Aquarian Age dynamic is our transformation into multi-sensory beings capable of communicating and working with other energies. There is an entire "devic" realm that includes universal devas,[7] such as the deva of Feng Shui, and specific, local devas, such as the deva of a certain house. Anything that has form: a house, a marriage, a car, a job, whether visible or not, has a deva. The deva of Feng Shui is the same around the globe, while the deva of each house is distinct.

Devas are higher energies that actively want to work with us. We can connect with any deva, or with the Universe itself, at any time, simply by stating the intention and requesting a connection. It is important to ask for help that is in the highest good and to be receptive to and give thanks for the answer. Answers may arrive in the form of events, synchronicities, obstacles, opportunities, or *knowing* something, as this example shows:

> *I was typing a fresh biography to accompany an article. I was still connected to certain devas and ended the paragraph with, "Cynthia currently works and teaches in Colorado," except my fingers added on, "and in New Mexico." I had never worked in New Mexico, so I checked this piece of information with kinesiology,[8] and it was confirmed. Still, on that day it was not true, so I deleted the extra phrase and sent out the piece later that day. The very next morning, the phone ran, I was booked to lead a seminar in Santa Fe, New Mexico, and have worked there regularly ever since.*

Trusting the answers can be the most difficult part of the process. It is important to act on whatever information is received in order to develop the capacity to receive. The more time and attention given to the process, the better the channels of communication and the quality of information are.

---

7    *Deva is a Sanskrit term used in Buddhism to refer to a heavenly being or a "shining" light being invisible to humans.*

8    Kinesiology or muscle testing makes information from higher and invisible energies available to everyone.

## Aquarian Age Feng Shui in Practice

The Aquarian Age principle that commonly arises during Feng Shui consultations is the idea of shifting from the parent/child mentality to the adult mentality. In our current culture, we train people to treat outside authority as superior to that from within; we constantly seek validation from others. People must break with this destructive habit and trust their own inner voice as the only viable authority, as this example illustrates:

*Barbara and her husband had moved their regulation-sized pool table into the main living room; they enjoyed the game as a way to unwind and spend time together.*

*She wanted to furnish and decorate the room, but she wanted a Feng Shui recommendation about having the pool table there. She was primarily concerned that people would think the arrangement was strange or irresponsible, especially her mother.*

*A traditional Feng Shui response might also have cautioned her against spending too much time playing pool or valuing recreation over other pursuits. But the energetic opportunity was for Barbara to create a house according to her own values, not those of a judgmental parent or anyone else. The pool table was symbolic of Barbara's validation of her own life as she saw it rather than through the lens of someone else.*

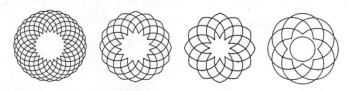

Feng Shui can also teach us to shift into a higher consciousness and gain a greater understanding that the power of our choices and intent will transform our lives.

*Sharon was experiencing indecision about how to market her new business. She had a free standing, arched trellis at the sidewalk end of a narrow path leading to her house.*

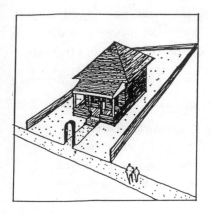

*The trellis clearly marked her property, which could be good for business recognition and identity, especially since the trellis was in the career area[9] of the lot.*

*On the other hand, since it was narrow, people tended to go around rather than through it, and new opportunities could be compromised. Sharon commented that since she had installed it a year ago, she still could not decide whether she liked it and constantly questioned it. This ambiguity was reflected in her approach to business. Within one month after removing the trellis, her vague plans turned into clear direction and she began attracting new clients.*

When working on a space, it is important to keep preconceived notions in check so as to not block the higher intuitive, energetic process, which is the true source of Feng Shui answers. For example:

---

9    *This refers to how the Bagua was overlaid on the site plan, see "The Bagua," p. 35 for more information.*

*During a consultation, I observed that the master bedroom of the house was outside the main Bagua.*

DINING  KITCHEN  BATH  BEDROOM

LIVING ROOM

BEDROOM

MASTER BEDROOM  GARAGE  ENTRY  DRIVEWAY

STREET

*My first impulse was to recommend cures such as mirrors or other connective devices. The client said that she and her husband loved the room, slept well there, and had a fulfilling relationship. The house did have a certain balance to it, and the master bedroom was in a power position on the property. Recommending a change here would attempt to solve a problem that did not exist, possibly communicating to the client that there might be hidden problems brewing, and doing so could create insecurity.*

## Feng Shui Cures as Energy Movers

### The Red Envelope, Please

The use of red envelopes[10] as a vehicle of payment for service is an illustrative example of working with energy and matter in either Piscean or Aquarian Age ways. The practice is intended to increase the energetic commitment of the recipient of Feng Shui information to a level that matches the energetic and psychic commitment of the practitioner. The envelopes *work* whether the client consciously understands the process or not; the act alone demonstrates an energetic commitment. This commitment is often extended or increased by using a greater number of envelopes and enclosing larger amounts of currency.

---

10    *Please refer to the "The Red Envelope," in the Glossary p. 427.*

## Mirrors

One common Feng Shui cure is to use mirrors to deflect intrusive energy. When the energy is impersonal, such as oncoming traffic or nearby oppressive structures, mirrors can be an appropriate and effective cure. When the energy involves people, there is potential for karmic complications through emotional involvement and attachment to outcome.

> *Jane was upset with a neighbor who harassed her, and she used a mirror to repel his energy and presence. She knew that it was important to see his energy as neutral, not as negative but merely as inappropriate for her space. She thought she could use the mirror from a place of neutrality. Her triumph at his subsequent eviction was a clue that this was not the case. Within one year, her building was sold, and Jane was looking for a new apartment.*

A recommendation to avoid karmic attachment is to send light to the offender when using mirrors as a cure to repel energy. The operative phrase of that cure is *send light*. In the Aquarian dynamic, if this principle is used, a mirror is not even needed. Another powerful way to transform personal energy is to breathe in and wish the other *peace, love, joy, and harmony* before exhaling.

## Mantra

The ongoing repetition of a phrase, the name of a divinity, or any other mantra is a practice called "japa." Japa can be used silently or aloud at any time to transform the energy of external situations and internal moods. It is mediation in motion and possibly the single most powerful spiritual practice because of its convenience and availability for use.

## Flower Power

The easiest way to clear negative energy and raise sensitivity to what is necessary and appropriate in a situation is the use of flower essences. They stabilize and clear the electrical and central nervous systems. There are also methods for using flower essences and various minerals for property cleansing and soil balancing. There is nothing mysterious or secret about the process. It simply requires the ability to focus long enough to do the work.[11]

## Guidelines for Thriving in the Shift

Following is a blueprint for moving into the new Aquarian age:

1.    Eat consciously. Whole grains, organic produce, and clean water create the biological quality that supports energetic work.

2.    Bless the food before eating. That connection to The Source energizes the food and improves your ability to be nourished by it.

---

[11]    *Please refer to "A Scentual Reminder of Feng Shui Remedies," p. 329, "Energy Fields, Feng Shui, and Fragrances," p. 339, and "Feng Shui and Children," p. 349.*

3.      Meditate or pray for at least twenty minutes per day. Develop concentration, learn to clear the mind, and make way for divine inspiration.

4.      Practice japa, the fastest way to transform the energy of any situation, including your own moods.

5.      Exercise daily. It is Feng Shui for the body.

6.      Use flower essences to reconnect and stabilize the electrical and central nervous systems.

7.      Spend time in nature. Breathe real air; get to know planet Earth.

8.      Act on intuition; learning to trust it insures a steady supply.

9.      Stop blaming. It undermines the ability to create a personal reality.

10.     Learn to release negativity and attachment to the past. Remember, focusing energy creates.

11.     Assume that everything happens exactly as it needs to.

12.     **Express joy and gratitude for everything and everyone in life.**

Everybody has an innate ability to create balance and harmony. The Piscean Age has created an abundance of specialists and experts in every field, from law to medicine. They jealously guard their positions and knowledge behind the pretense of authority and superiority. The rest of the people support this dynamic by giving their power away to these practitioners, turning to them to solve all their problems or filing lawsuits when things do not go their way. Consulting practitioners should be just that, a consultation. **The shift into the Aquarian Age means taking responsibility for your own well being. The power and responsibility for change and evolution lie with only one person, you.**

# The Bones of Your Home

## Carol Bridges

Feng Shui teaches that to be in harmony with yourself, you must be in harmony with your ancestral history. Your home gives you a unique opportunity to create this harmony by honoring its *bones*. Your body is built upon your bones, an inheritance from your biological ancestors and Mother Earth. Your house is also created from earth elements. The bodies of all living creatures that have walked the Earth before you have gone into making the natural resources and elements from which your house is made.

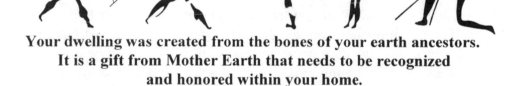

**Your dwelling was created from the bones of your earth ancestors. It is a gift from Mother Earth that needs to be recognized and honored within your home.**

To honor your ancestors and all that came before you, you might choose to set up an Earth altar in the ancestors area[1] of your home or room. Other good positions are the marriage area, which relates to the <u>I Ching</u> earth trigram, and the center area, which relates to the earth element.

On the altar, you might have a piece of wood or stone to honor the materials[2] from which your house is built. Perhaps, place a photo of the house during its construction and something to represent the land it is built on, like a pine cone or a stone from the backyard. You will intuitively know which objects are right.

---

[1]     *Please refer to "The Bagua," p. 35.*

[2]     *Please refer to "The Way of Beauty through Feng Shui," p. 267*

## Clearing Your Home's Energy

Energy from those who lived in your space before you may still be present. Clearing this leftover energy is vital. If the prior residents tried to make the home fun for children, lingering *childish* energy might impede your plans for a tranquil retreat. If the last tenants' marriage ended in divorce, or someone was very sick, patterns of this energy stay with the house until it is cleared.

Feng Shui offers many methods, from mundane to transcendental, for clearing the subtle vibrations left by past occupants.

Start with a simple, down-to-earth solution such as cleaning. Clean and scrub your house down to the bones; remember to *clean* with visualization and intent too.

Do a mental inventory of your possessions. Objects in your home and surroundings influence you deeply. Often you become accustomed to whatever is around and cease to notice their effect on you. Your consciousness receives millions of messages per minute about what is in your surroundings; make sure that all the messages are positive. Surround yourself only with things you love and truly need. Do not keep anything that intuitively feels bad to you. The desk passed on to you by a workaholic friend will not do you any good.

After a physical cleaning, perform a cleansing ritual. The following is a visualization you can perform to honor the past residents, neutralize any energy that may have lingered, and prepare your home for your specific energy.

*Imagine that you and a team of spirit energies (guardian angels, guardians, or however you choose to see these helping forces) are standing at the cardinal directions of the property; some north, east, south, and west.*

*Feel powerful energy gathering in your hands; you might imagine putting on energy gloves. Stretch your arms out in front and send strands of light across the property. Together with your team, visualize an energy blanket of light stretching from one side of the property to the other and reaching twelve feet underground.*

*Set the intent to clear all former energy patterns from the land which would interfere with your highest good. Then, lift the energy blanket, keeping it taut, moving it up through the house and property until it is twelve feet above the tallest point.[3] Now, visualize bundling the blanket, tying the ends, and letting the team of spirit energies take it away to be transformed. End by chanting: "gatay, gatay, para gatay, para sum gatay, bodhi swaha"[4] nine times, the most sacred number in traditional Feng Shui, or use a personal chant.*

---

[3]  *From Hermetic wisdom: "As Above, So Below."*

[4]  *From Black Hat Sect Tantric Buddhism Feng Shui, Please see the "Heart Calming Mantra" in "The Magic of Ritual and Feng Shui," p. 369.*

After your house cleaning and cleansing meditation, find an appropriate space in your home to perform *a renewal of the spirit* ceremony.

*Quiet your mind and visualize the hopes and dreams you want to manifest in your house. You are now setting the etheric pattern. You can use such things as a stick smudge of sage or cedar, a candle, and a bowl of water to represent the natural elements.*

*Call upon your ancestors whose help you need, recognizing their skills and experience.*

*Speak your intent, telling them how you want to live in relationship to this particular house and land. Invite the ancestors' assistance in manifesting your desires. When you feel complete, give thanks to your ancestral helpers and the spirits of the space. Then, Celebrate!*

## Honoring Your Ancestors

You can honor your family by continuing some of their traditions. You will feel more connected, rooted, and akin to the universal forces if you do a celebration exactly as your ancestors did. Or you might carry a cherished object forward in time, like an heirloom quilt, letting it be the thread that binds you to your history.

**Honoring the past puts you in touch with
the larger wheel of life.**

Create a special space to hang pictures of your parents and grandparents. One client put up a wall of photos of all of her women relatives at a time when she needed to recognize her female heritage to empower herself. What history can you joyfully acknowledge at this point in your growth? It could be your nationality or your religious history. Who are the wise ones of your tradition? Can you symbolize their presence somewhere?

## Using the Bedroom as the Focus

Keep in mind that even while you are asleep, you still receive messages about yourself from your environment and what you have in it. So, if you want good dreams, restful sleep, and a feeling that you are in charge of your life, Feng Shui has some suggestions.

Make sure your bed is across the room from the door, in a position where you can see anyone who might enter. Remove your computer, your business files, children's toys, or other things that keep your mind engaged in daily affairs. If you live in a studio apartment where space is limited, cover these items or keep them in cabinets or drawers. Make the objects you can see remind you of sleep, dreams, and the love appropriate to who you truly are.

**The bedroom is the perfect place to actualize
your dreams for the present.**

Your bedroom should provide total, relaxing comfort. Look around the room. What is the first thing you see every morning and the last thing every night? Do the items you see generate happy, peaceful feelings? Do they remind you of jobs undone? Irritations? Or can you say, "My space inspires me, lets me know I live a good life, helps me to remember my dreams and soul's desires." Your bed should support you well, telling you all night, *you are supported*. Make your bed, by its form and coverings, a place of total peace and a place where it is okay to let go.

The bedroom, usually relatively hidden and private, is a perfect place to live out your dreams in its decor. Be as creative as you wish. Learn from children. Their rooms often have fantasy themes that involve princesses, rock stars, or basketball players, planes and trains, or doll and animal families. Adult bedrooms do not have to be boring.

Allow yourself the space to dream. Provide sounds that nourish your spirit and textures that help you to experience sensuous pleasure. Create visual treats that you enjoy looking at each morning. Bring light to dull and dark corners. Clean up piles of anything; they are stagnating energy that drain your Chi. Build a meditation area or altar, put up pictures of a romantic interlude, and bring in plants to add more life force, whatever makes you feel good.

After a hard day in the world, come home to a place that reminds you of all that is good in your life. When you fall into bed, rest knowing that you sleep surrounded by the radiating love of your ancestors and the beauty and pleasure of your personal dreams.

You will find that your life takes root and flowers more easily than before after *getting down to the bones* of your house, recognizing its origins, and honoring your ancestors. The past has made your present place possible. Honoring this completed portion of the life cycle brings power to the place where you now reside.

# Zen Feng Shui
## Finding Place of Mind at Home

## Johndennis Kaiten Govert

"The most important thing for us in building our new house is to have it face southwest[1] because our relationship is our number one concern," said a couple as they considered site orientation of their house. "Of course," they added, "If we don't make enough money, it will damage our marriage, so we should face the house to the southeast to optimize our wealth. Then again, if our careers aren't highly visible, we won't make enough money to ensure that our marriage lasts, so of course we will construct the house with a red, double door to the south. That should make our goals very clear." After listening to my clients, I knew exactly what I had to do next: organize their scattered energies and determine their *real* needs.

The hardest part of Feng Shui is deciding what part of your life to improve first. Your house, office, or neighborhood are essentially mirrors of what you have chosen to do with your life. You may ignore these reflected images, thinking that they are something apart from yourself, when in fact your rooms and possessions are the most intimate reflection of your connection to the universe.

Modern Feng Shui practices are a collection of strategies to guide you on your life's path toward better health and longer life, greater riches, and happiness. The three Chinese gods: Wealth, Longevity and Happiness, are represented by statues or pictures in many Chinese homes because they collectively reflect the main aspirations in Chinese culture. A great deal of Feng Shui has been devised and tested specifically to help attain the treasures of the Wealth, Longevity, and Happiness triad.

---

[1] Within a space, specific compass points have corresponding life energies. Cures are implemented when that energy is not in balance. *For additional information, please refer to "The Bagua," p. 35.*

The Chinese place strong emphasis on the family: not only children, parents, and grandparents, but the extended clan as well. In China and all of East Asia, the value of the collective group is held in higher esteem than the individual. In Western culture, individual achievement has been pushed into the forefront. Romance, relationships, travel, career success, and having few or no children have become the most important life goals.

Whether these common societal values have an Eastern or Western flavor, each culture strives for something higher, something more transcendental, and Feng Shui is a bridge to get there. There are many types of Feng Shui inspired by Confucian, Taoist, and Buddhist teachings. Over the course of the last 3,000 years, Feng Shui has helped people reach higher goals: scholarly service to society, human heartedness, excellence in the arts, oneness with nature, radiant compassion, supreme enlightenment, and immortality.

There is a Feng Shui system, born of the union of Taoism and Buddhism, called Zen Feng Shui. In China, Korea, and Japan, Zen concepts were at the center of transforming music, art, and literature. Naturally, Feng Shui as an essential art of harmonious living was also transformed into a practice that uses forms, symbols, and energies to unmask the subtlest force of place, the mind.

Zen Feng Shui encourages everyone to elevate the goals they have chosen so that their aspirations are wiser, wider, more compassionate, more inclusive, and more aware. This can be accomplished by Zen meditation. It teaches you to look into your mind and watch it with fresh eyes. If you do not have direct instruction in this meditation, you may use the following Feng Shui contemplation:

> *Become aware of your surroundings. Explore each room in your home in detail. Make a descriptive list of what you find there, wall by wall. When you review this list, you will see patterns of what you are pursuing in your life. As you examine what you surround yourself with, you can discover just what parts of yourself you are cultivating: the common, the lofty, or the supreme. Once you see where you are headed, ask your parents, mentors, or friends to frankly deny or confirm what you have found. That is the beginning of honesty. The beginning of wisdom is when you decide to enlarge your aims to the next larger circle.*

This book has many insightful ways to improve your life through various Feng Shui techniques. You will find that some of the techniques may seem contradictory. However, if you experimentally apply them to your life you will verify that they work.

**All Feng Shui techniques have their root in the spirit of continually discovering where you are headed and adjusting your path.**

Zen Feng Shui is the moment-by-moment practice of making that journey more aware and more delightful. The following are six aspects to Zen Feng Shui, all of which are directions that can be used with any Feng Shui tradition, school, or technique:

## 1. Clarifying Your Aims:

This is simply the task of selecting the one tone to which you will tune your home or office. If you do not make this step, then anything you do from a Feng Shui point of view will only cause more scattered energies. Write down eight things you want to accomplish in your lifetime. Review the list, and select the top three that have had the most meaning to you now and for the next two years. Next, select one goal from this group that needs the most work over the next six months.

**That is your Feng Shui focus.**
**Everything that you do must advance this one noble aim.**

### 2. Emptying Yourself and Your Space:

Discarding everything in your life that you no longer need can further clarify your aims. Chinese philosophy and art point out that emptying your life is the prerequisite for filling it more swiftly with what  you really do want. This means simplifying your life. Get rid of 90% of the objects that you have not used in the last two years. Emptying also means purifying your space by cleaning the accumulated dirt of the past. Before you apply any Feng Shui technique, you should give your house a good spring cleaning. Do not hire someone to do it for you in order to shield yourself from what you may find. Do it yourself; it is *your* space and your mind you are purifying, not your maid's.

### 3. Energizing Yourself and Your Space:

This is rooted in the practices of Qi Gong. It means slowing down and systematically eliminating energy leaks. Examine whether water, heated or cooled, is being wasted. Are plants dying inside or in the yard? Is there anything broken or not working properly? Discover the reason and fix it.

On a personal health level, check that your own *Qi* or vital life energy is healthy and strong.[2]  If it needs improvement, consult a health care practitioner, personal trainer, or dietitian to help you change negative, energy draining habits.  Enhancing your Qi daily suggests that you be as straight forward as beginning or returning to a practice of Qi Gong, Tai Chi, Yoga, Gong Fu, or Zen meditation.

---

[2]  *Please refer to "Using Feng Shui to Create Health," p. 285, "The Energetic Basis of Good Health," p. 293, and "Five Elements for Better Health," p. 303.*

**You will know when you are making the right progress because
your vessels,[3] both your house and body, will have
the tranquil feeling and power of a sitting mountain.**

The last three characteristics of Zen Feng Shui are more difficult to practice, but they are indispensable if your aim is enlightenment or a well-balanced life.

## 4. Cultivating Daily Living as an Art Form:

As you move through life, regard each situation as an opportunity to express yourself artistically. Cultivate your daily life as an art form. When you serve tea, fruit, and cookies to a loved one or guest, arrange the food with as much presence as if you were painting a landscape scroll. Placing teacups purposefully on a tray, then onto a table is the prelude for properly placing everything in your house. As you begin to approach each situation and moment with this awareness, you will begin to rearrange furniture, rooms, yards, and walls with the same carefulness and attention. This practice will lead you on a path of discovering for yourself what is favorable and unfavorable Feng Shui because your own experience will be the judge.

## 5. Cultivate the Depths of Your Intuition:

The deeper you cultivate your intuition, the more effortlessly you will arrange things as they need be: be it an impromptu dinner party, a kitchen remodeling, or pruning the cedar in the side yard. Certainly all the fine arts are meant to cultivate accurate intuition. If you pursue oil painting, ikebana flower arranging, or bonsai, you will develop your artistic talents and train your intuition.

---

[3]   *Please note the description of the Anthology's cover in the opening pages.*

How well your intuition operates depends on how aware you are of all that surrounds you, however obvious or subtle. As your circular awareness widens, you will discover more interconnections between the universe and you. When pure intuition operates, any Feng Shui art you perform will be perfectly suited for you or anyone else you wish to help.

**Great Feng Shui will arise spontaneously.**

### 6. Resting Your Mind in its Original Place:

At the most subtle level, through meditative practice, you will encounter what is really your mind. You will encounter your original nature and how to rest your mind in its natural place without effort. As you practice, the enlightened mind will show itself as having been present from the beginning: completely, dynamically, and joyfully. At this stage of awareness, the conditioning of the specific places where you live and work dramatically diminish in their power to influence you in any negative manner. Everywhere you go, the places through which you travel, all serve to empower you with wisdom and compassion. This is the state of Feng Shui-less Feng Shui, and this is the aim of Zen Feng Shui as an art form.[4]

---

4    This calligraphy by Johndennis, pronounced "Hon Sho" in Japanese and means *"Original Place."*

# The Divine Plan

# Coming Full Circle

## Mary Buckley

The beauty of the world, which is so soon to perish, has two edges, one of laughter, one of anguish, cutting the heart asunder.
**Virginia Woolf**

My father was my first Feng Shui teacher. He would say things like, "Don't forget to plant a few white flowers in your garden; you'll see why when you do it," or "Have you ever noticed that the most colorful things in nature, like sunsets, and butterflies, or soap bubbles, have the shortest life? And things that last a long time, like rocks or wood grain, have a much less flashy kind of beauty?"

He was the first person to teach me, long before I had ever heard about Feng Shui, to pay attention to tiny details in the garden and woods, to notice subtle nuances in music or books, and to learn from things by noticing how they made me feel. It was a sort of meditative habit I learned from him. And it serves me well now. Feng Shui calls on us to notice how the subtlest elements of people's surroundings affect them: the sound quality in the room, the arrangement of colors, the air and light, the shapes and textures. As a sensitive gardener, nature lover, and philosophy professor, I suspect my father knew of this too.

He died about a year ago. I was fortunate to spend time sitting with him in his hospital room, doing anything that seemed helpful to make his transition easier.

I arrived with a lot of ideas and a few tools: a copy of <u>The Tibetan Book of Living and Dying</u> and our old Pentecostal hymn book filled with songs we had sung together. I brought photos of my daughters and stories of their latest adventures. I had quite a collection of questions I had always meant to ask him about his life, our family background, and so many of his feelings, actions, and choices that I had never understood

I came with my knowledge of Chinese medicine, Feng Shui, acupressure, massage, and subtle energy work. I brought a few sacred objects and Feng Shui baubles to brighten the room, adjust the energy, and make his experience more comfortable.

As it turned out, he did not want acupressure massage. He tolerated an occasional foot rub, but he was not really interested in being touched. He did not want to sing or be sung to. He did not even want to be read to. He ignored my attempts to brighten the room, and our family history was the last subject he wanted to discuss.

It was then I realized that my study and work with Feng Shui had been geared to creating an atmosphere to make people feel *more alive*. I had never been taught how to help someone become *less alive*. My father became my teacher once again. I gradually abandoned my crusade to brighten his existence, as I realized what he needed most was a silent witness to his death.

There were helpful things to be done: feeding him, shaving him, rolling him over, and holding his hand. But more than anything else, he just wanted me or one of my sisters to stay in the room with him, keeping him company as he slept or spoke about dying. He wanted someone to listen quietly when he said, "I'm dying, you know," instead of cheerfully dismissing it as a joke, or an old man's morbidity.

He seemed to know exactly what he needed, and it was much simpler and much more difficult than I could have imagined. I had to let go of all my urges to help him, to draw him out, or to create an enlivening atmosphere that all my training had taught me. I found myself inventing a kind of *negative* Feng Shui, a way of aiding my father by not interfering, as he progressively shut out the world and pulled his focus inward.

He gradually divorced his senses from this world; I realized that he was gathering energy for the impending burst needed for his transition. A sense of overwhelming awe overtook me as I watched him choosing death. He slowly opened himself to death as a desirable aim for his life, as something to be embraced as a natural extension of life.

My father fixed me with an extraordinary gaze at times, supernaturally steady and brimming with so much love and feeling that I could hardly bear to hold it for any length of time. My oldest sister said, "That alone was worth making the trip." I agreed. At the end of a week, I had to return to my home, my work, and my children. I said good-bye to him and told him I would be leaving the next day. He said a simple good-bye and told me he loved me. A few hours later he died, quietly.

For weeks afterward I traveled through my life with an exquisite sense of what it feels like to be alive.[1]

---

[1]  *With Mary's permission, I changed the title from "Death Bed Feng Shui" to "Coming Full Circle." Celebrating the joy of living is what life is all about, and Feng Shui is a proven path to manifest life's fruit. As our own cycle comes to a close, I myself want no regrets, no hesitation. I want to say that I experienced everything I could in the best and nicest way I knew how. And, most importantly, that I did it with my heart and with my eyes wide open. I want to be sure that I had a great time!*

*Can we "start over" right now.......*

I tasted food and felt textures with an incredible depth and sensitivity. Light looked different. I felt I had received the gift of appreciating the simple fact of being alive from someone who had chosen to forgo it. The sadness caught up with me only later.

I no longer tell my Feng Shui students that brightening up a room will improve it or that engaging more of the senses and representing all the five elements will make a place more habitable.

I tell them to pay attention to the unique realities of a person's life situation, to respect whatever presents itself, to stay flexible and receptive, to notice and honor their intuitive sense of what is appropriate, regardless of the rules.

I tell them that Feng Shui is something they will always be learning, and they will be making it up as they go along. Teachers and books will never really have the last word.

Graphics:     Courtesy of J. Ruth Gendler, PO Box 10153, Berkeley, CA 94709 ph: 510-525-7853.

# Starting Over

## William Spear

Feng Shui is a method of understanding the relationship between our external environment and our consciousness within. When properly practiced, this profound, ancient art creates a polarity between these two worlds, which stimulates movement and change. This sounds easy enough, but for anyone studying Feng Shui beyond the media sound bites and popular magazine features, one overwhelming truth quickly appears: There is a vast body of knowledge requiring many years of study, and confusion can easily conquer clarity.

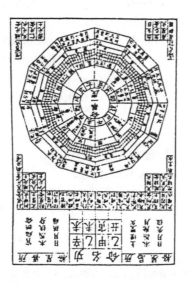

It has been said that no lesser sages than Lao Tsu and Confucius spent their whole lives studying the <u>I Ching</u> or Book of Changes, which is the basis of Feng Shui.[1] Indeed, their words are wise, but is their teaching practical in today's world?

More a philosophy than a science, Feng Shui defies description or a superficial approach. While it might be presented as a collection of universal principles, the wise student searches for deeper understanding by consulting the source, the guidebook, the <u>I Ching</u>. Posing the question, "What is Feng Shui?" more than fifty experienced practitioners around

---

1   *Please refer to "Energy Systems and Feng Shui," p. 275.*

the world recently sought guidance from the Book of Changes. The responses varied greatly, of course, but a consistent theme emerged which offers an essential teaching. Nearly every interpretation advised the *seeker* to keep a beginner's mind, to remain detached from any point of view, to let go of rigid thinking; simply, to *start over*.

The objections explode. "Go back to square one? Wait a minute, I'm no beginner. What's going on here?" Alas, our well-trained minds do not give up so easily. The ego would be out of a good job, the commentator replaced by the unsettling voice of "I don't know." We seem so sure of ourselves, so absolute in seeing the world the way we think it is, so fixed and determined in our interpretation that we call it *the Truth*.

Belief systems without challenge become the basis of a culture's unconscious destiny. It was only a few thousand years ago that we *knew* the world was flat. A literal translation of both the Qu'ran and the Holy Bible confirms it. People did not just believe this; it was an obvious absolute. Any fool could tell; just take a look out over that ocean. Get in a boat, lose sight of the shore, and you'll fall off the edge of the world. Why you might even go beyond the horizon! Imagine the surprise on the explorer's face when, with only water visible everywhere, Captain Courageous set sail and found himself smack in the middle of *nowhere*. The great adventurer had ventured into the unknown, experiencing the first, essential step on the road to any great discovery: doubt.

*Ubi dubium ib-I libertas*
**Where there is doubt, there is freedom.**
Latin Proverb

## The Inner Compass

It is heartening to know that many students and practitioners of Feng Shui want to make the world a better place, to contribute their understanding, and to make a difference where it counts. City planners as well as designers of health care facilities and schools are seeking input from experienced practitioners. The modern language of Feng Shui is cognitive ergonomics: how the physical environment reflects the way we think. Awareness of the invisible energies of electromagnetism has resulted in deep concern over the safety of advancing technology.

But the real change in the modern world is not happening outside us. We are in the midst of a major shift in consciousness. Research shows that most of us no longer see the world as a safe place, that each individual must move beyond chaos to order within. We are returning in large numbers to the guidance of *spirit*. Our inner topography is changing dramatically, and with it, our priorities and what we consider reality. We are finally recognizing that the illusions under which we have lived have become so big that we actually thought they were real.

*"Man experiences himself, his thoughts, and his feelings, as something separated from the rest, a kind of optical delusion of his consciousness. Our task must be to free ourselves from this prison by widening our circles of compassion to embrace all living creatures and the whole of nature in its beauty."*

Albert Einstein

## One Grain at a Time

Sand in an hourglass marks the passage of time in the same way we are changing. In the final analysis, Feng Shui is about changing ourselves.

Its teachings remind us of an order in the universe, a place where chaos theory stops and a cosmic design takes over. Feng Shui is about the individual, about each one of us in relationship to the finite world of time and space. It offers us the ancient view of an infinite perfection, the architecture of heaven embodied in the I Ching, and it allows us to examine more closely the assumptions we have swallowed whole about the way life works.

During such an inquiry, we find concepts that are powerful intoxicants for an aspiring ego. The mind's constant activity of bringing meaning to why things are the way they are is exposed as a full-time tyrant holding our gut feelings, instinct, and intuition prisoner. It is not until we surrender to a *higher power*, often in the face of great difficulty, that we are able to return to the teaching of the I Ching, that change is from the inside out.

Most educators in the field of Feng Shui readily admit that their personal abilities to teach, guide, and counsel emerge more from their intuition than their intellect. Those seeking consultation frequently comment that the advice given supported what they already felt but could not easily access. In Japanese, writing the word *intuition* results in the characters for *original ability.* It is the source of our own truth, our higher self, recovered from among the many messages of parents, teachers, friends, and learned behavior.

As children, like the people of *primitive* cultures, our view of the world was of *one big family*. Bringing two hands together to clap made a noise; unifying crayon and paper made a picture; placing one foot in front of the other moved us closer to where we wanted to go.

It was all so simple then. And as we remember to cultivate *a beginner's mind*, we are empowered to follow the words of Lao Tsu, to "give up learning and put an end to our troubles."

**Come forth, and bring with you a heart that watches and receives.**
William Wordsworth

Our role as teachers of this vast body of knowledge continues to be one of drawing out what is already there, not pouring in more. Listening, observing, and reflecting are our most valuable tools; gratitude to those who came before us is our most precious view. The *backwards facing path* may seem less enticing than the one that moves forward, progressing. But as our vessel[2] empties, energies like wind and water stream in. As we experience the energy within ourselves, nature constantly nourishes us. Rudrananda said,

> **"It is surrendering and stretching and reaching and taking in more energy that accomplishes the impossible."**

Every individual knows *the Truth*, and no one can possibly claim mastery of it for anyone but himself. His Holiness The Dalai Lama calls us to embrace a *spiritual democracy*, a deeply held reverence for the many different interpretations of the Way. The opportunity to study is not easily overlooked, however, by anyone seeking a life. Even Sir Isaac Newton attempted, at the end of his life, to reconcile biblical passages with astronomical occurrences. Modern physicists sound more like ancient mystics these days; great discoveries come from what Albert Einstein called "the feeling that lies behind appearance." It was his personal definition of *intuition*.

## The Oracle Points the Way

The main theme in the I Ching hexagram of Water over Wind is *self development;* the message is to return *to the origin.* Society is changing its direction, its journey. The symbol for this movement in the I Ching is Water. As we individually examine our path in life and collectively realign our innermost intentions, our thoughts and consciousness will be reflected in the external environment. Floods, tornadoes, hurricanes and torrential downpours reveal this shift within; they are similar to the way our goals of self-enlightenment and illumination change. Symbolized by the element of Fire, the outer atmosphere heats up with record temperatures and spontaneous combustion. Droughts, wildfires, and intense geological change reflect the inner tumult.

---

[2]  *Please refer to the explanation of the Anthology's cover on the opening pages.*

Could it be that instead of life moving from the outer environment to us that *we are the creators of our entire destiny,* that life moves from within us to nature, so that what is happening now in the atmosphere and society is the reflection of our collective consciousness? The organic opposites of Water and Fire, beginning and end, life and death, are manifest in our everyday world. Maybe we have more to say about our future than we imagine.

### A miracle, my friend, is an event which creates faith.
George Bernard Shaw

The principles of Feng Shui have inspired the spirits of thousands of people all over the world. Deep within each person lies the *possibility* for peace, health, and freedom. How we realize these endless dreams externally has little to do with the political agenda of the time, the religious doctrine of a particular sect, or the conceptual dogma of any specific culture. There are universal principles underlying all of what we do, a perfect order to this natural world of constant change. By cultivating the space within, each person reflects a different reality without. It is this place within where we will all meet. Songwriters and sages have long guided us toward such a reality. As we move forward, together, we will transform ourselves, and miracles will happen, from the inside out.

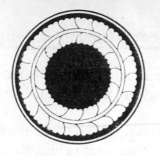

# The Divine Plan

## Jami Lin

When I asked my intuition how to close the anthology, the answer was the same as with <u>Earth Design: The Added Dimension,</u> which also concludes with "The Divine Plan."

### Life Is Your Divine Plan
### By Design.

It is a celebration that unfolds when you watch the magical coincidences of your daily experience. Whatever your destiny, Feng Shui and its spiritual energy can be your vessel for life's abundance.

As a slice of life, the magic and lessons I learned when working on the anthology were no different. In the early stages, very few of the contributors advised me on what subject they chose to write. As the articles started to flow, there was little duplication. Even similar articles provided unique information that added to the anthology's cohesion. Even without a specific plan, through their desire, their specific expertise, and hard work, each author magically filled in an integral piece of the puzzle.

At the final hour, several practitioners who had previously said, "no thank you," suddenly added their contribution, which I knew would provide you with great information. Just in time... perfect time!

The most interesting coincidences magically happened on the same day: Professor Lin Yun's foreword and Sarah Rossbach's introduction.

Professor had understandably asked to see the text before he wrote the foreword. The day *after* it was sent to him, the Temple called to say the foreword was currently being translated. Even though Professor previously had a table of contents, and yes he is an amazing individual, how did he write it so fast?

Could it be that Lin Yun connected to the anthology on the transcendental level? Did he feel the anthology's energy on the level of spirit connected by the earth meridians, on the web spun by the mythological goddess Spider Woman, or in Carl Jung's collective unconscious?

In the preface, I suggested that somehow "I was chosen" to facilitate this project. Did professor somehow know about my daydream? Did he plant the seed? In the spiritual realm, did he ask me to do it? After all, like all magical coincidences, it was just days after I performed *his* ceremony of tracing the nine star path[1] on my home while I asked "what should I do now," that I *knew* to start this anthology.

Wherever it came from, I was *supposed to* create a vessel in which practitioners could share their spirit, an anthology about expansion, a universal network, and how Feng Shui can make the planet a better place through the vessel of the authors' love.

A few hours after I heard from the Temple, the phone rang. It was Sarah, my first teacher, who had introduced me to the added dimension of design. After I expressed my appreciation, we giggled and shared life stories. She said she would try to write an introduction between juggling her children and the new book she was working on. More magic.

---

[1]  *Please refer to "Spirituality and Feng Shui," p. 357.*

Watch the magical coincidences of your day. Did the phone ring with the person you were thinking about on the other end of the line? How did you connect with them in that instant? What happened yesterday that magically lead you to plant the seeds to create the magic of today?

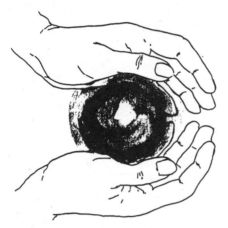

When you design your vessel to support you, your primary vessel, your essence, you ride the wave of joy, success, and wonder.

**Always take time to recognize and honor this magic.**

**You can make a difference in global harmony merely by happily living your dream.**

Again, I lovingly thank my Feng Shui friends, Maggie for her help, love, and support during every phase, editors, family, and most of all my very understanding husband Joel, for without them, *we* could not have shared this anthology with you.

# Glossary

**Acupressure** - the application of pressure to acupuncture points to stimulate/regulate Chi flow through the body's energy *meridians*.

**Bagua** - an octagonal symbol composed of the eight *trigrams,* which represent the eight primal energies of the universe. A note: the spelling of the names of the trigrams differ depending on the system of transliteration used. Please refer to the chart courtesy of Ho Lynn.

| Chinese Character | Trigram | Yale System | Wade-Gile System | Pinyin System | English |
|---|---|---|---|---|---|
| 乾 | ☰ | Chyan | Ch'ien | Qian | Heaven |
| 坎 | ☵ | Kan | K'an | Kan | Water |
| 艮 | ☶ | Gen | Ken | Gen | Mountain |
| 震 | ☳ | Jen | Chen | Zhen | Thunder |
| 巽 | ☴ | Syun | Hsun | Xun | Wind |
| 離 | ☲ | Li | Li | Li | Fire |
| 坤 | ☷ | Kwun | K'un | Kun | Earth |
| 兑 | ☱ | Dwei | Tui | Dui | Lake |

**Buddhism** - an religion of Indian/Asiatic origin based on the personal experience of Gautama Buddha; one of the great religions of the world.

**Chakra** - energy centers or vortexes that are located in the etheric body. They transfer energy between the subtle bodies and the physical body.

**Chi** (Qi) - the primal life-force energy that flows in all things.

**Chi Gong** (Qi Gong, Chi Kung) - an internal martial arts practice that integrates and transforms life force energy from the universe

**Command Position** - the most favorable position in a room for bed or desk placement; it should face and be across from, but not in direct line with, the room's entrance.

**Dharma** - the sacred law, the Buddhist cannon.

**Five Elements** -the five basic divisions of Chi or five forces of the universe; they are given archetypal names from nature: Wood, Water, Metal, Earth, Fire.

**Gua** - one of the eight *trigrams* or areas of the Bagua.

**Heart Calming Mantra** - "gatay gatay para gatay, para sum gatay, bodhi swaha" is used at the beginning of a meditation or Feng Shui cure to bring peace of heart and mind.

**Hexagram** - a symbol composed of two *trigrams* that represents a specific pattern of energy or human condition. It is the basis of the *I Ching* oracle.

**I Ching** - The Book of Changes; an ancient Chinese oracle and book of philosophy; it is based on 64 *hexagrams,* which represent all human and cosmic situations.

**Loupan** - a specialized compass used in Feng Shui that incorporates astrological, geomantic, and directional markings, among others. It is used by Compass School Feng Shui.

**Kabballah** - an umbrella term for the Jewish mystical tradition; a symbolic system of spiritual and philosophical wisdom.

**Mandala** - a circular, symbolic representation of the universe using geometric shapes and deities; it is used as a meditation tool.

**Mantra** - a sacred sound that is chanted or repeated during meditation or a Feng Shui cure.

**Meridian** - channels through which Chi flows.

**Mudra** - a sacred hand gesture used for energy transformation.

**Red Envelope** - a traditional symbol of exchange used when a transcendental Feng Shui cure is shared; the person who receives such a cure places a monitary token of acknowledgement inside and gives it to the Feng Shui practitioner. The purpose is to set the intent of the work and to protect the exchange from negative karma.

*Jami Lin honored the tradition for every transendental cure or blessing in this book. She asks that if they are used or shared, that you respect the tradition and send a red envelope to The Yun Lin Temple, the original source of the cures, or to your favorite charity.*

**Sefiroth** (sephirot) - the tree of life, a Kabbalistic symbol which illustrates the interrelated stages of the manifestation of God and/or creation.

**Sha** - negative or harmful Chi.

**Six True Words** - "Oh Man Ni Pad Me Hum" - literally translated: "Hail to the Jewel in the Lotus," used as a seal for Feng Shui cures and as a meditative *mantra*.

**Stupa** - a sacred structure built with the five elemental shapes which contain the five basic energies.

**Tai Chi** - the integration of *yin* and *yang* from which life emerges.

**Tao** - the Subtle Origin of the universe; the original energy of the universe that is incomprehensible. Creation is the expansion and polarization of Tao into *yin* and *yang*.

**Three Secrets Reinforcements** - the combination of body (*mudra*), mind (visualization), and speech (*mantra*) used to seal a Feng Shui cure.

**Transcendental Cures** - Feng Shui adjustments that lie beyond the rational realm.

**Trigram** - a symbol of universal energy composed of three lines; the lines represent combinations of *yin* (broken line) and *yang* (solid line) energy. The eight possible configurations form the eight basic energies of the *Bagua*.

**Yin** - a polarity of *Tao*; the feminine, negative, dark, static principle that exists only with *yang*.

**Yang** - a polarity of *Tao*; the masculine, positive, light, active principle that exists only with *yin*.

# Index

## Chinese Flutes:
Direct from tropical China, these fine instrument-quality bamboo flutes have the nodes and joints of true bamboo that give the flute its power. They are 21" long, and come with red ribbons for immediate use in your Feng Shui cures. They can also be used for meditative playing.
**See p. 375 for the Feng Shui Bamboo Ritual.**

___ Traditional Chinese Bamboo flute      $22.00 _____

## Ceremonial Joss Papers:
The "location clearing" package brings new energy to a location. These traditional, full color, ornate papers can be burned when moving into an new home or business, to drive away unwanted entities, and to invite protection. The "relationship/money" package enhances abundance. Includes: candles, incense and instructions.
**See p. 376 for the Feng Joss Paper Burning Ritual.**

___ Location Clearing Kit      $11.00 _____
___ Relationship/Money Kit      $11.00 _____

## Wind Chimes

___ SP: Spiral 22" long      Total of 15 chimes      $35.00 _____
     Gentle enchanting melody (Notes: A, B, C #)

## Fun Spirals:
Great looking Chi movers for your home or garden. Ideas: cluster them, hang at different heights, order different sizes, order the color of the element or Gua you want to enhance. Jami has 3 hanging in her garden!

___ 48 inch Spin      $14.00 _____
___ 25 inch Spin      $ 7.00 _____
(Please specify what color plastic: red, yellow, lime green, blue, hot pink, and purple.)

## "Feng Shui" Incense:
These are yummy and a fantastic value!

___ Temple Bundle: 30) 18"sticks that burn "forever"      $10.00 ____
___ Sandalwood Coils 10) 20-24 hour burn p/coil      $22.00 ____

## Sacred Geo-Toy:
It is an expanding(30")/contracting(91/2") sphere you can play with or enjoy as an object of art; it combines mathematics, geometry, and aesthetics into a magical motion of surprising simplicity, beauty and fun. A Blast! (Comes with a pulley for hanging)

___ Sacred Geo-Toy      $50.00 _____
(Please specify what color plastic: red, sliver, or blue.)

# Order now! Call toll free: 1(800) EarthDesign™
Please allow 2-4 weeks for delivery. See last page for Fax & Postal orders.
Please call (305)756-6426 for other inquires.
**Visit website for photos: www.gate.net/~earthdes**

## Feng Shui Jewelry:

| | | |
|---|---|---|
| ___ Physical Chakra Balancer Pendant | $25.00 | _____ |
| ___ Emotional Chakra Balancer Pendant | $25.00 | _____ |

7 traditional *"chakra"* stones: amethyst, lapis lazuli, turquoise, malachite, carnelian & jasper along with catalyst bead. (see electro magnetic devices) in physical balancer: green jade and rose quartz, in emotional balancer: tiger eye

___ Chakra Balancing Bracelet      $40.00  _____

Semi-precious stones, resonating to each Chakra are placed in "Chakra order" and repeated four times aligning with the moon cycles. Hematite beads at the ends ground the body to the earth while connecting to heaven energy. Jami wears one of these along with the next protection bracelet!

___ Quartz Crystal Protection Bracelet      $ 70.00  _____

Clear Quartz and semi-precious stones (carnelian, yellow & green jade, lapis lazuli and onyx-representing "Om Ma Ni Pad Me Hum" prayer) enhances aura and energy.

___ Good Luck Earrings:      $18.00  _____

4mm Austrian crystal stones-representing "Om Ma Ni Pad Me Hum" prayer- with antique brass Bagua. Sterling silver posts/hooks.

___ Bagua Pendant      $18.00  _____

Austrian crystal beads help neutralize effects of Electromagnetic fields and resonates with your aura. The Bagua charm wards off negative influences.
(Please specify wealth, relationship, career, or fame)

## Electromagnetic Devices: 
Dielectric resonators absorb and rebroadcast harmful electromagnetic radiation. Their molecular structure alters the frequencies of most harmful environmental radiations, neutralizing the damaging effects. Scientific brain wave tests confirm they also have a calming effect.

___ Crystal catalyst bead      $15.00  _____

Wear around your neck; a must for computer users!

___ Electric Smog Buster Tab      $12.50  _____

Place on your TV, computer, and any electrical devices that you have long term exposure to.

___ Cell Phone Tab      $15.00  _____

Place on your cellular phone. A must for cell users!

___ Tri-Pak Resonator      $44.00  _____

Neutralizes electromagnetic emanations associated with electrical systems and power line transformers.

## Astrological Charts: 
Please refer to *Feng Shui Today: Earth Design the Added Dimension* to learn how to overlay your local space chart on your home and office floor plan. Use your planetary energies!

| | | |
|---|---|---|
| ___ Natal birth chart | $15.00 | _____ |
| ___ Local space chart | $15.00 | _____ |
| ___ Natal & Local chart | $25.00 | _____ |

**Birth information:**    Date_____ Time_____ Location_____
**City/State for local chart :** _____

# Order now! Call toll free: 1(800) EarthDesign™

Please allow 2-4 weeks for delivery. See last page for Fax & Postal orders. Please call (305)756-6426 for other inquires. Visit website for photos: www.gate.net/~earthdes

# Crystal Prisms

**Crystals are used as traditional Feng Shui cures to disperse or direct Chi.**
**Tip: The size of the crystal should be proportionate to the area.**

## Octagonal

| | Size | | Each | Total |
|---|---|---|---|---|
| ____ quantity | 28mm | (.75") | $ 6.00 | _____ |
| ____ | 40mm | (1.5") | $13.00 | _____ |

## Sphere

Special Colors: **Rose:** *Romance* **Sapphire:** *Self-Cultivation*
**Emerald:** *Healing/Opportunity*

| ____ quantity | 20mm | Clear (.75") | $ 9.00 | _____ |
|---|---|---|---|---|
| ____ | 20mm | Sapphire (1.25") | $12.00 | _____ |
| ____ | 20mm | Rose (1.25") | $12.00 | _____ |
| ____ | 20mm | Emerald (1.25") | $12.00 | _____ |
| ____ | 30mm | Clear (1.25") | $15.00 | _____ |
| ____ | 30mm | Sapphire (1.25") | $20.00 | _____ |
| ____ | 30mm | Rose (1.25") | $20.00 | _____ |
| ____ | 30mm | Emerald (1.25") | $20.00 | _____ |
| ____ | 40mm | Clear (1.75") | $27.50 | _____ |
| ____ | 40mm | Sapphire (1.75") | $33.00 | _____ |
| ____ | 40mm | Emerald (1.75") | $33.00 | _____ |
| ____ | 40mm | Rose (1.25") | $33.00 | _____ |
| ____ | 50mm | Clear (2") | $53.00 | _____ |
| ____ | 60mm | Clear (2.5") | $85.00 | _____ |

## Mirrors

**Small mirrors direct Chi while not effecting your design when a decorative one may not be appropriate. Good for transcendental cures.**

| ____ quantity | 2" octagonal | $ 3.50 | _____ |
|---|---|---|---|
| ____ | 2" diameter | $ 3.50 | _____ |

## Crystal Beaded Hangers

| ____ quantity | All Clear | $7.80 | _____ |
|---|---|---|---|
| ____ | Rose/Clear-every other | $7.80 | _____ |
| ____ | Sapphire/Clear-every other | $7.80 | _____ |

Shipping: ($5.00, orders over $50, please add 10%) _____
Sales tax (Florida residents only 6.5%) _____

## Total

$ _____

($25.00 minimum please, prices good through 1/98)

*Use traditional* sparkle *in your Feng Shui Design!*

# Order now! Call toll free: 1(800) EarthDesign™

**Please allow 2-4 weeks for delivery**

See last page for Fax & Postal orders. Please call (305)756-6426 for other inquires.

# Feng Shui Today
## Enrich Your Life by Design

---

### The *third* of the EarthDesign™ series
*that brings practical Feng Shui home to the spirit.*

---

## "The finest Feng Shui video on the market!"
---Feng Shui Warehouse

Experience Jami Lin's "Chi" and spirit in this fun, jam-packed, how-to video that combines her expertise in Feng Shui and Interior Design.

Flow through a home, as if you were Chi.

Observe the right way to place your furniture.

See how-to decoratively use finishes, fabrics, accessories, and symbolism according to the Bagua and the 5 elements.

Your invitation to a consultation enables you to discover the relationship between Feng Shui and your own life experience.

ISBN# 0-9646060-6-9

Produced and directed by multi-Emmy award-winning team.

## Order now! Call toll free: 1(800) EarthDesign™
Please allow 2-4 weeks for delivery
See last page for Fax & Postal orders. Please call (305)756-6426 for other inquires.

# 𝒯eng Shui Today
## Earth Design The Added Dimension

**Deepak Chopra**: "*Feng Shui Today* draws from sacred architecture, geomancy and astrology, to the organic approaches of Frank Lloyd Wright, Corbusier, and Buckminster Fuller. Jami presents practical, inexpensive ideas for bringing harmony to your surroundings in a book that goes far beyond Feng Shui."

**Lin Yun Feng Shui Grand Master**: "*Feng Shui Today* captures the essence of ancient and contemporary knowledge. Whether you are a Feng Shui practitioner, architect, divinator, or environmental protection, *Feng Shui Today* is a valuable reference."

**Feng Shui Warehouse:** "*Feng Shui Today* is a major Feng Shui breakthrough. An absolute necessity to read!"

**Derek Walters**, Feng Shui author/expert: "*Feng Shui Today* is an elegant and cleverly assembled account of the various ways that buildings can be designed to maximize their potential for environmental harmony."

**New Leaf Distributing:** "*Feng Shui Today* is a self-directed spiritual journey, guided by our connection to substance and form. Approachable enough for beginners, it draws surprisingly new connections for even the advanced student of Feng Shui by tying in Jami's knowledge of architecture, interior design, and a variety of metaphysical subjects."

**International Miami Book Fair:** "Your presentation and command of the material is outstanding. Your architectural and interior design background provides practical Feng Shui."

**Intuition Magazine:** "*Feng Shui Today* is an impressive, informative guide to make your home or office more beautiful, functional, and environmentally safe....a wealth of information with a refreshingly original synthesis of Feng Shui, geomancy, and design."

**The Open Line: Spokane:** "I had no idea *Feng Shui Today* would cover your whole way of life. What a great book!"

**View on Design Magazine:** "*Feng Shui Today* is an excellent handbook on the science and mysticism of a practice as old as man's need for shelter, dedicated to the improvement of the human spirit and living condition."

## Order now! Call toll free: 1(800) EarthDesign™
### Please allow 2-4 weeks for delivery
See last page for Fax & Postal orders. Please call (305)756-6426 for other inquires.

# Earth Design

**Telephone orders:**      **Order now! Call toll free: 1 (800) Earth Design**
Please have your Visa/MasterCard/Amex ready

**Please call (305)756-6426 for all other inquiries**
**Fax orders:**      (305) 751-9995
**Postal orders:**      Earth Design, P.O. Box 530725
Miami Shores, FL 33153

\_\_\_\_\_copies    *F*eng Shui Today (book)      $18.00 _____
Earth Design the Added Dimension

\_\_\_\_\_copies    The *F*eng Shui Anthology (book)    $22.50 _____
Contemporary Earth Design

\_\_\_\_\_copies    *F*eng Shui Today      $24.93 _____
Enrich Your Life by Design (video)

\_\_\_\_\_copies    The *E*ssence of Feng Shui (book)    $12.95 _____

**(10% off for 2 Items, 15% off for 3 or more! _____)**

U. S. Shipping: book rate         _____
($3.00 for first book, & $1.00 each additional, $5.00 minimum for products, orders over $50.00 add 10%)
Sales tax      (Florida residents only 6.5%)      _____
**Total**        $ _____

**Please allow 2-4 weeks for delivery**

**Please mail to:**     Name _____
Address_____
City/State/Zip_____

**Payment:**      o Check (enclosed)    o Visa    o MasterCard    o Amex

Signature: _____
Print name on card: _____
Card number: _____ Expiration: \_\_\_/\_\_\_

*Free mini Feng Shui kit with orders over $75.00!*

## Please visit our website: *www.gate.net/~earthdes*
**New Ideas, Practitioners Training Certification, Classes, & Products!**
(or request our product information: Chakra/Bagua Essential Oil Blends,
crystals, chimes, mirrors, EMF reducers, and much more!)

**Call, write, fax, or E-mail your address and/or E-mail
to receive information on upcoming events & free newsletter.**